AFTER THE COLD WAR

Also by Arthur I. Cyr

* BRITISH FOREIGN POLICY AND THE ATLANTIC AREA
The Techniques of Accommodation

LIBERAL POLITICS IN BRITAIN

* US FOREIGN POLICY AND EUROPEAN SECURITY

* *From the same publishers*

After the Cold War

American Foreign Policy, Europe and Asia

Arthur I. Cyr

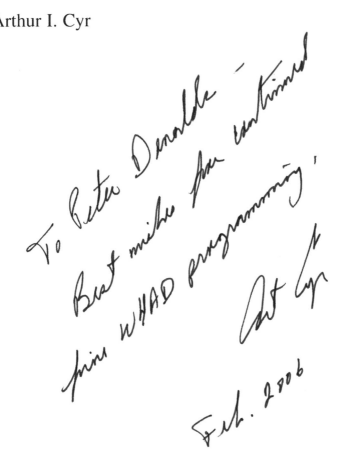

To Peter Donolfe –
Best wishes for continued
fine WHAD programming!
Art Cyr
Feb. 2006

Published 2000 by
MACMILLAN PRESS LTD
Houndmills, Basingstoke, Hampshire RG21 6XS
and London
Companies and representatives
throughout the world

First edition 1997
Reprinted (with new Preface and Epilogue) 2000

ISBN 0–333–67211–9 hardcover
ISBN 0–333–80392–2 paperback

A catalogue record for this book is available
from the British Library.

This book is printed on paper suitable for recycling and
made from fully managed and sustained forest sources.

10   9   8   7   6   5   4   3   2   1
09   08   07   06   05   04   03   02   01   00

Printed and bound in Great Britain by
Antony Rowe Ltd, Chippenham, Wiltshire

To the memory of my father
Irving A. Cyr

Contents

Contents

Preface to the 2000 Reprint

The publication of an updated edition of *After the Cold War: American Foreign Policy, Europe and Asia* has provided a welcome opportunity to review and reflect upon the volume. I believe the basic themes and contours of the study have stood up well, at least over the short term of the several years since the manuscript was completed in 1996. Certainly the steadily growing importance in contemporary international relations of both the mass media and the private commercial realm has been confirmed. The spread of both representative democracy and relatively open competitive markets has now reached a point where any broad global reversal of the trend is difficult to conceive.

Very different, however, is the view, especially popular currently in the United States, that the business cycle and recessions have been abolished and that – by implication – the world has somehow become relatively easy to manage. The difficulty of perceiving emerging problems on the horizon of policy, especially in the midst of a relatively stable and extremely prosperous age, underscores the basic challenge confronting leadership at the national level and for that matter other levels, including not only multinational corporations but virtually all organizations, large and small. Anticipating surprise, or even the full implications of partially anticipated developments, is at the heart of successful leadership, whether the chief executive attempting to guide a nation or the individual attempting to manage a career. After literally decades of anxiety, combined with periods of outright fear, the Cold War has been replaced by an era in which complacency, excessive self-confidence and occasional hubris encourage misperception and miscalculation. President Bill Clinton, in his self-indulgence and self-righteousness, personifies this era to an unnerving degree. The crucial variable of leadership, therefore, is emphasized in the Epilogue as in the original body of the text.

From high policy to immediate work environment, Carthage College in Kenosha Wisconsin has provided a most congenial environment for reviewing and updating this work. Initial contacts with President F. Gregory Campbell and Dean Kurt Piepenberg were followed by a series of conversations with other administrators, faculty and staff, concluding in appointment in April 1998 as the A.W. and Mary Margaret Clausen Distinguished Professor of Political Economy and World Business. Alden W. 'Tom' Clausen is former Chairman and Chief Executive Officer of Bank of America as well as President of the World Bank. He and his wife Peggy have very generously supported student scholarships as well as the academic chair I occupy at the College. After years in nonprofit administration, involving helping to build the Chicago Council on Foreign Relations and a successful turnaround of a nearly bankrupt World Trade Center Association, a change of context was very much in order. The honest, warm and friendly community at Carthage provides an ideal setting for effective teaching as well as sustained scholarship.

Continuing involvement with the Chicago Council on Foreign Relations, where I worked for many years, has also been a source of professional insight as well as substantive information useful to this study. My friend John E. Rielly, President of the Council, asked me to participate in the 1999 edition of the Council public opinion report. Information from that publication is highlighted in the Epilogue. Working to build an effective educational and service organization over a long period of time has been a source of very great satisfaction as well as a worthwhile professional experience, and I appreciate the opportunity to continue involvement there.

A new edition of the book provides an opportunity as well to acknowledge individuals not previously mentioned. Professor David E. Bell of Harvard University provided an outstanding professional example years ago at the Ford Foundation, following his service as Director of the Bureau of the Budget in the Kennedy administration and later as Director of the U.S. Agency for International Development in the Kennedy and Johnson administrations. Several years ago, he was a source of very helpful, insightful advice on what to do – and what to watch out for – in the vortex of strengthening a troubled world trade association. Any individual worth mentioning should have integrity; Dave fulfils this requirement to a remarkable degree. The role of nongovernmental organizations in mediating between the public and private sectors is one I hope to develop at greater length in a succeeding volume. During the past several years, I have been fortunate to continue involvement with the Ditchley Park program, thanks to the good will of Director Sir Michael Quinlan and Deputy Director Heather Weeks in England and Administrative Director John J. O'Connor in the US. Ambassador Hong-koo Lee of the Republic of Korea in Washington DC, as well as Consul General Jong Kyou Byun in Chicago, have been very helpful, especially in increasing the visibility of the volume in their country. Consul General Michael Hodge of Great Britain in Chicago likewise has helped round out ideas for this updated edition.

Finally, my three sons – David, Tom and Jay – have provided welcome companionship and in each case a good example of the importance of sustained focus in accomplishing a goal.

Northbrook, Illinois   ARTHUR I. CYR

Preface to the First Edition

The genesis of this book has been my long-term fascination with the inter-play of domestic and international factors in the development and conduct of foreign policy, plus work on international affairs and politics in Europe and, more recently, Asia. The revolutionary developments in the interna-tional system in recent years have provided rich material for analysis; there is a challenge simply to understand what has been happening as great powers have both collapsed and reunited. Likely consequences of the end of the Cold War and the implications for leaders in the United States, and elsewhere, inform the discussion in these chapters. The collapse of the Soviet Union, the unification of Germany, the end of the Cold War as a diplomatic and military competition, the related failure of communism as a secular religion, and other developments have profoundly altered the social and intellectual as well as political atmosphere and landscape of international relations. No single volume, even a much longer one, could possibly fully analyse all of these changes, and my own hope is that this particular perspective or 'take' on these events will encourage debate and discussion in policy and scholarly circles as well as being of interest to the general public.

Even in a revolutionary period, important elements of continuity can be found. The nation-state is still the basic unit of the system, and par-ticular allies of the United States are worth special attention in addressing a world which we cannot, and never could, manage alone. Despite the great changes which have occurred, Europe remains the principal source of the cultural heritage of the United States, including our political prac-tices and institutions. We maintain a relationship with Britain that tran-scends and endures beyond passing disagreements over policy, the economic and imperial decline of the older power, and the vagaries and unpredict-ability of democracy in both nations, especially our own boisterous polit-ical arena. For these reasons, and also because of a history of exceptional diplomatic experience and skill, Britain is given special attention in the course of this volume as a nation with lessons for others in the post-Cold War world.

Asia provides a dimension for comparison and also a region that can no longer be neglected in discussing political as well as economic influences on America, Europe and Atlantic area relations generally. To some extent, this has of course always been true. A classic old cartoon in the *New Yorker* showed two prosperous middle-aged couples, in evening dress and immersed in social chit chat. One smug gentleman is saying that the other is forgetting one thing in his remarks: '. . . Asia'. Only the fatuous would ignore, or underestimate, the impacts of this enormous region. However, only in recent years have Asian nations beyond Japan become notable engines of industrial development along with traditional roles as sources of raw materials. In an earlier era plausible analysis could deal pretty exclusively in geographic terms with Atlantic area nations alone. During the height of the Cold War, we were concerned with Asia primarily in military security terms with the perceived threat of 'Red' China, wars in Korea and Vietnam, a Soviet–American arms race that was global in nature, and other related developments. Asia today is leading economic growth in the world, becoming more democratic, and undercutting earlier ideological and imperial divisions.

The Republic of Korea receives special emphasis for several reasons. The success of South Korea has been spectacular in vaulting over a short period of time from very low income and economic underdevelopment to become a powerhouse of productivity and commercial effectiveness. This success has in very recent years been married to transition from dictatorship to representative democracy. The Korean War cemented our special relationship with that country, whereas histories of Cold War as well as war still create some distance between the United States and the other great powers of Asia, China and Japan.

This book is not designed exclusively for those who concentrate on international relations but also for the interested general reader; a principal ambition in fact is to provide a sort of handbook or outline to assist thinking and reading about unfolding American foreign policy in regard to Asia, Europe and in general. The Notes section is designed to provide useful background and suggestions for further reading to the serious generalist. The same ambition is reflected in a relatively comprehensive bibliography. The current world involves a new interplay between traditional diplomacy and a drastically changed international system, dramatic growth in public participation and involvement in foreign affairs, the influence of interests previously seen as largely or wholly domestic, and pervasive electronic media providing instant information – both true and false, accurate and inaccurate. Revolutionary doctrines of communism and fascism have been defeated, democracy is more widespread than ever in history, and international relations are being transformed. Communication between specialists and generalists in consequence is of high priority.

I am indebted to a number of individuals for advice, commentary and insight. Some have read parts of the manuscript. Most have been helpful over the years in more informal conversation and interchange, in some cases simply by providing the right sort of example concerning how to go about serious research and analysis, especially in an age when specialized divisions of labour, pressured schedules and pervasive media all encourage a superficial approach to the great matters of our time. They include among faculty professors William James Adams of the University of Michigan, Byung-joon Ahn of Yonsei University in South Korea, McGeorge Bundy of New York University, Bruce Cumings of Northwestern University, Lawrence Freedman of the University of London, Jonathan Galloway of Lake Forest College, Charles Glaser of the University of Chicago, Roy Grow of Carleton College, Donald Haider of Northwestern University, Russell Hardin of New York University, D. Gale Johnson of the University of Chicago, B.C. Koh of the University of Illinois, Edward Kolodziej of the University of Illinois, Andrzej Korbonski of UCLA, Richard Kosobud of the University of Illinois, Ho-Youn Kwon of North Park College, Phyllis Lyons of Northwestern University, Peter Merkl of the University of California at Santa Barbara, Joseph Nye of Harvard University, Benjamin Page of Northwestern University, Stephen Szabo of the School for Advanced International Studies in Washington DC, and Charles Wolf of the Rand Graduate School.

Others generous with advice and assistance have included Tom Boodell of Rudnick and Wolfe, Lord Carrington, Dr Gary Geipel of the Hudson Institute, President Noboru Hatakeyama of the Japan External Trade Organization in Tokyo, former Prime Minister Duck Woo Nam of South Korea, Executive Vice President Russell Phillips of the Rockefeller Brothers Fund, Dr John Steinbruner of the Brookings Institution, Dr John Stremlau of the Carnegie Corporation, and Dr Francis X. Sutton of the Ford Foundation and a whole array of non-profit and service organizations. Sir John Graham, Director of Ditchley Park in Oxford and his predecessors, along with Charles Muller of the American Ditchley Foundation, have provided a wonderful opportunity over the years to examine the Anglo-American relationship in fine style.

Professor Samuel H. Beer of Harvard University more than any other single individual set me on the right road of scholarship many years ago and has remained a valued and wise friend as well as mentor.

Professor George Yu, Director of the Center for East Asian and Pacific Studies at the University of Illinois at Urbana-Champaign, has become a friend as well as collaborator in directing an ambitious project of the Chicago Council on Foreign Relations on American foreign policy in Asia after the Cold War. Participating with him and the other authors in that project has contributed greatly to my education on Asia. Mr. T. M. Farmiloe of Macmillan has over the years been exceptionally receptive to both ideas and manuscript, and understanding as well concerning unexpected delays and changes. His courtesy and professionalism set a fine example.

Work at the Chicago Council on Foreign Relations has provided a foreign policy education and the experience of general public education beyond the college and university world. I have appreciated collaborating with Council President John E. Rielly on the public opinion reports cited in the text, the Atlantic Conference series which he directs, the Asia project cited just above, and all the other matters great and small associated with our work together in building one particular institution. Any effective organization is more than one or two individuals, and other colleagues at the Council over the years have contributed, each in a helpful way.

All these people contributed in a helpful, positive, often very distinctive way, to my efforts to bring Asia and Europe together within analysis of American foreign policy.

Northbrook, Illinois   ARTHUR CYR

Part I
America and the World

1 Incentives for Analysis

FIRST EFFORTS

The purpose of this book is to provide perspectives on, context for and analysis of United States foreign policy in the contemporary international system. This study follows and is conceived as a companion to an earlier volume, *U.S. Foreign Policy and European Security*, which was designed to be a straightforward treatment of Atlantic area relations since the conclusion of the Second World War. The earlier volume was essentially though not exclusively descriptive in nature, undertaken to address the false but widespread assertion that Nato (North Atlantic Treaty Organization) and related crises in the Atlantic region in the 1980s were somehow either unprecedented or more threatening to Alliance cohesion than those in earlier decades. Entirely too much alarm was being generated by Alliance conflicts in the 1970s and 1980s; in fact the disputes which did occur were hardly unprecedented and in some ways seemed, at least from my perspective, less consequential and threatening to unity than some of the events of the 1950s and 1960s.[1] The present study builds on that earlier one and is conceived primarily as an extended analytic essay, placing current and relatively recent political and economic developments in wider historical context, providing some of the reasons for policy choices, especially on the part of the US government, and endeavouring to describe ways in which the international system is changing in tandem with as well as because of the end of the Cold War.

I believe the first volume achieved the primary purpose of placing the conflicts animating Nato in the 1980s in suitable perspective. The tensions over deployment of cruise and second-generation Pershing nuclear missiles in Europe, the Soviet gas pipeline commercial arrangement with West European nations, and other matters that generated intense controversy in that decade were hardly mild misunderstandings. Yet in relation to such developments as the Suez Crisis of 1956, the intense competition of the early 1960s – involving image, ego and personality as much as policy – between Presidents John F. Kennedy and Charles de Gaulle, the extended Berlin crisis of 1958–61, the Cuban Missile Crisis of 1962, and others, these difficulties were hardly unprecedented in nature or sentiment.

The earlier work, like all books, had shortcomings; these became increasingly apparent and troubling to me with the passage of time following publication. First, despite some very preliminary discussion of Japan,

3

especially in the initial pages, there was an absence of systematic integration of that nation, already an economic superpower, in the body of the analysis. This was so despite reiteration in the text of the increasingly significant political and social as well as diplomatic roles of economic factors in international relations. A backward-looking examination of Atlantic area Alliance matters was by definition not only geographically restricted but focused on years when Japan was still only beginning to emerge from post-Second World War devastation to a major international role, and even then the role was more purely economic than was the case for any other main industrial power. This explanation, however, does not change the fact that the end product was too circumscribed. A major goal of the present volume is to relate traditional Atlantic-area concerns to evolving relations in the Pacific region, with comparative analysis of how the balance between Atlantic and Pacific interests defines and should be addressed by American foreign policy.

Second, the concluding discussion in the earlier volume regarding the evolving course of the international system quickly became dated. Here the main problem was timing. The volume appeared in 1987, at the start of genuinely 'interesting times' in international relations. The rise and decline of Mikhail Gorbachev in the Soviet Union, the end of the established communist regime and collapse of the structure of government, the growth of uncertain democracies in the former Eastern bloc, and the unification of Germany were extraordinarily significant, indeed profound developments. The map of Europe literally was transformed as Germany came together and the Soviet Union fell apart. The relentless ongoing economic growth in Asia – not just Japan – and the political as well as economic implications thereof, the impacts of the emergence of relatively conservative governments in the USA and in West Europe generally are other developments inadequately addressed in the earlier book. Conservative domestic political regimes in the Atlantic area have been important not only for pursuing a generally hard line in foreign policy during the Cold War years, at least directly *vis-à-vis* the Soviet Union, but also for heavily favouring the private sector, through both active promotion of 'privatization' at home and emphasis on free trade internationally.

If the main theme of the initial study remained valid, and the Alliance relations of the USA had been at least as severely strained in the years before as during the 1980s, the extraordinary pace and character of recent international developments provided an incentive to retest the proposition while catching up with events. Because the Cold War so powerfully influenced and shaped international relations and American foreign policy, the sudden end of that fundamental conflict has provided an opportunity to address a host of new questions, not least the future of the Alliance strategies which had been designed to handle the earlier international system. The first volume may have become rapidly dated because of profound transformation of the international system in the late 1980s and the 1990s; likewise any useful contemporary insights concerning that system are especially desirable. This is particularly the case since the sea changes affecting our foreign policy and the world of nations were foreseen by very few observers in government, scholarship, journalism or elsewhere. Self-criticism is useful only when not overdone; there were genuinely revolutionary changes coming in the 1980s which would provide a positive incentive for a second volume even had the first been more sensitive to the seismic shifts that were about to occur.

Third, the earlier work could and should have been more explicit in analysis of the manner in which the relative importance of economic and military factors was changing. Common perspective holds that the economic sphere has become more significant, especially since the late 1960s. The earlier volume generally reflected this viewpoint yet did not fully elaborate the theme, including the specific implications for US foreign policy.

Having emphasized these limitations, the earlier effort also contained some strengths. The case was developed that more recent difficulties really are not so monumental when considered in the light of crises in the past. This in turn resulted from the emphasis on the long train of time, the environment in which particular events unfolded, the inevitable bearing of the past on the present – and the future. There was a realistic and pragmatic emphasis, which the evidence of crisis and controversy generally reinforced, on the nation-state as the main component in the international system. This element remains pre-eminent, despite the growth of an increasingly complex tapestry of relations among a range of public, private, subnational, and supranational organizations. International relations are still mainly relations among states, though the argument is developed in the text that non-state entities are becoming ever more consequential.

THREE-WAY ANALYSIS

This examination of international relations is also linked to an even earlier volume, *Liberal Politics In Britain*, which addressed party politics and public policies in that country, with particular attention to the growth of third party movements, not just the revival of the Liberal Party, and the closely related expansion of social service and reform organizations.[2] A threefold division of the subject was used to guide the research and writing;

distinctive but related prisms were employed to go over the same material from different perspectives. Specifically, the British Liberal Party and associated political and social developments were examined through attention to intellectual, structural and sociological dimensions. 'Intellectual' refers to the philosophical underpinnings of Liberal thought in Britain, the main policy currents in the Liberal Party old and new, and the ways in which Liberal ideas were reflected in the policies of the two major parties, Conservative and Labour.

'Structural' refers to the organization of the Liberal Party, with particular attention to the defining theme that active hostility to modern party discipline and elaborate administration are characteristic of the party. This is an important reason why certain kinds of activists have joined the Liberals, and is also a factor in the continued small size, limited electoral appeal, and distance from power of the party. These characteristics also account for the general frustration of more pragmatic activists within the party. Often structure is treated as passive context or the frozen stage upon which political action occurs, yet this factor proved to be a source of insight into the Liberal paradox of party decline yet continued survival.

'Sociological' refers to the broad social environment in which the Liberal Party has existed, including but going well beyond the dimensions included in what the political scientist normally refers to as political culture. A fundamental argument of the book is that very broad social changes taking place in Britain are moving the nation in basically Liberal directions, even if the Liberal Party has not been profiting from that development with sustained increased popular support.

The decline of class in Britain has reduced somewhat the intensity of partisanship between the two major parties, or at least altered the tone of their debate, while providing each with a more middle-class image. The growth of electoral volatility over time demonstrates a loosening of class holds on public sentiment, and again a waning of the stark confrontation between Tory and Labour. The study also included discussion of the rise of voluntary associations, both social service and social reform groups, of the sort that flourished during nineteenth-century British politics – the Liberal Age, in the terminology of Professor Samuel H. Beer. This dimension was especially important for analysis of the contemporary Liberal Party.[3]

There are no direct parallels in substance between an analytic approach used to study almost purely domestic politics, and a rather small third party at that, and large-scale changes in international relations bearing on American foreign policy, but approximately the same scheme can be usefully applied. Ideas, even when implicit rather than explicit in form, influence policy. Even the most self-consciously pragmatic operators have a set of values which underlie their actions. As Hans Morgenthau demonstrated with great impact, pragmatism can itself become a highly complex and elaborate guide to policy. Concern in the chapters that follow is primarily with ideas and concerns influencing US foreign policy, especially during the Reagan years in the 1980s. In addition, there is attention to ideas influencing European policymakers, especially in terms of the very persistent effort to construct significant regional integration above the level of the nation-state, which contrasts with the situation in and context of Asia. In any democracy, and perhaps particularly in the United States, domestic political dynamics have a very significant influence on foreign policy, and the American domestic political debate is given considerable attention in the analysis. This is also designed to be a practical guide, of use to the interested citizen as well as the professional engaged in foreign affairs, and there is an assumption that a large proportion of the readership will be American. Those who are not Americans have a strong incentive in any case to understand the forces, practical as well as thematic, shaping our national policies.[4]

'Structure' in the arena of US foreign policy includes at least potentially a very large number of different organizations. Political parties can themselves have a distinctive impact on the foreign policies of our own country and most others. Arguably in the case of the United States, the end of post-Second World War bipartisanship in foreign policy, yet one more casualty of the Vietnam War, has resulted in a situation of marked and actively debated differences between the Democrats and Republicans on major foreign policy concerns. Attitudes toward defence spending and the use of military force overseas contrast dramatically. The very intense manner in which these topics were debated following the Vietnam War indicated the end of the earlier bipartisan era. The Gulf War victory, a policy though not political success for President Bush, and the Bosnian peace accord, a policy and perhaps also political victory for President Clinton, may mean that a more secure America in a post-Cold War environment is returning to relative bipartisanship in foreign policy.

While the post-Vietnam national security debate underscored cleavages between American parties on fundamental foreign policy choices, the point must also be kept in mind that the role of party is limited. Parties aggregate some interests and foreclose others, spotlight some issues and ignore others, mobilize activists and pressure officials in ways that have important policy impacts. They are not, however, the principal structures for the final definition or actual implementation of foreign policy. They are removed at least one step from decisions on the use of military force. They do not have the last word in foreign policy.

With this in mind, for our purposes 'structure' will be defined as primarily, though not exclusively, the intergovernmental, largely regional, economic and military security organizations that serve as arenas for discussion and debate, mechanisms for co-ordination, and to some extent initiators of policy, plus large multinational private organizations. Arguably they are the main instruments for building coalitions and aggregating interests between nations in the areas of most concern to this discussion. After all, this study and its predecessor are concerned with the condition of the Atlantic Alliance. Of course, regional alliances are not repositories of fundamental political loyalty or policy authority. They depend fully on the goodwill of their constituents. Consequently, any effort to analyse Alliance relations without consideration of the constituent nation-states is guaranteed to be artificial, partial in scope, and ultimately limited in providing satisfactory conclusions. The nation-state, including very specific arrangements for foreign policy within a government, has to be included in any effective discussion of structure.

Worthwhile analysis of the politics of Alliance relationships must include attention to the role of other private international organizations, including the modern corporation. If the political is by definition in the *public* realm, the actions of private groups as well as individuals comprise that realm, and in our day there is no way for the serious student of international politics to ignore the world of international commerce. Arguably the period from the end of the Second World War to the end of the 1960s, when international politics experts in the academy could successfully ignore the commercial marketplace, was highly unusual, an era when the combination of enormous American economic power and the related stability of trade and monetary affairs guaranteed by Bretton Woods kept the global economic order unusually orderly.

President Nixon's decisive action in 1971 finally to separate the US dollar from gold, and at the same time restrict imports, not only signalled clearly a change in our foreign economic policies, but also provided dramatic confirmation that the international system was fundamentally changing with the relative waning of American economic power. A comparatively less influential United States created a situation in which students of international relations as well as some policymakers could not so easily ignore the role of trade and finance in political interplay. Economic strength could no longer be assumed or taken for granted in the calculations of foreign policy in the government, or in foreign policy critiques or suggestions emanating from the academic world.

Concern with economics on the part of students of politics is in one sense nothing new. As Joan Edelman Spero notes at the start of her admirably clear treatment, *The Politics of International Economic Relations*: 'The interaction of politics and economics is an old theme in the study of international relations. From seventeenth-century mercantilists to twentieth-century Marxists, students of relations among states have dealt with the problems of international political economy.' She assigns much of the blame for the modern separation of economics and politics to the sociology of academic disciplines in the West.[5]

The multinational corporation is to some extent a creation of the free-trade atmosphere of the Bretton Woods agreements and the long post-Second World War economic expansion that continued through the 1960s. Though business is from time to time the whipping boy of politicians, and the political/media atmosphere is from time to time punctuated by news of allegations of corporate complicity in controversial political developments, much more consequential for serious analysis is the growth of the modern multinational corporation as an independent entity with control of considerable capital resources. Between 1971 and 1986, for instance, the book value of US-owned overseas investment grew from $86.2 billion to $259.9 billion, while between 1971 and 1984 the comparable figures for the Federal Republic of Germany went from $7.3 billion to $51.1 billion and for Japan from $4.4 billion to $71.4 billion. As a result, the capacity of the multinational corporation for action independent of any one government, and to influence various developments beyond the national borders of headquarters, has become much more significant. These means are commercial in nature, but only the most committed business booster – or theoretician – would deny they have political implications as well. To quote Spero again:

> Multinational corporations are not simply large corporations that market their products abroad; they are firms that have sent abroad a package of capital, technology, managerial talent, and marketing skills to carry out production in foreign countries. In many cases, the multinational's production is truly worldwide ... Marketing is also often international. Goods produced in one or more countries are sold throughout the world. Finally, multinational corporations tend to have foreign subsidiaries in many countries.[6]

A flurry of active political-scientist interest in the roles of multinational corporations took place in the 1970s, reflecting perhaps belatedly but certainly clearly that the political dimensions of international economics should not be neglected. No doubt the rise of the New Left in foreign policy and international relations circles, a direct result and continuing legacy of the Vietnam War, was an important spur. But the modern giant corporation was also an immediate, very tangible factor. As the end of the twentieth century approaches, as the aftermath of the Cold War rather than a generally accepted conceptualization of a new system continues to characterize discussion of international politics, as the USA tries collectively to come to grips with a new international role, what exactly are the influences of the multinationals, and what opportunities exist for collaboration between them and nation-states and regional intergovernmental organizations?

'Sociological' is the hardest term to apply to this environment but it is potentially the most insightful. For our purposes, the word is intended primarily to draw attention to the wider context of international relationships and developments, beyond governments and other institutions public and private, and will refer to the broad popular dimensions of international affairs. This includes activities beyond the realm of, or only loosely linked to, traditional diplomacy, the nation-state, and such instruments of policy as regional alliances, military forces, and other entities under the direct control of governments, international corporations or other non-governmental institutions. Migration, tourism, communication as a process, the media as a distinct force in international affairs are all factors under this heading. The sociological dimension is, if you will, the human environment that fleshes out the structural dimension and reflects at least partially the drives, desires and goals articulated by political ideas and ideologies. Leaders define and promote ideas and manipulate structures; publics at large inspire and respond to ideas, and confirm or reject structures through their participation, especially but hardly exclusively in the context of political democracy.

The great human migrations which are having such profound impacts on both sides of the Atlantic and the Pacific certainly qualify as one such component. Variations on this theme are numerous and perhaps endless; two migrations of recent times have a particular bearing on this examination of the US in the international system. One is the tremendous influx of Asian and Latin American immigrants into the United States. The other is the equally massive movement of peoples from East to West Europe, and in particular the Western part of Germany.

Another component of the sociological dimension of the international system is the impacts and roles of public opinion on the foreign policy process. In the United States and Britain, both well-established democratic polities, public opinion is almost by definition an inherent part of the dynamics of policy development and implementation. With the increasing spread of democracy in both the industrial and developing worlds, a phenomenon which clearly predates the end of the Cold War, the role of public opinion, and the importance of study of the phenomenon, continue to grow. This particular work, partly for reasons of convenience, also because of more objective substantive considerations, will rely heavily on the studies of American public opinion attitudes carried out every four years since 1974 by the Chicago Council on Foreign Relations.[7]

The threefold conceptual division described above can be employed usefully in analysis of international as well as domestic political concerns, although the former environment arguably is more uncertain and more permeable, if not more complex, in terms of the number of variables and the interplay among them. The international system is always most clear and pristine when conceived at a highly abstract level. Even in terms of regional relations between Europe and the USA, the analyst has considerable freedom to be arbitrary in the choice of factors and developments to highlight. This is even more true in the contemporary period, when events in Asia, including Japan, but also in particular China, as well as other countries, have a particularly strong economic impact on the Atlantic region.

From the perspectives of the more conventional diplomat, the collapse of the Soviet Union and the Warsaw Pact has fundamentally changed the psychological and political contours of Europe, and also provided great freedom in defining the borders and limits of US–European regional relations. From a different perspective, the very point that the new system represents such a transformation means that there are good reasons to experiment with various analytic perspectives, to order facts in different ways that may help in encouraging insights.

CARTER AND REAGAN

In overall policy emphasis, the Reagan administration represented a major departure from the Carter administration and indeed from much of the post-Second World War evolution of US foreign policy. The Carter administration, seemingly President Carter most of all, was actively engaged in a whole range of policy areas, foreign and domestic. There was a commitment to arms control negotiations and accords with the Soviet Union, resulting in the SALT II treaty, that was continuous with American diplomatic priorities since the Eisenhower administration. There was also, at least at the beginning of the administration, a declared interest in giving more attention to relations with major European allies and Japan, which some argued had been short-changed as a result of the focus on great power relations among the USA, the Soviet Union and China during the years when Richard Nixon and Henry Kissinger were managing US foreign policy. Leadership as detailed management was a defining much-discussed characteristic of the Carter years, and human rights, the international economy, the environment, plus arms control and other topics, usually linked to ambitious plans for policy and institutional reform, crowded the presidential in-box.

By contrast, President Reagan ushered in a regime that for the first time since the Second World War gave main sustained attention to domestic rather than international initiatives, with a president who seemed to take some satisfaction from his relative inattention to policy details. Reagan was animated primarily by the goal of limiting US federal government activity, and ultimately he and his associates achieved at least a slowdown if not a reversal in the expansion of public sector social services, primarily through the long-term drag effect of relatively large federal fiscal deficits. Deficit reduction as the main preoccupation of federal public policy is the principal, and very important, tangible Reagan legacy. President Reagan from time to time shrewdly referred to his personal admiration for President Franklin Roosevelt. In preference for the relatively familiar, and therefore comfortable, domestic political milieu over foreign policy, Reagan was similar to FDR during the New Deal years, before the pressures of world war became unavoidable.

To be sure, Reagan is no old-fashioned isolationist, his administration developed foreign policy as well as domestic policy priorities, and in the national security field in particular major initiatives were taken. The very great expansion in defence spending which occurred, combined with aggressive anti-communist and anti-Soviet rhetoric early on, recall the Truman or Kennedy administration rather than early Roosevelt and certainly reflect a concern with foreign policy. However, this arguably was not associated, at least in Reagan's first term, with many major specific policy initiatives overseas. Again, in terms of action rather than rhetoric, even in the sensitive realm of covert operations, the Reagan administration seems not particularly risk-prone or hard-line in action in comparison, for example, with the militant Truman, adventurous Kennedy, or even Johnson and Nixon administrations. Each of these administrations was involved in war, which the Reagan people avoided. That avoidance may have been due to luck and circumstance, but for whatever reason makes the case that the Reagan administration was especially hard-line or militaristically difficult to develop. The Reagan defence buildup was not linked to any broad international initiatives related to our European allies, again in contrast with the Kennedy administration. In contrast to the Nixon years, there were no major diplomatic initiatives toward Cold War adversaries during Reagan's first term. There was no broad international 'Grand Design'. Truman, Eisenhower, Kennedy, Johnson, Nixon, Ford and Carter all were at least to some extent associated with such institutional themes, which varied in the nations, structures, and other policy specifics involved. In this intellectual/policy sense, the Reagan administration during the first phase was decidedly different from what went before.[8]

The point should not be overdrawn. As usual, reality is more complex than a set of comfortable pigeonholes. Lyndon Johnson's policy preferences were decidedly domestic in nature, and the Vietnam War tragedy could only have vastly reinforced his personal wish to spend his policy time elsewhere. The Reagan foreign policymakers found ample opportunity for intervention beyond US borders, in Grenada, Iran, Lebanon, Libya, Nicaragua and elsewhere. These activities, however, were not a function of one consistent foreign policy theme articulated by the President and his most senior representatives on a continuing basis. The USA can hardly avoid global involvement or overseas crises given the range and reach of its power, interests and concerns. Nevertheless, the fact remains that during Reagan's first term there were no significant initiatives *vis-à-vis* Europe, the Soviet Union or China. During his second term, as in FDR's third, dramatic events beyond US borders drove him to take a more active role. The Iran/contra scandal was certainly a major foreign policy development, but the principal point is that this covert action was not linked to any broad consistent publicly articulated policy of rollback or overthrow of established Communist powers. The intensity of the Cold War conflict, at least in global and even in specific European terms, was waning. Presidential rhetoric and policy declarations reflected this changing world. Hard-line American conservatives were still anti-communist but were no longer compelled to lead a public anti-communist crusade. The much-discussed 'Reagan Doctrine' of supporting anti-communist movements in Nicaragua and elsewhere reflected the President's views but did not originate in the Oval Office, but rather with journalist Charles Krauthammer. Krauthammer coined the term in the course of a *Time* magazine analysis of the President's 1985 State of the Union message. He was describing a range of initiatives emanating from various sectors and levels of the administration, often pressed by ideologues, not driven directly by the President or by conservative political opinion in the country.[9]

Conservatives and Republicans have had to address the New Deal legacy whenever they have achieved national power. When the Republican Party returned to the White House, and control of the Congress, under the moderate Dwight Eisenhower in 1952, some informed observers anticipated an abolition of the New Deal/Fair Deal welfare state along with the new panoply of international commitments, represented most significantly and centrally by the Nato Alliance. Eisenhower in fact did nothing of the sort, instead confirming the permanence of the modern welfare state and the commitment of the Republican Party's dominant wing to internationalism. When Reagan took office, there was much less of this sort of concern despite his very conservative political credentials. Yet arguably he did more than any of his recent predecessors to change the course of presidential policy back toward a domestic focus, and to shift the dynamics of public policy toward a restricted role for the federal government.[10]

For US–European relations, this was not an undesirable development. A less active United States was arguably a more realistic superpower in an era when American economic influence was in relative decline. If the Cold War still provided the main definition of conflict in the international system, the intensity of the conflict had cooled from the supercharged 1950s and 1960s. The Soviets might build a new strategic capability to project conventional forces relatively long distances by sea and air, intervene in Southern Africa and Nicaragua, and launch a blatant *coup* and invasion in Afghanistan, yet for all that the old imagery of a well co-ordinated international communist camp relentlessly seeking expansion was no longer persuasive. Even American conservatives reflected the relative decline of both our national power and the international ideological conflict.

Moreover, conservatives have some special advantages in the political calculus of diplomacy. Because of his clearly established commitment to anti-communism, Reagan had unusual independence to seek and accept agreements with the other side. Just as Richard Nixon was free to open the diplomatic door to China because he had been such a prominent spokesman for the most extreme and strident anti-communist factions in the USA, including the old 'China Lobby' of supporters of Chinese Nationalist leader Chiang Kai-shek, so too Reagan's pro-military credentials combined with his anti-communism provided a strong position from which to pursue arms accords with the USSR during his second term.

FAMILIAR INSTITUTIONS

Beyond the intellectual currents of policy, and moving to the second dimension, the international structural environment which has unfolded from the early 1980s is noteworthy for the continuity of inherited institutions, which may be testimony to the fundamental effectiveness of those arrangements. Europeans in practical discussion of current crises and other international developments, off the record as well as more publicly, are noteworthy for the degree to which they take refuge in the known quantities of the European Community (EC), now the European Union (EU), as well as the

North Atlantic Treaty Organization. The Western European Union (WEU), revived for a time at least rhetorically, especially during the Bush administration, has not become in reality a principal source of co-ordination among the powers of Western Europe, despite the obvious difficulty experienced by the European Union in implementing initiatives to address the ongoing warfare in the Balkans. The United Nations, while severely tested by the Balkan war, has also been provided with new opportunities for a greater international diplomatic role.

Both Nato very explicitly, and the European Union more implicitly, have received legitimacy and direction over time as a result of the military threat of the Soviet Union and the Warsaw Pact. Nato was designed specifically to confront and mitigate the perceived military danger of the other side in the early days of the Cold War. The European Community was above all a reaction to the dreadful costs of nationalism gone berserk in the two world wars. Yet a more indirect incentive as well for seeking the Community, perhaps especially for Washington, was to use an economically prosperous Europe as the primary bulwark to counter the threat of communism. The military alliance structure was designed to resist a military threat; the economic community structure had the result of cementing commercial market practices that by example undercut the appeal of the Soviet bloc. The latter collapsed mainly thanks to internal weakness, but external events also had a role, at least of positive comparative example.

There are at least three considerations, however, that change the context of these two fundamental structures for West European and, in the military sphere, transatlantic collaboration. The environment in which they operate has changed considerably in recent years, and not just because of the end of the Cold War or the relative decline of American power. First, there is continuing evolution in the forms and composition of both organizations. The European Union has already moved well beyond the established full regular members and West European geographic base. All the details of association of a diverse group of potential East European members, to say nothing of the European Free Trade Association, have yet to be hammered out. Yet the very fact that the Community is willing to entertain such a shift argues implicitly for the same point illustrated by the failure of the effort at full currency integration: the commitment to strong central institutions, especially in banking and related financial services, is not strong enough among current member states. 'Broadening' the European Union is a tacit admission that 'deepening' has not taken place in any really meaningful sense.

The urge to expand the European Union also clearly reflects implicitly considerable concern over German power. If failure to go all the way to the projected 'Europe 1992' world of full integration shows that Europeans are unwilling to accept a single central bank which, in *de facto* terms, would be a mirror image of the Bundesbank, expansion in the number of Union members is a device to reduce the market power of Germany, at least temporarily. If the destructive nationalism of an earlier period was a principal reason – indeed the key reason – for forming the Community of the Six in the mid-1950s, more traditional calculations of power and influence among states that fuelled European diplomacy historically has re-emerged, though this time so far thankfully mainly in economic rather than military terms.

Likewise the Nato Alliance is undergoing important change. Although US Secretary of State Warren Christopher stated early in the Clinton administration that expansion of the Alliance membership was probably on balance not desirable, Nato Secretary-General Manfred Woerner nevertheless at approximately the same time began the process of bringing the Czech Republic, Hungary, and Poland into the fold of the organization. If current trends continue, Nato will enlarge to encompass former Warsaw Pact members to the east, reinforcing moves by the European Union to expand to include smaller economies on the borders of Western Europe. The much-discussed Partnership for Peace of the Clinton administration is at heart an effort to smooth, finesse and facilitate the great shift represented by Eastern European participation in what had been the Western military Alliance.[11]

Second, the Asian region impinges to an unprecedented degree on developments in the Atlantic area, primarily economically but also politically. Japan, despite the long-term very severe recession, is a heavy investor as well as competitor within the large American and European markets. European nations, in particular but not exclusively France, have taken dramatically restrictive steps against Japanese goods. The Asian region, going well beyond the specific role and impact of Japan, has become increasingly important as trader and investor for the industrial nations generally. Since 1981, US trade volume with the Pacific region has surpassed that with the Atlantic, and the differential has steadily grown. Commercially and industrially, Asia has come to the fore as a region of tremendous economic activity, more and more the rival, and in some areas the superior, of Western Europe.

Asia, however, remains very distinctive *vis-à-vis* Europe in the absence of the very organizational structures that give life to regional communication and policy co-ordination in Europe and the Atlantic region. In the realm of military security, the Southeast Asia Treaty Organization is dead, in a truly tangible sense never really seemed to exist, and more vital organizations such as the Australia–New Zealand–USA pact are far more limited than Nato geographically and psychologically. The most important security arrangements are bilateral – USA–Japan and USA–South Korea. In economic dimensions likewise there is no parallel to the European Community, although there have been growing efforts at regional institution building, most comprehensively in the awkwardly titled Asia Pacific Economic Co-operation (APEC) association. This organization has made a firm, comparatively recent commitment to free trade, but so far has undertaken no effort at a continuing fundamental integration of markets comparable to that of the European Union. If the organization surpasses anything that has been achieved in trans-Atlantic economic co-operation, that underscores how much remains to be done, and the absence of on-going comprehensive administrative arrangements has to be viewed as a major disadvantage in terms of institution building in the Asia/Pacific region.[12]

Third, the environment of European and Atlantic regional institutions has been changed by the expanded role of the United Nations as a result of the end of the Cold War. The organization may yet prove to be very badly damaged by ineffectiveness in the Balkan war of the 1990s. Given that the region invites historical analogies, allusions and reminiscences, one can even envision a UN that founders in this conflict, much as the League of Nations was destroyed in the 1930s as the result of inability to stem fascist aggression. On the other hand, the UN has been notably effective in other arenas, most dramatically in the 1991 Gulf War, and also in promoting greater stability and reduction of violence in such areas as Cambodia, El Salvador and Namibia. The end of the Cold War means that the old stalemate between Washington and Moscow which stymied UN action, and enhanced the influence of militant Third World nations, has disappeared. The UN, despite frustration in the Balkans, has a range and reach of influence not previously available.

To some extent, the current period is reminiscent of the Truman and Eisenhower years to the degree that both of those American presidents seemed to turn almost automatically to the UN forum to vet major world crises and tensions. In those years the pro-Western working majority in the Security Council, when the Soviet veto was not imposed, and also in the General Assembly was very useful. From the 1960s, the USA turned less to the UN, at least in part because the reliable General Assembly support disappeared as new Third World nations joined the body, in part perhaps because a later generation of American foreign policy leaders were less inclined to try to work within the institution. With the Gulf crisis and war of 1990–1, George Bush returned the United Nations to a priority position in US global foreign policy. In the organization and legitimization of the military action to drive Iraq out of Kuwait, Bush secured both US Congressional authorization to use force and UN co-operation in implementation, thereby returning to an emphasis on institutional legitimation that had been badly damaged by secretive American policies during the Vietnam War.

More broadly, there has been a passing of the energizing sense of mission which played an important role in the initial formation of the United Nations, the Nato Alliance and the European Economic Community. Hopes during the Second World War that the world body would become a kind of world government, on either democratic terms or through the special influence of the victorious leaders of the anti-Axis coalition, were quickly revealed to be utopian. The end of the Cold War also has terminated the role of the UN as an arena in which that Soviet–American contest was engaged. Nato also has been primarily a creature of the Cold War, although here one of the great unfolding ironies is that Europeans seem increasingly to look to the military organization as a mechanism to keep the Americans involved across the Atlantic. The European Union has become frustrated with the potential role of peacemaker. This has taken place at a time when nationalist sentiments, a main incentive for creating the Community institutions in Western Europe in the first place, have been given new life in Eastern Europe as a result of the end of the diplomatic as well as military bipolarity imposed by Moscow and Washington. A principal challenge to any American president therefore is complex institutional management of and morale in organizations not directly under US national control. In each case – the UN, Nato and the EU – limited success and new opportunities with the end of the Cold War have been closely linked to specific frustrations and problems, in each case in the European arena.

FOREIGN RELATIONS AND HUMAN RELATIONS

The third broad area of analytic focus, in addition to the intellectual and structural dimensions, is 'sociological'. In an earlier examination of British domestic politics, the term was used to refer to broad social changes in the population, namely the decline of socioeconomic class and related strong identification with class-based Tory and Labour parties – or with any political party on a continuing basis. The main result was increasing electoral volatility as strong long-established partisan ties waned, along with measurable revival of interest, as was noted earlier, in voluntary social service and social reform associations typical of those prominent in nineteenth-century British politics.[13]

The sociological dimension refers to focus very explicitly on people, with emphasis on groups and collective actions rather than on the ideas that motivate them or the structures *per se* through which they operate. To some extent this distinction is artificial, which is not the same as being inappropriate to analysis. How can political activists, especially radicals at odds with the domestic and international orders, be understood in total apart from the ideas which motivate them or the practical party or other organizational structures through which they operate? At the same time, social and political movements and broad currents of public behaviour go on in dimensions removed from the concerns and drives of committed activists – or professional diplomats. This is especially true in our age of relatively great prosperity in the industrial nations, spreading democracy and absence of totalitarian threats previously represented by communism, fascism and nazism.

Emphasis on social as well as political movements is also one way of trying to gain insight into the behaviour and attitudes of the great mass of the population beyond the rather small groups that participate in party politics, government policy implementation, and international commercial and other organizations, public and private. The recent large-scale movement of people from the eastern to the central and western parts of Europe, unprecedented since the even larger – and much more tragic – human migrations at the conclusion of and after the Second World War, powerfully draws attention to this dimension of international 'relations'. From this perspective, the imagery of international interplay within the Atlantic area can be described as dual or 'double imagery'. Great migrations of refugees from the east, from political as well as economic collapse in that part of the world, are moving steadily into Western Europe, mingling with active commercial enterprises large and small, which are simultaneously spreading, albeit unevenly, into Eastern Europe and the former Soviet Union.

While one result is considerable social unrest, and some nationalist backlash, another very important result is to create a genuine common market in human terms, one which includes but goes well beyond the current membership of the European Union. A source of instability in the short term given the dislocations and disruptions attending any great movement of people, this migration also holds the promise over the longer term of binding different parts of the European continent together. Likewise, the continued magnetic appeal of the United States as the proverbial 'land of opportunity' argues that there is a fundamental strength to the US economy, society, and approach to life that is reassuring in the face of, and somewhat contrary to, its focus on domestic social problems, especially crime and drugs, and political dilemmas, especially the federal fiscal deficit and related debt.[14]

A different dimension of the sociological influence on international relations concerns the attitudes of people in the aggregate – that is, the direct and indirect influence of public opinion on the policy processes of the nations of the Atlantic area and of the industrial nations more generally. This factor is of special obvious importance in a democracy. Here, available data is both rich and uncertain. Public opinion surveys in the United States, including those carried out every four years since 1974 by the Chicago Council on Foreign Relations, can be read as reassuring from various perspectives. Recent surveys reveal no growth in support for protectionism on the part of the public and broad recognition that the world is genuinely interdependent, especially in economic terms. While such sentiments are commonplace among international relations specialists, for such perceptions to be widely held among the public represents a fundamental change in attitude from earlier generations of Americans, especially those which predated the Second World War. There is also public commitment to an active international role for the United States. Finally, there remains a fundamental aversion to the use of military force overseas except in certain highly selective and relatively clearly defined circumstances. The American public is internationalist, not isolationist or protectionist, yet that internationalism is of a decidedly cautious variety, especially regarding the use of force.[15]

The 1990 public opinion survey conducted by the Chicago Council on Foreign Relations revealed growing hostility to Japan, though this had waned by the 1994 survey. To a degree, this is a direct result simply of the absence of the Soviet Union as primary rival and antagonist. With the collapse of that nation, and the attendant fading of the Cold War between two reasonably coherent, ideologically opposed blocs, attention individually and collectively was freed to focus on other areas of conflict. The principal international power in economic terms outside of the United States has been Japan. The enormous international trade surplus of Japan, a constant focus of the American news media, is one source of friction. The frustrations attending American foreign policy is another, especially in an era when Japan still seems comparatively uninvolved internationally beyond the enormously powerful and wide ranging economy. Finally, while the USA has been pursuing an international order which is global, broadly under the auspices of the United Nations, Japan appears to have been more regionally focused. This has especially been the case in recent years, as

Japan's capital, including human capital, has been steadily redeployed from elsewhere, especially the North American region, to a more explicit focus in Asia.

Comparative discussion of opinion trends in Europe and Japan adds an important descriptive dimension, and is essential for any effort to define the public influences and parameters on policy for the Western Alliance structure as a whole. Here, evidence and information is decidedly uneven. Concerning Europe, there is a lot of reassurance to be had in the clear long-term trend in Germany of movement in liberal directions. Opinion polls taken in the Federal Republic of Germany over time show decided growth in democratic sentiments, especially among younger people, since the Second World War. Germans under forty, in contrast to Germans over sixty, strongly believe in the value of democracy and decisively reject Hitler and the Nazi past. Concerning Japan, the picture is considerably more murky, reflecting much greater reticence on the part of both public and pollsters, and a national culture which is much more isolated from the rest of the world – still – than is the case with any other major industrial nation in the late twentieth century.[16]

DIVERSITY

What can be concluded for future US policy, at least in tentative terms, as a result of this broad survey of different factors which appear to influence current foreign policies of the industrial nations? First, leaders in the democratic West must make do with a situation in which there are no large-scale, highly emotive concepts around which to attract public support. Communism versus freedom, Soviet bloc military power versus Nato military power, even the relatively benign and uncontroversial goal of European economic integration, have all been challenged in a world which has not been turned completely upside down, but has been significantly changed as a result of the end of the Cold War. Outside of the realms of the demagogue and the dictator, the world is a complex place to try to describe in terms which are both realistic and appealing to democratic electorates. Consequently, we may well be in for a relatively long period – if we are lucky – of government by management rather than inspiration.

Second, there is simultaneously a demanding requirement for imagination to define and implement policies which will draw upon a number of resources, private as well as public, informally as well as formally. Private enterprise, a cornerstone of the political and social as well as economic culture in the USA, little used in dramatic public terms by politicians, will have a large role to play in the future of international relations. In fact the multinational corporation is playing a very large role now. A US government burdened with a relatively large fiscal deficit has comparatively little freedom for manoeuvre in terms of foreign assistance. The USA, which has declined in relative terms as the international economy has expanded beyond US post-war domination, is in great need of policy partners. The realities of budgetary life at home and economic life abroad make such collaboration absolutely essential.

Therefore – and this may be a very tangible lasting legacy of Reagan's stress on the virtue of the private sector and tolerance of buildup of the federal debt – future American leaders will have to be attentive to the new ways in which US-based, and for that matter other, multinational corporations are operating in the international system. Can and should government encourage private investment in particular countries or regions of the world? Can and should public–private partnerships be arranged to develop policies, for example, which both foster economic development and discourage military weapons proliferation? In responding to such questions, Democratic presidents may have some special advantages over Republicans, just as Republicans historically have been able actively to seek accommodation with the Soviets (Eisenhower, Nixon, Reagan) and open doors to mainland China (Nixon) because they had less fear of being termed 'soft on Communism'.

Private structures, always diverse and influential, are becoming even more essential to effective policy as various public structures become more constrained and restrained. Emphasis on such specifics as foreign investment tax credits, and more broadly on the unavoidable global nature of our economy, might or might not work to combat protectionism, but would surely address the validity of such pressures, which are undeniably important in the context of the American economy. There is clearly a movement toward three great blocs in the international trading field: the European Union, North America, and Japan and China in Asia. Greater public–private collaboration could be one way of reconfirming commitment to internationalism broadly conceived, in the spirit of the years which immediately followed the Second World War, and perhaps limiting the effects of regional protectionism, along lines the American public broadly supports.

In a global marketplace private decisions are essential to the success of public policy. The markets simply have not been ready to accept a single currency in Europe, no matter what the designs of public-sector bureaucrats and visionaries might dictate. At the same time, the relentless drive toward commercial market integration in Europe, and indeed in the Atlantic area generally, continues. In a practical trading sense, in a buying-and-selling sense, in a human migration sense, Europe 1992 has been a major success, however frustrated some European Union officials, advocates and theoreticians in Brussels and elsewhere might be that true supranational political integration still remains elusive.

Co-operation between the two cultures, government and business, is always difficult but there are promising factors today encouraging co-operation. The private sector has the economic resources to make a difference, in a time of relatively heavy debt restrictions on government in the USA. The multinational corporation has proven to be a remarkably durable and increasingly influential factor in a steadily more global, integrated economy. The US government remains a banker of unusually broad capacity. The long tenure of Republicans in the executive branch of government from 1981 to 1993 implies, among other things, that earlier public hostility to business has been waning, with presumably greater opportunities for politicians to be adventurous in co-operation rather than just regulation.

Finally regarding the human dimension of foreign policy, there is a need to analyse and understand the social as well as purely commercial results of such policy initiatives as the North American Free Trade Agreement (NAFTA) and the continuing, if now more cautious, effort to achieve comprehensive integration of the European Union in the 1990s. Effective democratic political leaders on both sides of the Atlantic are challenged to define ways in which NAFTA can encourage environmental and social welfare goals, beyond simple references to the automatic benefits of the free market; ways in which the European Union can be strong at the centre while relatively inclusive of the geographic peripheries of Europe; ways in which a co-ordinated Western Alliance structure can turn from opposing communist military power to furthering human rights and human welfare goals in former communist nations. Each of these efforts has significant public as well as policy impacts.

There is a need to co-ordinate and expand social service and social welfare efforts internationally. Despite setbacks, the United Nations on balance has been revitalized in the wake of the Cold War, but so far the world organization has focused rather explicitly on international peace-keeping exercises. Especially in the light of the growing controversy over involvement in the Balkans, the UN should be encouraged to find more effective roles in the less military aspects of international policy. The same approach could be used in the context of Europe. This emphasis could dovetail with the President Clinton's demonstrated interest in detailed public policy reform which involves, and ideally improves, the social and economic infrastructure at home.

There is a tendency, especially in intellectual circles, though probably less so in America than in Europe, to argue that government–business collaboration is at worst destructive, at best rather simple-minded; yet this perspective arguably is itself increasingly distant from reality. Likewise, the sociological dimension of foreign policy outlined herein may seem awkward or distant from power to observers who are used to the perspectives of traditional diplomacy, which emphasize the outlooks of elites, decisions of diplomats and politicians, and such explicit instruments of influence as trade and military policies. Yet the more 'human' dimensions of policy have already had a profound impact in our own immediate international world. The end of the Eastern bloc, the collapse of the Soviet Union, and the disappearance of Communism as a genuine, influential, at the core consistent ideology in Europe and much of the rest of the world has been a direct result of human action, of a wave of popular resistance, which even well-established police states proved unable to defeat.

Reformers and researchers from time to time produce works, varying widely in quality, which argue that a totally new international system has arrived. The argument in this book is different – I hope. The sociological dimension to international relations has been strongly present and at times highly influential at least since the democratic revolutions in America and Europe in the eighteenth and nineteenth centuries. In the contemporary period, popular and populist sentiments have proven to be especially important, and played the decisive role in bringing down the Soviet empire and thus transforming the map of Europe.

In very practical terms concerning popular opinion, one great advantage for American foreign policy as noted above is the basic support among the American public for the United States to exercise broad leadership on the international front. Save for direct commitment of US military forces to combat overseas, there is generally broad support for an active role in the world. This provides attitude capital, if you will, which must be husbanded, but should also be invested for growth. There is an opportunity for imaginative presidential leadership, without great worry about being restricted by domestic political considerations.

AMERICAN FOREIGN POLICY

With these varied considerations in mind, the principal foreign policy challenges facing President Clinton or any American president in the post-Cold War world can be boiled down to essentials which are briefly stated but exceptionally difficult to implement:

(1) Articulate not necessarily a 'vision' but a set of principles and goals which are understandable and supported by a majority of Americans. In this age of democratic progress around the world, the theme of freedom is easier to develop and defend in comprehensive global terms than at any other period in history. Such efforts seem less utopian now than ever before. At the same time, the end of the Cold War has created a much more uncertain, complex environment which cannot be described through one or even two or three axes of conflict, and is almost impossible to sum up with catch phrases or slogans. This may be beneficial for policy but is challenging for political leadership.

(2) Emphasize structures for foreign policy and international co-operation which are practical and workable, implementing both military and economic policies through the United Nations, which became more central and legitimate under George Bush, despite US financial arrears. This approach is appropriate to a world in which blocs have broken down. As the frustrating US experience in intervention in Somalia demonstrates, however, the UN is no substitute for clear national goals and detailed national policies. An important challenge is evaluation of existing structures which might be strengthened because tasks are growing (for example, should there be a genuine permanent staff structure for the Group of Seven – the G-7?) or downgraded because tasks have faded or disappeared (for example, how can and should Nato best survive when the principal incentive for creating the Alliance, the Cold War and Soviet threat, is over?).

In particular, the current time may be especially promising for partnerships between those two antagonistic cultures, government and business. The private sector has the economic resources to lubricate international relations, governments plan and implement the foreign policies which directly affect the international system of trade and finance. The US government, despite the restrictions imposed by a comparatively heavy fiscal deficit and heavy debt, remains a uniquely capable banker, thanks to the size and scale of assets and influence to guarantee as well as encourage loan and investment activity in virtually any part of the globe.

(3) Seek to involve the popular dimensions in national and international policies. Opinion polls indicating fundamental strong public support for active American involvement in the world do not define policies for leaders, but do provide a solid base of support for policy-makers. The human, populist component of foreign policy can be harnessed in part through emphasis on humanitarian goals, in part through

emphasis on encouraging democracy, in part through further promotion of market capitalism. A US president is on safe ground, for example, in drawing parallels between a nation of diversity and a world of diversity. American leaders, including but going beyond the president, have to be skillful at using the mass media to communicate with foreign as well as domestic publics. This also creates opportunities for imaginative leadership involving direct communication with large publics. Here, Clinton's active interest in appearing on television overseas, in contrast to Reagan's general media caution outside the USA – and, on occasion, the USSR – may prove instructive for various European and Asian democratic politicians.

This is a full foreign policy agenda, which requires leadership which can strike a balance between urgent domestic political demands and long-term international interests. The alternative of focusing on the former and ignoring the latter will be a good way to foster a new international disorder, a new crop of dictators and demagogues in other nations who use mischief and adventure abroad as a means of providing gratification while ignoring their own problems at home. The history of the twentieth century still teaches this basic lesson in a dramatic and bloody way.

In efforts to understand the evolving international system, and especially the balance between Asia and Europe, Germany and Japan are often the focus. This is understandable given the economic and related political influence of these two great powers. Yet such an emphasis can be deceptive. Both are distinctive nations especially because of their histories of aggression in the Second World War. Thanks to history, both are cautious about the use of military forces beyond their borders, though in recent times they have become more willing to engage in intervention of a broadly international variety, for Japan in Cambodia and for Germany in the Balkans. Both major economies have some distinctive problems, in the case of Germany related to high labour costs, the burden of integrating eastern Germany, and a lack of job creation; in the case of Japan, an exceptionally long-term recession exacerbated by a crisis of political authority and effectiveness, and the fundamental ill effects of a heavily protected and institutionally distorted economy. For these reasons, other nations should be selected for possible fresh insights on the future of relations with Asia and Europe. Britain and South Korea are emphasized in this study.

During the height of the Cold War, some commentators tried to draw parallels between the international great power role of the United States in the second half of the twentieth century, and that of Great Britain in the nineteenth century. Modern air power was comparable with traditional sea power, the great economic resources of the British empire were related to the economic dynamism and reach of modern industrial America, and so forth. The most obvious problem with this analogy is that the United States in the Cold War did not hold sway globally, without challenge, in the same way that imperial Britain was able to do following the defeat of Napoleon. The United States' unprecedented economic dominance nevertheless did not lead to the sort of control over vast territories that the British were able to achieve at the height of their empire. Rather, international stability was maintained in part through the nuclear balance of terror, which was in turn a function of the momentous conflict between the two nuclear superpowers, the USA and the USSR.

Now, however, the United States is in a global position which can be compared favourably with that of Great Britain in the earlier age. No other power is on the same level with the United States in terms of exceptional military reach and economic scale. No other power in the world rivals the American capability to project enormous military destructiveness, and therefore political influence, over very long distances. No other power has the philosophical, and practical economic and political, commitments to a range of involvement around the globe. This is not to argue that the USA should become a contemporary 'imperial' nation. In an age of powerful nationalism outside the Atlantic area, and expanding democracy around the world, there is virtually no likelihood of demonstrating the sort of imperial role perfected by the British. Even if Americans wished to operate in this manner, arguably alien to their culture, the nature of modern international relations would frustrate them. Rather, the point is that we have to come to grips, in the details of our policy, with the diversity of the contemporary international system, combining prudence with commitment, restraint with assertiveness, and basic principles of freedom and stability with a sense of realism in how we pursue those goals in the world. We are not an imperial nation, but we cannot avoid an especially powerful role. A variety of British-style balance between engagement and fatalism is a very helpful approach to the pursuit of a more stable and more democratic world.

In the case of South Korea, spectacular economic growth and success in increasing *per capita* income in the years since the devastation of the Korean War of 1950–3 have been combined with a transition from dictatorship to political democracy that so far has been successful. Britain dominated a Europe-centred international system in the nineteeth century that was basically stable, co-operative and in many respects benign. South Korea is a notable representative of political as well as economic success in an Asia region which increasingly is the centre of gravity in the world's economic activity.

IMPLICATIONS FOR THE USA

The United States remains the world's largest economy, and an unrivalled strategic global military power, yet in relative terms its economic power is declining and in any case its international political influence is invariably limited. The USA accounted for fully half the total gross product of the industrial world during the period immediately after the Second World War; admittedly this was an unusual, indeed unique, time, but nevertheless it became a psychological reference point in the future. The relative decline of the USA in economic terms, combined with reluctance and limits concerning the use of military force, means that imagination must be employed if its foreign policy is to have maximum influence on other nations and be truly effective in encouraging stability in the world. We cannot avoid great influence; even if we abdicate world leadership, that will constitute a policy choice with broad repercussions.

A principal argument developed through the course of this volume is that partnerships, not unilateralism, are the keys to future international success for the United States, along with encouraging regional powers with which it is especially congenial. Such partnerships should be constructed in various ways, employing different dimensions, not just bilateral or multilateral in the realm of nation-states; combinations of both sorts of relationship should be encouraged, built and maintained. American leadership should also be employed in encouraging other nations to follow examples of foreign policy styles past and present which seem effective, benign and beneficial for the international system. Here the examples of Britain and South Korea are especially germane. Britain's past practices are instructive for contemporary great powers and aspiring influential powers. South Korea's current practices are instructive for third world nations aspiring to economic and political development.

Partnerships must transcend the government realm, however, and include new relationships between the public and private sectors. The multinational corporation remains a durable, indeed expanding, international institution, less directly associated than in earlier decades with American leadership and American capital, for that very reason extremely important for the future of international economic relations. The USA should be much more actively pursuing relationships in which the security guarantee capabilities of the government are wedded to the investment and production capabilities of international business. The business of America is hardly only business; yet the gap between the two cultures, public and private, could be reduced to the benefit of both. Along with defence and economic issues, the right combinations of partners can and should be addressing social policy and social services questions of the sort that are always high on the domestic agenda and will become increasingly international as processes of migration and economic integration continue to expand.

This leads into the final, most fundamental theme of the analysis which follows. In myriad ways, domestic and international concerns are becoming intertwined and entangled. Diplomacy in a democracy is never comfortably the preserve of a traditional, removed social and educational elite. Such characteristics of the American foreign service, for example, have made that institution a ready domestic political target over the years, and not only for ambitious demagogues. The changing character of international relations provides an urgency and high importance to the task, always present in more implicit form, of finding the right combinations of foreign and domestic policy concerns. Addressing this theme will not provide a complete conceptual framework for American foreign policy after the Cold War, but will help partly to respond to the question of the most appropriate and effective role for the United States in moving into the twenty-first century.

2 A Reagan Revolution?

A REAGAN STYLE 'REVOLUTION'

President Ronald Reagan and partisans of his administration often talked, with enthusiasm and sincerity, of a Reagan 'Revolution' in American politics. There can be no doubt that he had a profound personal impact on the electorate, and a lasting, very significant influence on the federal government as well, especially regarding fiscal policy during his first term, and foreign policy during his second. In retrospect, he was particularly effective in solidifying and confirming the gains of a conservative movement which had been growing in political strength and public appeal since the early 1960s. The campaign of Republican presidential nominee Barry Goldwater in 1964 ended disastrously for the candidate and for the Republican political right which supported him, in a landslide for President Lyndon Johnson and the Democrats. The experience seemed to many, including liberal media observers, a quixotic and eccentric throwback to a dead conservatism of the past, one which had been overwhelmed at the polls with a reconfirmation of public support for the New Deal legacy of 'affirmative', ambitious government. The enormous LBJ victory was followed by passage through Congress of a huge range of new federal programmes, with expansion of the number of government departments dealing with social services matters.[1]

With hindsight, clearly the campaign, which gave Ronald Reagan genuine national prominence in political terms, a professional dimension different from though also related to his background as a Hollywood actor, was not a fundamental defeat for conservativism but rather the initial stages of a groundswell. By early 1969, the Republicans, albeit of the more moderate Nixon variety, were in the White House. The executive branch remained in Republican control for the next twenty-four years, save only for President Jimmy Carter's single term in office. The undeniably conservative Reagan and associates won a sweeping presidential victory in 1980, capturing control of the Senate along with the White House. Steady Republican Congressional gains, and sometime control of the Senate, was followed by majorities in both houses of the Congress in 1994. Both Carter and President Bill Clinton qualify as comparatively conservative Democrats, neither associated with FDR–Truman–LBJ style expansive government. Moreover, the Clinton health policy proposal, the only significant example of old-style Democratic social policy initiatives in either administration, was stymied almost from the beginning. Goldwater should feel a strong sense of personal satisfaction and vindication in representing the vanguard of change in American politics, a very appropriate state of mind for a senior political figure – or anyone.

The significance of this Republican resurgence is a good deal more clear in the domestic affairs field than in foreign policy. In an earlier era, the Republican Party was more isolationist than the Democratic Party, but that has not been the case for more than forty years, and policy differences are much more visible on domestic than on international matters. The 1952 competition between Dwight Eisenhower and Robert Taft for the Republican presidential nomination brought a decisive victory for not only Eisenhower but also the internationalist wing of the party. Arguably in recent years the Democratic Party has been more the home of isolationism, beginning with the alienation of intellectuals and others as a result of internationalist commitment leading to the Vietnam War, and more recently encompassing those in the labour movement and elsewhere who tend to equate 'free trade' with undercutting the position and long-term gains of the American worker.

That is an important but perhaps still debatable proposition; less debatable is the argument that the resurgence of the far right in the Republican Party may have brought greater commitment to unilateralism in international affairs but so far no victory for isolationism. Presidents Eisenhower, Nixon and Ford all pursued arms control agreements with the Soviets, as indeed did Reagan after his initial emphasis on a purely rigid, pro-defence spending, hard line toward the 'evil empire'. The Committee on the Present Danger, and related conservative individuals and centres of policy agitation, no doubt provided some underpinning to the new hard line in Washington. However, there was no foreign policy revolution comparable to what happened on the domestic front with the 'supply side' emphasis on tax cuts, and the elusive goal of using greater economic growth to shrink budget deficits, which came to fascinate many conservatives and rationalized the budget deficits that grew as their party controlled the executive branch throughout the 1980s.[2]

Ronald Reagan deserves to be remembered as the first President since Eisenhower to complete two terms in office, a major accomplishment, and like that predecessor he was exceptionally adept at public relations, evidenced by the capacity to accomplish relatively long tenure in the White House with strong public support intact. President Reagan's completion of his terms with broad popularity provided a sense of continuity, and perhaps renewed legitimacy, after two decades of social and political instability and turmoil. His generally high approval ratings in polls over the years, reflecting perhaps the greatest ability to communicate persuasively with the people on a continuing basis since Franklin Roosevelt, all contributed to his influence while in office and the acceptance by the general public of his policy initiatives. Much criticized, at times ridiculed, by political opponents for inattention to detail and a relaxed work schedule, President Reagan nevertheless established strong credentials as an effective, indeed the dominant, player in the most important, and arguably most difficult, political role in the American system.

Often dismissed by sophisticated observers – as well as unsophisticated observers, and by professional politicians themselves, Reagan was for that very reason given an opening to gain political advantage. He won smashing electoral victories, including the ultimate prize of the White House, through the capacity to marry his considerable skills at public relations with the tactical advantage of surprise. His massive 1980 presidential victory provided an opportunity to solidify and confirm the gains of the conservative movement which had been growing in political strength and public appeal since the early 1960s. Reagan in fact had been a prominent and successful television spokesman for the Barry Goldwater campaign of 1964, by so doing helping to launch his own political career. In 1980, as in his first race for Governor of California in 1966, he was assisted by a desire on the part of important Democratic Party leaders to have him get his own party's nomination, in the mistaken assumption that he would be easy to defeat. Influential Carter supporters in 1980 hoped their man would run against Reagan; Democratic Governor Pat Brown in California made the same mistake in 1966, and was buried in an electoral landslide similar to Carter's defeat fourteen years later.[3]

When Ronald Reagan finished his second term in the White House, opinion polls showed clearly that Americans felt stronger, more confident, more capable in the world than had been the case eight years before. He had in this dimension a reverse impact from that of his predecessor Jimmy Carter. That previous president, exceptionally hard working and knowledgeable about the details of policy, was notably unsuccessful in communicating assurance or broad direction to the public, precisely the capabilities Reagan was able to demonstrate in office. Reagan's ability to build confidence as well as popularity justifies parallels between his impact and that of Franklin Roosevelt.

Reagan, confirming the proposition that perceptions and image are crucial to political success, at least in the short term, within his administration was arguably considerably less active than Eisenhower, yet the public did not seem to focus on this fact. President Eisenhower, himself extremely effective at maintaining public support, with a leadership style that communicated a sense of reassuring competence, confronted in the later years of his administration a sentiment among informed observers, not all of them Democrats or representatives of the largely critical academic community, that he was not vigorous or aggressive enough in confronting a Soviet Union and related international communist movement that were seen as on the offensive in global terms. Eisenhower toward the end of his tenure was beleaguered by the same intense Cold War that had provided the fundamental challenge to foreign policy, and certainly domestic tranquillity, at the start of his administration. Reagan's tenure was capped by the dramatic reforms of Mikhail Gorbachev in the Soviet Union, moving the nation away from Communism and the Cold War, by so doing opening the door to a vast international transformation and an enormous American foreign policy success.

PATTERNS OF CONTINUITY

In foreign policy, the Reagan administration represented a very great departure stylistically and substantively from the Carter years, but more broadly there was ultimately considerable continuity with the past. There has probably always been more continuity than change to American foreign policy, at least since the period just after the Second World War and the emergence of the new postwar international consensus. The Eisenhower administration came into power in 1953 on a tide of ferociously emotional anti-communism, fed by the insecurity of a people still recovering from world war suddenly saddled with a frustrating and seemingly endless conflict with the Soviet Union, as well as 'international communism' at a more abstract level. Yet that administration in practice, while rightly credited with some notable departures in foreign policy, including a different sort of emphasis or set of emphases in defence, as well as ending the frustrating Korean War, basically confirmed the outlines of containment as a guiding doctrine that had been firmly put in place by the Truman administration.[4]

Likewise, representatives of the Kennedy administration pridefully underscored, especially in communicating with the intellectual and journalistic communities, the differences between their approach and that of the Eisenhower administration. Anti-communism remained the motif of the American foreign policy establishment, the main challenge balancing restraint and credibility of forces, the main approach deterrence. If Kennedy foreign policy officials were more interventionist than their predecessors, that was also broadly continuous with a more assertive foreign policy, in levels of defence spending and engagement of force overseas, that had already been reflected in the last phase of the Eisenhower presidency.[5]

Reagan had a very powerful influence on US foreign policy, and also arguably on the international system more generally, not always in positive or beneficial directions, yet his administration also was burdened with a series of specific frustrations and failures. These included early in the administration, for example, an inability to transform hostility to the Soviet Union, publicly described as an 'evil empire', into practical support for an important dissident movement in Poland. Declared hostility – some would argue belligerence – toward the other side translated in implementation ultimately into the costly tragedy of the American military intervention in Lebanon, and the consequent large loss of life when a US Marine barracks was demolished by a suicide bomber. United States' intervention followed explicit successful encouragement of Israel to invade Lebanon. The inability of the administration, despite strenuous clandestine efforts, to bring down the Sandinista regime in Nicaragua, and the bizarre trading of arms for hostages in the Middle East, must also be counted on the debit side of the foreign policy ledger.

Yet in spite of all this, the President also enjoyed successes, including especially major arms agreements with the Soviets. Arguably relations with Western Europe, Japan and China were no worse when he left office than they had been at his inauguration, despite a whole series of policy and stylistic frictions. In some ways, especially in personal relations at the top, the atmosphere among the allies seemed to improve. Indeed Reagan, however derided by some, including Europeans in politics as well as the media, managed to develop extremely good personal rapport with British Prime Minister Margaret Thatcher, German Chancellor Helmut Kohl and, ultimately, Soviet President Mikhail Gorbachev. Probably more important than the fate of specific policies was the perception of consistency to Reagan's overall foreign policy. Whatever his shortcomings, he had the general qualities of decisiveness and ability to inspire loyalty and confidence that are essential to successful political leadership at the most senior level. Especially after the vexatious conflicts and policy shifts that characterized the Carter years, within Washington and among close allies overseas, this change in tone and overall direction was refreshing as well as effective.[6]

The enervating, seemingly endless Iran hostage crisis of Carter's final months in office, entangling a President who psychologically could not let go of the issue, stood in marked contrast with the sense of strength and confidence that developed during the Reagan years. The Carter years, which included intense personal friction between the President and German Chancellor Helmut Schmidt, and policy reversals on such matters as missile deployment in Europe, were succeeded by an environment in which policy differences continued to exist but were not compounded by changes in direction in Washington or serious personality conflicts.[7]

Broadly in line with the continuity of post-Second World War American approaches to international relations, the Reagan administration did represent something of a break with the past, but this was very partial in terms of specific policies, much more basic in terms of the style and tone of government as defined by the leader. There was much more dramatic priority given to national defence, a renewed emphasis on the dangers represented by communism in general and the Soviet Union in particular, and an attenuation of co-operation with multilateral institutions. The administration seemed in many ways a throwback to a harsher, more confrontational state of mind characteristic of the height of the Cold War rather than the more recent years of *détente*. Reagan, like Kennedy in the early 1960s, was notable for drastically increasing defence spending. This very comparison, however, makes the point that Reagan did not represent a total departure from the past in foreign policy.

If Reagan was in some ways comparable to JFK in emphasis on expanded defence, and a broadly assertive anti-communist foreign policy, he was very different from the earlier president in terms of his attitude toward government. The Kennedy years had been a high point of commitment to 'public service' as a worthy ideal. Emanating from the New Deal, but also the earlier Republican Roosevelt, Theodore, who consistently emphasized the role of government as positive good, the Kennedy administration seems in retrospect a sort of symbolic high water mark for favourable leadership and popular sentiment about public service. The cynicism of more recent times has been very much in tune with conservative denigration of public sector activities in general and government employees in particular. Reagan returned more than once to the theme that individuals appointed to posts in his administration would have to have worked for a living in significant jobs in the non-government sector; government service was seen as a step down, not a step up.[8]

Yet beyond the specific similarities and contrasts with earlier administrations, an important point to reiterate, given the strength of contrary impressions, is that the Reagan administration involved no basic break in the continuity of US foreign policy in the Cold War. There was the overall shift, discussed earlier, toward domestic over foreign policy, and an intellectual shift as well toward the rhetoric of the right. Foreign policy itself, however, ultimately was continuous with the past. Anti-communism was fiercely expressed at the start of his regime, which appeared to be a return to the harsh tension of the early and mid-Cold War, and a departure from the years of *détente* and arms negotiation under Nixon, Ford and Carter. But by the end of Reagan's White House tenure emphasis was being given to arms control accords, and major agreements were reached as well, along with important personal rapport between the American and Soviet Presidents. This remarkable changing, shifting series of events in US foreign policy and relations with the USA's principal adversaries and allies began with the presidential campaign of 1980.

THE RACE FOR THE WHITE HOUSE

Ronald Reagan may have made political campaigning look easy, and governing easy as well, finding positive humour rather than negative insecurity in gibes from opponents and the press that he was insufficiently hard working, indifferent to detail, too disengaged from the practical demands of his office. To be sure, from time to time the President would demonstrate a startling lack of information – for instance, in his ignorance of names of individuals visiting him, a lapse which is extremely unusual in a leading American politician. He did not pretend to extensive substantive learning. In 1986, he tried to make a virtue of this gap through the proposal at the Reykjavik summit meeting with Mikhail Gorbachev to abolish 'all' nuclear weapons, without waiting for staff support to develop or considering the significant complications that could result, including the roles and suddenly enormous influence of such third parties as Britain and France – and China. Unburdened by the conceptual and policy baggage of the arms control and defence communities, he could try to make dramatic policy leaps. Rather than any technical expertise, an instinctive rapport with a solid majority of the voting public, and a related grasp of the imagery and psychology of issues of consequence to that population, were sufficient to bring him two smashing electoral victories, and a position of steady dominance of the political landscape for two presidential terms.

His 1980 presidential election victory, however, was by no means guaranteed, and despite the familiarity of his face and voice from two terms as California governor from 1967 to 1975, to say nothing of his long tenure as Hollywood actor, commercial pitchman and sports announcer, he was not initially seen by most Americans as a natural political leader. Several factors helped him to hurdle the barrier of prejudice against someone whose experience seemed still to be heavily related to the 'lightweight' entertainment world, despite eight years as the chief executive of the largest state in the union. First were his instinctive gifts of political timbre and timing, more in evidence as candidate than governing leader, but for that very reason significant to electoral success. Reagan knew what people wanted to hear.

Second, what they wanted to hear was congruent with his conservative approach, and no politician packaged the message of less government, less 'welfare', a stronger defence and other conservative benchmarks more effectively. The country was moving steadily to the right, a course begun in the late 1960s with the strong public reaction to urban riots, campus unrest, and crime, aided by frustration over the Vietnam War, fuelled later by growing long-term resentment of affirmative action programmes. Reagan addressed this unhappiness more dramatically, and in a more persuasive tone, than any other candidate. Criticism of Reagan for sacrificing 'substance' to 'style' is highly unfair, for he used his unusually effective gifts at communication over television to promote a consistent policy line in which he strongly believed. Opinion surveys in the 1980 presidential campaign are clear in giving Ronald Reagan high marks for sincerity, consistency and clarity in communicating an understandable, effective political message. This rating stood in stark contrast to George Bush, who was perceived in ambiguous or cynical terms as a political leader who did not have a consistent message.[9]

Third, though Carter's defeat was by no means guaranteed, his vulnerability was apparent, both abroad and at home, and Reagan was extremely skillful at exploiting the general portrait of weakness associated with the Democratic incumbent. The long-term, enervating Iran hostage crisis had become a personal fixation with Carter, a demon he kept holding aloft, in full public view. The situation played out longer than might have been the case had Carter been able to distance himself emotionally and the events clearly benefited Reagan's campaign. The broader sense of international weakness in the world also helped the Republican cause. Finally, the economic recession at the time played to the Reagan camp as well.

In the campaign itself, Reagan was probably most effective in asking people rhetorically whether they felt better off or worse off compared with four years earlier. He also used the continuing controversy over the SALT II arms control treaty to weaken Carter, though on foreign policy he was understandably more cautious than on domestic matters. The fact that this important strategic arms control agreement, which Carter himself had made a very high personal as well as policy priority, had been caught up in fatal political controversy, provided enormously effective political ammunition for Reagan in the presidential debate devoted to foreign policy. Just as in discussing the economy the Republican candidate was able to ask people if they really felt 'better' or 'worse' than had been the case four years earlier, so in evaluating international relations before the cameras he was able to home in on the Carter image of weakness and ineffectiveness that had dogged the President throughout his term, especially though by no means exclusively after the inception of the Iran hostage crisis.[10]

President Reagan in office immediately began a campaign of rhetorical hostility to the Soviet Union which was dramatic, extreme and certainly successful in alarming public opinion. He described the Soviet Union and satellite states as an 'evil empire' and made his hostility to the other superpower, and Communist ideology, very explicit. His rhetoric was reminiscent of other American political leaders, but generally not of other presidents of the United States. Richard Nixon had been a ferocious anti-communist, at home and abroad, during his years as Congressman, Senator and Vice President, but he became considerably more restrained after inauguration as President in early 1969. Secretary of State John Foster Dulles was inclined to view the world of international relations as a contest between good and evil, but he was not the President, and his commander-in-chief Eisenhower assumed a rhetorical stance that was both more removed and more restrained.

Opinion polls showed that Americans during the course of 1981 and 1982 became increasingly concerned about the dangers of war, and more specifically nuclear war. When asked spontaneously to cite their most serious concerns in thinking about the world, notable numbers of Americans mentioned the danger of war. The public anxiety on this important matter became more intense, and fuelled the nuclear freeze and related anti-nuclear weapons agitation that was already part of the political debate during the closing phases of the Carter administration. So pronounced did this concern become that President Reagan came under increasing pressure to tone down his rhetoric; there was clear indication that he was responding to this pressure by the second year of his administration.[11]

Interestingly, the Caribbean played a significant role in terms of Reagan's specific foreign policy statements during the campaign, somewhat reminiscent of the intense debate over what to do about Fidel Castro and Cuba that gripped John F. Kennedy and Richard Nixon in the 1960 race. Kennedy outflanked Nixon to the right by advocating a hard line toward Cuba and a much more aggressive policy than was apparently being pursued, according to public information. There is still uncertainty about just how much candidate Kennedy knew about the Cuban invasion then being planned by the Eisenhower administration. Nixon may have been disingenuous in stating that responsibility forbade him from talking as tough on the issue as Kennedy. More likely he calculated, erroneously in retrospect, that a harsh line would backfire as he cast himself as the reassuring, restrained heir to the exceptionally popular Eisenhower. Reagan made one major foreign policy speech in the 1980 campaign, at the Chicago Council on Foreign Relations. At that time, he focused on the Caribbean in general, Cuba in more specific terms, and Grenada in most specific terms. In retrospect, given that the USA invaded that small island after Reagan's inauguration, this president was certainly characterized by consistency in concern and advocacy.[12]

President Reagan's foreign policy rhetoric, however, while extreme, did not indicate that foreign policy was becoming a relative priority for the administration. Jimmy Carter suffered from the problem that there seemed to be no priorities to his administration. By contrast, Reagan clearly had a few well-defined goals, the balance of which tilted in favour of domestic concerns and priorities. Carter was ambitious to make a substantial policy difference in Washington, fascinated by the details of policy, and apparently challenged by applying his considerable intelligence to the solution of a myriad of public policy priorities. Energy conservation, environmental improvement, transportation deregulation, arms control, international economic stability – all these goals and more received presidential attention, with no clear sense either within the administration or in public pronouncements that there was going to be a set of a few priorities over all others. The administration was frustrated further by the fact that circumstance and fate imposed one very significant foreign policy priority during the last year of Carter's tenure – the American hostages taken in the US embassy in Tehran, Iran, and the long, seemingly endless, tortured, tormented efforts to obtain their freedom. The release of the hostages came at literally the end of the Carter administration, as Ronald Reagan was being inaugurated, providing the outgoing President perhaps some personal satisfaction but no political benefit.

Stylistically and substantively, the Reagan administration provided a dramatic contrast to the predecessor regime. The President would rightly never be accused of focusing too heavily on the details of policy, yet even critics of the new conservative regime had to concede that there was a sense of priorities and relative urgency among issues. Of these, the most substantial was trying to reduce the expansion of federal spending. The Reagan administration is rightly credited with significantly increasing the federal deficit and total federal debt, as a result of tax cuts that went deeper than any spending cuts. The question remains open concerning whether or not Reagan and associates sought both spending and tax cuts and were only successful with the latter or, the less straightforward explanation, the administration was realistic, indeed cynical, enough to understand that cutting spending directly was virtually impossible in the interest-group dominated atmosphere of Washington. In the latter scenario, they concluded that the best to be hoped for was jacking up the deficit in order to put a significant drag on established programmes and stifle new spending proposals before they got off the ground. Lack of resources for federal spending initiatives, thanks to the load of debt that was a fact of life by the end of the Reagan administration, remains a very significant conservative legacy.

MILITARY PRIORITY

Reagan while in office had basically two foreign policy goals. First, he wanted to return initiative to the USA in the Cold War competition with the Soviet Union and with communist regimes more generally. Second, and closely related, he wanted to strengthen the defence position of the nation. The two goals were not only associated in direction but mutually reinforcing. A stronger America in sheer defence capability would have greater policy leverage *vis-à-vis* the Soviet Union. The perception of more assertiveness of a successful sort in turn would justify the greater defence spending.

The Reagan administration moved quickly to expand US defence spending. Analysis therefore is altogether fitting in giving early emphasis to this primary dimension of traditional measures of world power. Any full evaluation of the administration must be done in terms of the degree to which this defence and security emphasis made sense, and the effectiveness of the Reagan people in addressing this priority goal. The defence budget moved up as a share of the federal budget and approached about 7.5 per cent of gross national product by the third fiscal year of the administration, compared with 6.2 per cent during Reagan's first year in office. In contrast to the Kennedy administration, the Reagan people seemed to support defence spending across the board. There was especially strong emphasis on the Strategic Defense Initiative (SDI) anti-missile programme, new strategic systems, and expanded conventional military capabilities. There was even support for the special forces of the US Army, an unconventional arm strongly favoured by the Kennedy administration but shunned by the earlier Republican Eisenhower regime. Reagan in his memoirs leaves no doubt concerning the priority he attached to defence spending, even though the approach is couched in the imagery of responding to the concerns of others that he – and many politicians – have used to beneficial effect. 'Pentagon leaders told me appalling stories of how the Soviets were gaining on us militarily, both in nuclear and conventional forces; they were spending more than fifty percent more each year on weapons than we were . . .'. He adds, theatrically, that some military people were on welfare because of low pay, and others would shed their uniforms as soon as they left post and put on civilian clothes. 'I told the Joint Chiefs of Staff that I wanted to do whatever it took to make our men and women proud to wear their uniforms again. . . .'[13]

STAR WARS POWER

A particularly noteworthy priority of the administration was the Strategic Defense Initiative – Star Wars. This was by all accounts a personal interest, indeed fascination, of President Reagan. Ultimately the goal of a range of exotic, new technology weapons was unsuccessful and abandoned. Yet for virtually all of the Reagan administration this remained a major emphasis of the defence effort. In pursuing this initiative, the doctrine of 'mutual assured destruction', which had been a cornerstone of American defence strategy since the 1960s, was at a minimum undermined. The rationale of nuclear force profiles was to maintain the ability to destroy the society of the other side in a general nuclear exchange, while avoiding efforts to make missile forces themselves more secure. Arguably a programme of missile defence, at least one involving cities rather than just retaliatory missile forces, would appear to be preparation for an attack, a first strike, on the opposing power, and therefore destabilizing.

An important source of support for the Reagan candidacy as well as administration was the Committee on the Present Danger, a conservative group established by those who explicitly rejected the conventional wisdom in arms policies. The Committee contained Democrats who had been active in the strategic studies community and had come to believe that the wrong approaches and goals were being pursued. They rejected the prevailing conceptual wisdom of mutual assured destruction as too abstract and intellectualized an approach to strategy. They also generally rejected notions of nuclear 'sufficiency' in favour of driving for actual strategic superiority over the other side. A clear and decisive move away from what had been accepted conventional wisdom in strategic matters was one of the most important foreign policy departures of the Reagan administration.

The charisma of the President was fully effective in the promotion of this foreign policy initiative. His own personal 'vision' was clearly of primary importance in moving his administration in the direction of SDI. The vocal opposition of the Committee on the Present Danger to traditional arms control was one thing – a debate carried out and circumscribed very strongly in the parameters of traditional defence conceptions. Star

Wars was something else entirely, a radical departure from the foreign policy status quo driven by a popular, committed President who had been emotionally captured by this highly complex, utopian and drastically expensive weapons system. No longer were the established ballistic missile technologies to be emphasized. There was also an abandonment of the conceptions which had dominated the nuclear strategy of the United States since the McNamara years.

The administration was driven by a new vision of military strategy in which Hollywood imagery rather than known applied science was entirely appropriate as descriptive metaphor. 'Star Wars' emphasized defensive systems over nearly exclusive reliance on offensive missile capabilities. The latter approach had been defended as more stabilizing to the nuclear military competition of the superpowers. The new strategy also relied upon a variety of extremely exotic advanced technologies distinctive from ballistic missile characteristics. Only the star quality and popularity of this particular President drove the programme through the executive branch as well as the Congress to achieve notable research and development funds, if not actual deployment. A less popular, less effective leader in terms of public support would have had to answer much harsher questions concerning the adequacy of his military/strategic clothes.[14]

Reagan also made the decision, more symbolic than tangible but with great political impact, to go beyond ceilings in the number of launchers established by the SALT II treaty. Almost immediately upon completion of negotiations during the Carter administration, the treaty had come under intense criticism from conservatives, and in particular from disaffected members of the strategic defence communities who were active in the Committee on the Present Danger. The agreement, never ratified in Congress, symbolized the weak political position of President Carter, who suffered energetic attacks on an arms accord he clearly valued very highly. During the 1980 presidential campaign, Reagan described the understanding as 'fatally flawed'.

On 27 May 1985 President Reagan formally announced that the United States would no longer abide by the terms of SALT II. At the same time, the President decided to dismantle two ageing submarines, thereby keeping the national nuclear arsenal within the limits of the treaty for the time being. Nevertheless, there was a fierce reaction from Congress and also Nato allies. Secretary of State George Shultz implies in his memoirs, *Turmoil and Triumph – My Years as Secretary of State*, that this was related to the more general perception of the administration as aggressive on the military front: 'the feeling of confrontation created unease'. He also states that the harsh reaction was generally not foreseen:

I expected the uproar from our Nato allies (including Margaret Thatcher) and Congress, not to mention the Soviets. But I am not sure the president and [Defense Secretary Caspar] Weinberger were prepared for the magnitude of what hit them. I defended the decision, I felt, more effectively than its advocates.[15]

The Reagan administration combined an enormous military buildup with considerable caution in the actual use of force, but did take action to secure the island of Grenada, which as indicated had received specific attention from the candidate during the 1980 campaign. Stressing alleged dangers faced by American students on the island, and clearly mindful of the presence of a Cuban military force, the administration carried out a low-cost successful invasion and occupation in 1983. There was considerable negative reaction to the invasion from partisan Democratic political circles, and to some extent more widely, within the USA. The island hardly seemed a major threat to the national security, and given that state of affairs, why invade? However, Cuba still had a special irritating resonance in American political discussion and debate, and there could be no doubt that the regime was allied with Castro and could be used as a means, however modest, for furthering the goals of the Cuban revolution.[16]

TENSIONS WITH EUROPE

US–European relations, which increasingly had been characterized by the intense feud between President Jimmy Carter and German Chancellor Helmut Schmidt, were immediately relieved of this sort of interpersonal frictions, but other policy problems arose. One of the earliest and most serious was controversy over a projected European energy project. The Reagan administration reacted particularly strongly to a plan to build a natural gas pipeline from the Low Countries to the Soviet Union. That, plus the more comprehensive anti-communism of the new administration, seemed to put distance between the USA and Europe. In the context of what became a major controversy over the pipeline plan, Secretary of State Alexander Haig made a very positive contribution. Ironically in light of his ultimate fate, he provided a foundation of urging prudent caution which was very useful to his moderate, less confrontational successor, George Shultz. Western European nations, led by France and Germany, had been spurred by the oil producer nations' embargo and energy crisis which began in 1973 to seek alternative sources of fuel. This resulted in a highly ambitious venture in which the Soviets agreed to sell 1.37 trillion cubic feet of gas annually for twenty-five years. The price was attractive to the Soviets, and Europeans agreed to pay the costs of pipeline construction. Conservatives in the Reagan administration were alarmed that the arrangement would lead to excessive dependency on the Soviet Union for a basic resource, while supporting the headquarters of the evil empire. The crisis ultimately was defused by Shultz through linking greater flexibility on the pipeline to renewed commitment to the Co-ordinating Committee for Multilateral Export Controls (COCOM), the multinational agency set up to regulate goods of potential military value to the Soviet Union and other communist nations.[17]

The rise to the top as Secretary of State, and consequent rapid fall, of Alexander Haig in the Reagan administration meant that personalities overshadowed policy in the first months, and the latter seemed inextricably tied to the former. Very early in the regime, the new Secretary of State was on the cover of *Time* magazine, resplendent in the trappings of office, looking surely baronial, possibly imperial, in demeanour. When Reagan was shot in an assassination attempt in his first months in office, Haig was before the cameras even before all the facts were in, stating that he was 'in charge' in a tone of tension that could only be the reverse of reassuring.

Al Haig was also a rather belligerent Secretary of State, a man metaphorically still in uniform, viewing the Soviet Union with the wariness of the warrior rather than the insight of the senior diplomat. Knowledgeable and as a result relatively insightful concerning allies, he was unyielding in his hard line toward opponents. He writes early in his memoirs, *Caveat*, that

> Statesmen and others often speak of preventing World War III. One might instead suggest that World War III may actually have begun on that winter day in 1948 when Jan Masaryk was defenestrated in Prague, and that it has been going on ever since in a ceaseless testing of wills and exchange of blood . . .

That combative style was carried directly into the top job in the State Department, reflected in interpersonal dealings, and proved rather quickly to be his undoing. In great contrast to General George Marshall, a military predecessor as Secretary of State, or for that matter Dwight Eisenhower, Haig never really overcame a state of mind involving the most combative instincts of the professional soldier.[18]

Reagan had a reputation for informality and to some extent modesty, at least compared with conventional Washington-style politicians. Yet no president of the United States welcomes being upstaged by subordinates. Haig's penchant for the limelight, combined with a series of explosive confrontations with others in the administration, meant that from the start of his tenure as Secretary of State his days were numbered. He clashed repeatedly with others at the top of the administration, without the basis of long-standing personal rapport with Reagan that his rivals, such as Defense Secretary Caspar Weinberger and White House counsel Ed Meese, brought to the fray. Eventually, one of his relatively frequent threats to resign was accepted. The coalition of very senior White House staff members who combined against him – James Baker and Michael Deaver along with Meese – proved far too powerful in terms of overall influence and, especially, personal rapport with the President for Haig to prevail.[19]

Yet the Secretary in his brief tenure did have considerable influence on policy, with both positive and negative consequences. The gas pipeline imbroglio is only one example among a variety. The Israeli military strike in Lebanon in 1982 was without doubt encouraged by a major foreign policy address Haig delivered in Chicago. The extraordinary long-distance shuttle he undertook between London and Buenos Aires, in an effort to stave off war over the Argentine invasion of the Falkland Islands, was unsuccessful in policy terms and did nothing to encourage a reputation for calmness or stability. However, the Secretary also brought experience and sophistication to policy circles that was helpful, especially to a President in a new administration which really was in a fundamental sense heavily weighted toward Washington 'outsiders'. Concerning Europe, the administration very early lifted the grain embargo of the Soviet Union, despite Haig's efforts to maintain the policy given Moscow's threats against the incipient democratic movement in Poland. He is on strong ground in arguing that the very abrupt change in course, so early in the new administration – and, he might have added, a hard-line administration at that – sent the wrong signals to the Soviets, giving them openings unforeseen at the time to press for new economic advantages.[20]

MIDDLE EAST ADVENTURE AND DISASTER

This was followed by a more substantial military adventure in the Middle East. The administration, following very extensive internal debate, decided to send a force of United States Marines on the ground in Lebanon as a peace-keeping measure. The adventure ended in disaster in October 1983 when 241 Marines were killed by a truck bomb driven into the barracks where they were quartered. The heavy loss of life and retreat from the region seemed to belie efforts of some in the Reagan administration to provide an image of being tougher or more forceful than predecessors in international affairs.

One additional consequence of the disaster was to continue to fuel the growing conflict between Secretary of State George Shultz and Secretary of Defense Caspar Weinberger. The conflict, which apparently dated from the years both served as senior executives in the Bechtel Corporation, and perhaps earlier, from their service in the Nixon administration, became one important source of cleavage on foreign policy matters. Just as the conflict between National Security Adviser Henry Kissinger and Secretary of State William Rogers in the Nixon administration, and between National Security Adviser Zbigniew Brzezinski and Secretary of State Cyrus Vance in the Carter administration, had been a source of frustration and discord in these earlier periods, so the conflict between Shultz and Weinberger provided at times distracting dissonance in the Reagan administration.

In this case, the style of a President who remained generally aloof from the daily policy battles in the administration served to reinforce the conflict. Some have argued that President Reagan consciously modelled his presidential style on that of Dwight Eisenhower. Overtly genial, collegial, with a stance above the fray, Reagan did provide an echo of the former President. However, where Eisenhower, as we have become increasingly aware, was a president who actually intervened quite actively in the day-to-day problems and challenges of his administration, Reagan appears to have been genuinely disengaged from detail, however consistent in pursuit of the most central and fundamental policy goals of his administration. Hence the Shultz–Weinberger feud, reminiscent of others in recent times in Washington, but in great contrast to the much stricter discipline Eisenhower imposed on his own team, became an important source of policy division and interpersonal dissonance in the administration.

The two senior advisers were stylistically and temperamentally quite different. Shultz, by nature conciliatory, contrasted with the more obviously aggressive, and at times combative, Weinberger. At the same time, Weinberger, perhaps reflecting the institutional perspectives and interests of the military after the Vietnam experience, remained much more reluctant to commit force overseas. Shultz tended to be more willing to undertake such missions. Reportedly the disaster experienced by the Marines in Lebanon was especially difficult for Shultz, himself a combat veteran of the Pacific theatre in the Second World War. Both men demonstrated considerably more staying power than Alexander Haig, remaining until virtually the end of the administration.

If the Reagan administration became rhetorically more restrained over time, there remained a willingness to use force, albeit cautiously and selectively. In April 1986, the administration launched a sudden air strike against Libya in retaliation for dictator Muammir Qaddafi's support of terrorism around the world. As with other such moves, the strike was unilateral and underscored US distinctiveness rather than being a more collective effort that underscored Alliance co-operation. Indeed, France refused to permit the strike force to fly over national territory on the way from bases in Britain to bomb Libya. Colonel Qaddafi was not killed in the attack, though some speculated that he was in fact a target. However, following the incident he appeared to become considerably more restrained in deed as well as word and faded as a visible force on the international stage.[21]

RELENTLESS ECONOMICS – TRADE AND FINANCE

The Reagan administration came into office committed to make big changes in military affairs but to try as much as possible to remain uninvolved in economic affairs. Broadly true to the contemporary American conservative vision, the President was not at all reluctant to use power and influence for anti-communist ends, though the waning of a focus on domestic communism in American political life meant that energies were focused overseas. In this context, the image of a robust and assertive Soviet Union clearly spurred the administration on to acts of covert action as well as the very visible across-the-board military buildup.

In economic matters, the administration may have been committed to *laissez-faire*, but circumstances compromised that desire. Almost from the beginning, the Reagan administration was confronted with the problems and realities of heavy debt loads in the Third World and growing trade frictions among the industrialized nations, especially the constantly vexing US trade deficit with Japan. Regarding these matters, the administration very quickly established a strongly activist style, spearheaded not by the State Department but rather by the Treasury, especially after James Baker became the Secretary. The Baker Plan was created for management and eventual reduction of debt of Third World countries that had become overextended in the inflationary 1970s. The initiative relieved considerable pressure in Third World markets.

Issues of international trade and finance continued to grow in importance and complexity, as the predictable stability of the Bretton Woods system receded into history. The global economy gradually moved out of the severe inflation of the 1970s and there was continued growth in trade. The severe recession of the early 1980s gave further impetus to protectionism in terms of practical pressures on policy, but there was no broad retreat from the principles of freer trade. The administration addressed the situation in part through firm institutionalization of the economic summits among the great powers which had become increasingly important during the Ford and Carter years. These regular consultations among ministers, and at times heads of government, of Britain, Canada, France, Germany, Italy, Japan and the USA became defining instruments for communication as well as co-ordination of policies in the monetary and trade areas.

The large fiscal deficits of the Reagan administration, which began almost immediately with the new regime, changed the calculus of issues and policy. Combating the deficit increasingly became a major theme of the domestic US political debate. At the same time, the resulting higher interest rates, plus more abstract factors, led to a general movement of capital to the USA, a perceived safe haven. This in turn funded the US deficit and fuelled a comparatively large amount of domestic economic activity.

There was also a general movement away from the sort of managed financial arrangements that had been a preoccupation of the Carter administration. The commitment to a free market and floating exchange rates in retrospect arguably is one of the major differences between the two administrations, although the long-term trend, confirmed by the general stance and approach of the Clinton administration, has been toward a more open, less regulated market. At the same time, there was some continued intervention. The Baker Plan was joined by the Plaza Accord of 1985 among the main industrial nations to reduce the value of the dollar over time.[22]

RE-ELECTION

The outcome of the 1984 presidential campaign was no foregone conclusion, yet Reagan by the end of his first term had established such a strong political position, a direct function of his personal appeal to the electorate, that any Democratic candidate was assured of having an uphill battle. This was a fundamentally different state of affairs from that which confronted Reagan in 1980, when Carter was clearly vulnerable to attack, and much more comparable to the situation in 1956, when Eisenhower was the obvious favourite despite, and partly because of, the intensity of Cold War tensions between East and West.

The Democratic nominee, Walter Mondale, Carter's Vice President, was not the most conservative of the major contenders in the party. Senator John Glenn, who had the aura of the astronaut as well as his own political base and success in Ohio, was a strong challenger who had on balance a position more to the political right on a number of issues. The former Vice President was nevertheless relatively conservative, and very much a traditional Democrat. Yet he proved unable to surmount the very powerful appeal Reagan had demonstrated in 1980 to Democrats and independents among the electorate. Mondale launched a three-part campaign theme, outlined in a major speech at the National Press Club in Washington in early January 1984. He emphasized economic issues, trying to link the growing US government deficit with the perception that the nation was falling behind in the intense international economic competition. 'First we'll be deciding what kind of economy we'll have', he declared. 'Will America get its competitive edge back and lead the world economy again? Or will we saddle our kids with debt, second-rate jobs, impossible interest rates, and a falling standard of living?' But here the challenger had the problem that the economy was in fact improving.

Mondale also addressed traditional Democratic hostility to privilege: 'Second, we must decide what kind of people we are. Will we restore a sense of fairness and decency in American life? Or will it be the rich against the rest?' Yet the recession was over, and bashing the rich simply reinforced Mondale's image as an old-fashioned Democrat. Class appeals had been used successfully in American politics, notably by FDR in 1932 and, in particular, 1936, yet then the country was immersed in the enormous suffering of the Great Depression, arguably on the verge of genuine revolution. That was hardly the case in the early 1980s.

Foreign policy was Mondale's third main theme, and here he might well have been on more sure and politically profitable ground. He tried to combine emphasis on the dangers of war with the President's apparent disengagement from detail. International challenges were to be a principal theme of the Mondale campaign. He was obvious in trying to adopt and reverse Reagan's tactic regarding the economy of asking whether or not people felt better or worse off in 1980 compared with four years earlier. This was Mondale's most aggressive line of the Press Club presentation: 'Do we live in a safer world than we did three years ago? Are we further from nuclear war? After a thousand days of Mr. Reagan, is the world anywhere less tense, anywhere closer to peace?' He went on to describe continuing wars in Central America and the Middle East, the ongoing growing arms race, the dangerous competition between the USA and the Soviet Union. He linked this range of problems to Reagan's lack of experience and expertise. 'When the globe is a tinderbox, we need a President who knows what he's doing.'

Mondale to his credit was notably specific in his policy proposals during this campaign. He advocated updating and resubmitting the Salt II treaty, seeking deeper strategic arm cuts within the framework, reviving

the agreement that was tentatively reached between US and Soviet nego-
tiators on intermediate range nuclear forces during their famous 'walk in
the woods' in Germany, redoubling efforts in the fight against nuclear
proliferation, terminating the MX missile and going ahead with the smaller
Midgetman, terminating the B-1 bomber programme, renewing the fight
against nuclear proliferation to include a verifiable freeze on nuclear
weapons, and reaffirming the national commitment to the Anti-Ballistic
Missile (ABM) treaty. Mondale was also against what he called 'poison
nerve gas'. His support of the ABM treaty, designed severely to restrict
missile defence systems, was important as a dramatic contrast to Reagan's
Star Wars programme, with attendant enormous emphasis on post-ballistic
missile defence concepts.[23]

Mondale met with Soviet Foreign Minister Gromyko in late autumn,
shortly before President Reagan met with the durable official. The meeting
left him vulnerable to the charge of interfering with foreign policy, a realm
of fundamental presidential authority. Mondale in self-defence declared
that the USA has 'only one President at a time' and that 'I was not negotiating'. The President's meeting by contrast was politically helpful. This
was Reagan's first direct encounter with any Soviet leader and was widely
considered a plus, even though Shultz said only that the two governments
had agreed to 'stay in touch' and there was no agreement or break in the
existing negotiating logjam.[24]

SECOND TERM AND IRAN-CONTRA

Reagan's second term brought in foreign policy both his most substantial
accomplishments and his greatest failures. The arms control accords with
the Soviet Union, signalled though in excessively simplistic fashion by the
personal interchange with Gorbachev at the Reykjavik summit, dramatically reconfirmed the appeal and importance of the arms control process to
fundamental US interests, further linking the President's priorities and
policies to those of previous administrations, despite the campaign rhetoric
about fundamental departures. At the same time, the Iran-contra controversy reflected the degree to which the administration was willing to go
to extreme lengths both to free hostages, in this case individuals held
in the Middle East by Islamic fundamentalists, and to fight a traditional
anti-communist battle. The President himself was clearly emotionally committed to the cause of liberating the hostages. Secretary of State Shultz in
his memoirs states emphatically that he was opposed to such efforts. By

the amount of heat as well as space he devotes to the subject, he makes clear just how significant was the battle within the administration and the degree to which this was given a very high priority at the very top.

The controversy over arms sales to Iran and diversion of money to support the right-wing contras in Nicaragua may have presented the administration with a very serious crisis, but, in considerable contrast to Watergate during the Nixon years, this threat did not linger and grow until the President was brought down. Unlike Watergate, the crisis did not seem to become a preoccupying fixation of the executive branch. To some extent, this reflected the fact that the crisis was not nearly so multifaceted, and did not lead into a whole range of domestic law violations. In addition, the positive public image and personal popularity of the President meant that partisan opponents were not reinforced by a large phalanx of personal enemies and just could not generate the energy in Congress, the media or public opinion that played such a crucial role in bringing down Nixon.

The Iran-contra scandal is revealing as much for what did not happen as for what did. First, the administration was not destroyed by the experience. Arguably, the Reagan presidency was not even particularly weakened. Predictably the controversy became a major source of distraction for the President and others at the top of the administration. However, there was no implosion, no sharp neglect of all other business in a desperate effort to stave off political – and legal – disaster. In short, this was not Watergate. Second, and related, the administration was able to pursue at the same time notable arms control agreements with the Soviet Union and other international affairs business. If anything, Iran-contra demonstrated that the weakened, ultimately terminated presidency of Richard Nixon was a function of problems peculiar to that administration, not a Congress which was unavoidably and inherently dominant over the administration. Finally, the crisis, as indicated, revealed the intensity of the anti-communism of the administration, the lengths to which decision-makers, starting at the very top, were willing to go in the effort to combat the Soviet Union and groups and nations elsewhere in the world perceived as allies of the opposing superpower.[25]

This is not to argue that the public was accepting of Iran-contra. Quite the contrary was the case; the scandal hurt the administration. Opinion polls revealed a sense of disillusion with the administration and unhappiness with the events. On balance, people were particularly upset with the fact that business had been done with a terrorist regime, Iran. There was much less alarm in the body public over diverting arms and funds to the contras, the specific source of the illegal activity which provided the opening for Congressional prosecution. The most fascinating point is a related but different one: how the President, unlike Nixon, survived a scandal which continued even after he left office. Perhaps this important incident demonstrates more dramatically than any other the remarkable finesse, public relations flexibility, and sense of political timing that brought Ronald Reagan to the very top of American politics, from a professional background not previously seen as a recruiting ground for the White House.

Reagan pleads innocent to any direct involvement in or encouragement of the Iran-contra effort, emphasizing in his memoirs that 'private citizens' in 'churches and various groups around our country' were the prime initiators of assistance to opponents of the leftist Sandinista regime in Nicaragua. He states explicitly that he was unaware that any NSC staff members were actively involved in the process until later, when the Tower Board and the Congress brought such evidence to light as a result of investigations. On Oliver North, the main Iran-contra operator, Reagan was very explicit:

> I knew Oliver North only slightly when he worked for the National Security Council. What impressions I did have . . . were favorable . . . Although press reports claimed that he told others that we met together privately many times, I knew little about him personally and never saw very much of him at the White House. I never met with him privately and never had a one-on-one conversation with him until I called him on his last day at the NSC to wish him well.

Secretary of State George Shultz provides a very different perspective in his memoirs. As indicated, he states he was outraged at the very conception of arms for hostages exchanges, fought the notion as soon as he learned about it, and describes a President who was very much involved in the exercise, though also not fully comprehending.

> My overriding responsibility would have to be to get the President to understand the true nature of this terrible operation and to order it stopped. That would not be easy, for President Reagan simply did not seem to grasp what was actually going on. I would have to marshal my arguments carefully and powerfully so that he could not brush them aside.

He also provides blunt insight into the fundamental motivation for the operation: 'The Iranians must have learned, no doubt with help of media hype, that the President would do just about anything to get hostages released.' [26]

DÉTENTE REVISITED

Yet for all the hard-line, hard-core anti-communism, in rhetoric and in action, the core conservative doctrines and pro-military policies of the Reagan administration co-existed increasingly, especially in the second term, with efforts to come to terms with the Soviet Union in the realm of arms control agreements. Reagan and his allies had used the image of Henry Kissinger, a Secretary of State allegedly 'soft' on communism, to attack incumbent President Gerald Ford at the 1976 Republican convention, nearly wresting away his renomination. By 1986, Reagan was himself pursuing a course very similar to the denounced '*détente*' of the earlier period. In that year, the Reykjavik summit between Presidents Reagan and Gorbachev provided the opportunity for dramatic demonstration of the degree to which the American President had become persuaded that arms control, especially of a comprehensive nature, was extremely important. As noted, there was even an effort as part of the summit to issue a declaration banning all nuclear weapons, a step which was fraught with dangers political as well as technical in nature. By all accounts, this was a very personal initiative on the part of Reagan. Important policy concerns resulting from such a dramatic step would include verification that all nuclear weapons had been destroyed, managing strategic imbalances which might result, heightened importance of conventional military forces, and the dangers of cheating. A primary dilemma from such a dramatic disarmament would follow from the extraordinary power that would be given to any nation that had just a few nuclear weapons, or even one. Another, noted above, is how to involve, especially after the fact, such third nuclear powers as Britain, China, and France. These complexities by all the evidence were not seriously debated or apparently even considered in advance. Reykjavik, a near-disaster of the sort that has preoccupied serious diplomats when reflecting on the pitfalls of summits, was also a public relations success. Reagan's alienation from the strategic studies community facilitated such utopian approaches once he embraced the goal of arms limits.

Ultimately the proposal went nowhere in terms of actual policy; Secretary of State George Shultz and others sidetracked the initiative. President Reagan, reflecting his extraordinary domestic political good luck, profited from the image of being an arms controller and man of peace, thereby finally undercutting the warlike image that had plagued the earlier phase of his administration, without having to grapple with the endless practical difficulties involved in the actual abolition of all nuclear weapons. Reflecting his international relations luck as well, the crisis within the Soviet system brought forward in Mikhail Gorbachev a leader who recognized the necessity for change impelled by the failure of the communist regime.

If relatively technical arms considerations revealed the President to be vulnerable to utopian schemes, his interpersonal relations with other national leaders on the world stage demonstrated his one-on-one skills to be extremely effective. Like every American president going back to Franklin Roosevelt, Reagan felt the need to deal with his counterparts around the globe in very direct and human terms, taking the risk of miscommunication and misunderstanding in order to have the benefit of face-to-face discussion and becoming familiar with both allies and opponents in the most direct possible manner. Like FDR, he practised a highly individualistic, idiosyncratic style of diplomacy and relied heavily on personal relationships to maintain ties of alliance and break through barriers of opposition and confrontation.

The personal rapport the President was able to establish with British Prime Minister Margaret Thatcher and Japanese Prime Minister Yasuhiro Nakasone was probably beneficial concerning specific policy matters, and was certainly worthwhile for broad understandings between the two leaders involved. A traditional American ally and former great power, a bitter American opponent in the Second World War and emerging great power in political as well as economic terms, were both brought closer to the USA through the chemistry of interpersonal relations. Likewise, though in more muted terms, there was no doubt an element of friendship between two men in the overall working relationship with Mikhail Gorbachev that led the Strategic Arms Reduction Talks (START) to the very far-reaching nuclear weapons agreement that concluded President Reagan's tenure in office. Elected as an opponent of the established *détente* process, Reagan by the conclusion of his two terms had become committed to arms limitation.

EVALUATION OF REAGAN

President Reagan, disdained by intellectuals and many elements of the media, underestimated on a consistent basis by a wide range of partisan opponents and many in his own party, was successful for eight years with the people, where it counted. The fact that he became the first president since Dwight Eisenhower to complete two terms in office should be underlined, because this happened in spite of a general long-term trend in American politics toward increasing public cynicism about and hostility to politicians. He did not succeed on every agenda item; the Strategic

Defense Initiative is particularly notable as a major, and impractical, consumer of resources that would not really endure beyond Reagan's period in office. On the spending fronts, a very substantial increase in the US defence budget, and the expansion of the fiscal deficit and overall federal debt, effectively restricted the actions of future presidents and administrations. His overall impact on public policy and the political process was therefore very great.

President Reagan also presided over a time of momentous change in international relations in the direction of American interest. Elected to office with a strong commitment to anti-communism and hostility to the Soviet Union, his watch saw the end of communism in the Soviet bloc and of the Cold War. Shortly after he left office, the collapse of the Berlin Wall and the reunification of Germany changed the political and strategic maps of Europe in fundamental ways.

Reagan stands out in this context as a President who was much more clearly and explicitly concerned with domestic policy matters. His first term may have involved a very substantial military buildup, but this was a unilateral activity. There were no major multilateral international initiatives involving the tapestry of international relations, a mixture of nations, a comprehensive policy blueprint. Anti-communism of a very traditional – critics would say simple-minded – sort was the single note to the policy theme of the first term of the administration. The focus rather was highly domestic. The President's own main interests were in trimming the federal budget, and that involved by the 1980s overwhelmingly domestic concerns, the defence budget consuming only about 20 per cent of the total federal budget.

This began to change during his second term, with the emphasis on arms accords with the Soviet Union, as well as the increasingly controversial Iran-contra imbroglio. The administration, previously concerned with unilateral international involvement, undertook more complicated moves. Arms control was to some extent an antidote to the negative imagery, secretive and hostile, that seemed to characterize Iran-contra. At the same time, there can be no doubt that the President himself had a strong personal interest in an arms accord.[27] What is remarkable in fact is the sense of continuity with the past, despite the expectations of committed conservatives that Reagan would bring a major departure from the restrained containment that had defined US Cold War policies. Arms agreements with the Soviets were achieved, the existing alliance structure was maintained. Even this notably domestic President was compelled by ambition and circumstances to have an international impact not drastically different from the approaches of his predecessors.

Some, not just conservatives and Republicans, argued that the strength and assertiveness demonstrated by the Reagan administration were vital to the collapse of the Soviet Union, in particular that the arms race drove the Communists to self-destruction through economic burdens that their system could not maintain. While this is a plausible argument in retrospect, an even stronger case could be made for the proposition that American foreign policy during the entire Cold War period was most important to the collapse of the Soviet bloc, buying the time necessary to reveal the fundamental structural weaknesses of the system. There is some difficulty in detecting specific elements in the Reagan foreign policy that demonstrably brought about the collapse of the other side. Arguably the pressure created by significant expansion of the US defence budget during the Reagan years was one factor, though not the only one, in a process of development and events that contributed to the final disintegration of the Soviet system. There were also factors at work in the Soviet Union which were decisive. If the Soviets could not maintain a burdensome arms race, that reflected the weakness of their economic structure across the board.[28]

He was, like all political leaders, a product and reflection of his time, and here the electronic revolution, meaning television but also other means of communication, are of special importance. By the 1980s, a comparatively large percentage of the American population had travelled overseas. The world was becoming literally more familiar and figuratively smaller for the population at large, not just those at the top of the income scale. The imagery of television was especially important as a mechanism for political communication between leaders and the people. Television had defined the brutality of the Vietnam War in people's living rooms, and had borne witness to the political assassinations – and attempted assassinations – of the 1960s and 1970s in American politics. Reagan was hardly the first 'television president'; Kennedy had been at least equally effective in his use of and impact on the medium, and Eisenhower was very skillful, and underestimated, in that arena. Reagan's great advantage was to come to power when television had become pervasive, as the principal and dominant vehicle for seeing the political and social environment in broad terms. Newspapers, and certainly newspaper pundits, were fading. Radio remained a source of commentary and entertainment, but not the primary medium. Television was paramount, and Reagan was exceptionally adept of putting himself centre stage and staying there, throughout his term as President.

President Reagan, by his success from professional origins far removed from conventional politics, a background rather in radio, the movies and then television, demonstrated by his very person the degree to which the media had come to dominate American politics. He was underestimated as a politician in part because he was so adept at playing the 'innocent abroad' version of the non-politician, a contemporary Will Rogers, with perhaps a wit less droll, but an equal effort to project an American 'original', unpretentious and homespun. Abraham Lincoln was a political actor in a different age, with efforts to mask his professional standing as a prosperous corporate railroad lawyer through presenting the picture of a simple rustic railsplitter. Reagan, likewise, was not purely a genial lightweight, not simply a product of the television and movie studios. Earlier in his career, before seeking the governorship of California, he was successful in the very rough world of movie union politics, and demonstrated genuine toughness in intensely vitriolic union conflicts at the same time as he was playing generally upbeat roles on television and in films.

Yet Reagan was peculiarly a creature of the media, a man whose career was formed by that vehicle, with no external professional credentials to speak of, except for the politics of a union that was itself closely tied to the entertainment world. Other politicians did not have such distinctive careers. Lincoln had years as a professional politician battling through electoral struggles, usually unsuccessfully, before reaching the White House. Likewise FDR had considerable political experience of the conventional variety. Eisenhower had the ballast of leadership of the enormous allied coalition in the North Africa and Europe campaigns during the Second World War. Reagan's lack of previous credentials beyond his media persona before running for governor of California in 1966 means that he would have been almost certain to fail in the political environment before the electronic media age.

Reagan's rise was in some ways very similar to the Kennedy family. Joseph Kennedy said Hollywood was the future, his fascination with the movie game as well as the big money to be made was self-evident, and his sons, especially JFK, inherited his fascination with movies – and movie stars. He also gave his due to the closely related business of modern marketing when he declared that Jack, his surviving oldest son after the Second World War, would be a successful politician along the lines of a popular consumer product – 'We'll sell him like soap flakes.' Reagan's success confirmed the predictions of the patriarch of the other party, the father ultimately of an especially tragic set of political experiences. Reagan is therefore both distinctive in background and representative of the steady growth in influence of the electronic media.[29]

In this sense, the Reagan years represent an especially appropriate confirmation of the politics of modern democracy. The mass media have provided an opportunity for the national leader to communicate to the general population with a drama, directness and effectiveness never before available. Radio represented one giant leap forward in this regard, film another. The advent of modern television has carried the process much farther. The most important single observation about the electronic media is the fundamental moral neutrality of what is involved; the revolution has occurred in the realm of process, not substance. Charles de Gaulle, Adolf Hitler, John F. Kennedy, Franklin Roosevelt, and Reagan all represent modern leaders with a special skill, recognized during their tenures in office, for using the media to communicate with the people. Hitler's legacy was to become the paramount symbol of evil in the modern twentieth-century world, thanks to a capacity to destroy as well as to communicate that was magnified and extended by modern technology.

Charles de Gaulle as President of France was also able to harness the media to facilitate both the symbolism of his dramatic role and communication with the people in crisis, by so doing building a new long-term political stability for his nation. He was both a radical, in rewriting the nation's constitution and cutting enervating old colonial ties, and a conservative in his military background and respect for the heritage of the nation. Appearing on television, in uniform, to rally the people to his cause against his own military comrades, summed up the flexibility, immediate broad communication, and high drama, which television provided even the most traditional leader, as long as that leader was gifted at exploiting the opportunities for communication. The French President also symbolized the degree to which the media is only a set of tools, with judgement and moves on the political chessboard still the responsibility of the leader. His decisiveness in ending the bloody, corrupting colonial war in Algeria, and his persistence in stressing the primacy of the nation-state against such supranational organizations as the European Economic Community and Nato, demonstrated a consistency of insight concerning at least the durability of the nation-state that has been confirmed.[30]

REAGAN AND THE PUBLIC

Reagan's greatest accomplishment was probably in the realm of confidence within the United States. During the Reagan years, opinion polls clearly demonstrated that people in the USA began to feel more positive about the strength of their nation and about their own future in the world. This built steadily, and was sustained even after the President left office, further reinforced by the end of the Cold War and the collapse of the Soviet Union. Public opinion polls conducted by the Chicago Council on Foreign Relations with the Gallup Organization indicated that over the course of the Reagan administration, people steadily expressed much more positive attitudes about the international position of the USA and its relative strength and influence *vis-à-vis* the Soviet Union. This was in great contrast to opinion in an earlier poll in this series, conducted in late 1978, about half-way through Jimmy Carter's term, which reflected a sense of weakness and ineffectiveness concerning the influence and role of our nation in the world.[31]

This is no small accomplishment. Arguably Franklin Roosevelt's most significant single positive contribution was to provide Americans with a feeling that they could cope in the midst of extraordinarily frightening economic realities and seemingly endless crisis in employment and production represented by the Great Depression. After the assassination of John F. Kennedy, CBS commentator Eric Sevareid predicted that the President ultimately would be remembered primarily for an 'attitude', a contagious spirit that all things, or at least many things, including conquest of the Moon, were possible for Americans if we could only mobilize enough determination and will. Reagan certainly ranks high in this most general, and perhaps most important, dimension of democratic presidential leadership.

His relative influence and standing in the realm of leadership as public confidence-building was no doubt further enhanced by the relative absence of equally popular leaders in the other industrialized nations. Margaret Thatcher in Britain and Yasuhiro Nakasone in Japan were both well-defined on the public world stage, and relatively popular in the United States, especially the former in the wake of the Falkland war of 1982, but neither was very popular at home. President François Mitterrand of France was increasingly beleaguered, German Chancellor Helmut Kohl a durable but not dominant presence. In this environment, Reagan was essentially a reassuring and collegial figure for allies, especially since the USA was, despite some initial belligerent rhetoric, fundamentally cautious in the use of military force during these years. The advent of Gorbachev and domestic revolution in the Soviet Union only reinforced this impression of an influential and reliably stable United States.

The Reagan administration concluded with Americans certainly more confident, and the USA perhaps more effective, than at the beginning of his tenure. He did not change the basic structure of US foreign policy or international relations, but he did personify more significantly than any of his predecessors the power and impact of the media as stage for political 'acting' and instrument for political leadership. Implicitly, the role of the public and public opinion in the formulation and actual conduct of foreign policy was greater than ever before.

Reagan in sum by his style, emphases and empirical career path demonstrated that Washington-style politics, and what had been an important conventional political path to the White House, did not really seem to matter so much anymore. In one sense, the Republic had been moving in this direction for a very long period of time. The populist movement of the later decades of the nineteenth century showed that the government was to some extent separated from large sectors of the population. The Great Depression furthered a broad sense of alienation from the status quo. The recovery after the Second World War only concentrated attention more fully on the private sector, the personal and family preoccupation of everyday life for most Americans, as a realm very distinct from that of the public business. The people did not identify easily or effectively with what the government was doing, despite the great increase in federal social spending as well as large defence budgets during the Cold War. The shocking examples of twentieth-century totalitarian dictatorships only reinforced this feeling that government was suspect.

Reagan also broke any remaining ties between conservatism and isolationism. The Republican Party by the 1980s had become at the national level the standard bearer of free trade. The modern multinational corporation has replaced the protected national industrial interests which used to define the economic policies of the Republican Party. The global marketplace has absorbed the national marketplace. Reagan, despite his homespun style and appeal to the average American, was more than able to accommodate and voice this new international economic order. The isolationist tradition is a thing of the past. The Reagan administration, not grounded in complex foreign policy doctrines, wrought nevertheless notable accomplishments in relations with our adversaries and our allies. The President was at the centre of a new constellation of forces, free trade economic policy was combined with expansive military budgets in a manner which gave initiative to the commercial/competitive strengths of the United States while placing enormous pressure on the Soviet Union.

Finally Reagan personified the feeling of American exceptionalism amid danger of a hostile world that characterized an earlier generation. Professor Richard D. Challener, in an essay on John Foster Dulles contributed to a comprehensive volume on the history of diplomacy since the start of the Second World War, drew a fundamental parallel between his subject and this very successful President when he wrote that Dulles, 'like Ronald Reagan a generation later . . . possessed a unique ability to preach the gospel of American exceptionalism, the mission of the United States to spread its institutions and its democratic ideology as a fitting model for a deeply divided world.'[32]

This was the remarkable tenure which Reagan brought to a close in 1989, after completing two full terms in the White House. Just as Eisenhower did not transfer his popularity directly to Vice President Richard Nixon, so George Bush was not the complete beneficiary of Ronald Reagan's strong popularity, though Reagan in some apparent contrast to Ike had been sympathetic to his Vice President. In 1960, Nixon started out ahead in the polls and ended in a virtual 'dead heat' with John Kennedy. In 1988, Bush was far behind Democratic nominee Michael Dukakis in opinion polls, then came surging ahead in a striking victory that brought a solid electoral college and popular majority. Foreign policy may have played a role in this success, especially given Bush's extensive international credentials and Dukakis' lack of anything comparable in his own experience, yet there is a striking contrast between the colourful discussion of foreign policy matters in the 1960 campaign and the general absence of these issues from the partisan interchange of 1988. To some extent, this reflected a set of positive developments, including improved relations with Japan and Germany. The Cold War was ending as Gorbachev pursued his reformist course. Yet there also was cause for anxiety among those who believed a lively foreign policy debate was essential for the political health as well as international effectiveness of the nation. Were the American people in fact turning inward?

3 Asia and Europe, Emergence and Change

Ronald Reagan, patronized and dismissed by many during his tenure in the White House, dominated the national political landscape in a manner equalled by relatively few American presidents. The first president since Eisenhower to complete two terms in office, he was a reformer out to make basic changes in the system, whereas the other leader had been essentially a consolidator. The popularity both he and Eisenhower maintained throughout their terms contrasts with the experiences in office of the very unpopular (though now redeemed) Harry Truman, discredited Lyndon Johnson, disgraced Richard Nixon, and frustrated Jimmy Carter. Initially a hard-liner toward the Soviet Union, Reagan ended his tenure comparable to Eisenhower and Nixon as a notable foreign policy leader who was seeking stability, and to some extent achieving accord, with the Soviets. For both George Bush and Bill Clinton, this important predecessor has been in unusually literal terms a 'hard act to follow'.[1]

President Bush employed the term 'new world order' to describe the transformation in the international system, yet neither the Bush administration nor to date the Clinton administration has fully come to grips with the new state of affairs. This is true in foreign policy overall, as well as in relatively specific relations with Asia and Europe. Alleged shortcomings have different permutations and emphases depending upon the particular critic, but generally can be described as twofold: an absence of effective conceptualization and public explanation of the primary features of the 'new' international system, and a failure to implement policies to foster stability and deter or reduce the threat of war.

Reagan, by contrast, maintained his standing and popularity despite initial lack of emphasis on and some reversals as well as successes in foreign policy. This does not mean his policies were superior; certainly the intelligentsia did not love him more than Bush or Clinton. Reagan rather was aided by the Cold War environment, which was dangerous but also clear-cut, with a principal, indeed preoccupying, opponent – the Soviet Union and associated Soviet bloc. The fundamental military, ideological and diplomatic contest between the two superpowers coloured all other international involvement of the United States. The comparatively simplistic approach of President Reagan was more appropriate, and perhaps more effective, in this environment than in one not ordered by such an overshadowing, preoccupying contest. Given Reagan's popularity at home, difficulties abroad in Lebanon and Central America were more easily addressed or evaded in the always-intense domestic political debate.

BUSH: FAILURE TO INSPIRE

Reagan's successors have confronted a more complex environment. The Cold War indeed had become so familiar, the related atmosphere and assumptions concerning policy so pervasive, that there was even a reassuring quality to the dangerous but stable system which melodramatists early on had termed the 'balance of terror'. Any president would have difficulty in coping with the end of that competition. Uncertainty about the best course of policy should not therefore be surprising. Reagan was able effectively to employ standard hard-line rhetoric early in his administration, and later to adopt the *détente* themes previously associated with less conservative predecessors, with considerable success, but arguably he faced a less frustrating, less slippery policy environment.

In the case of President George Bush and his administration, the world was quickly becoming much more complicated and unpredictable, with Germany coming together as well as the Soviet Union coming apart during the course of his one term in office. Even a very gifted political leader would have been hard-challenged to address this revolutionary change effectively with comprehensive new policies and effective presentations to the public. George Bush was never known for rhetorical skill, and his leadership talents proved to be highly operational and organizational, not thematic or structural. There was a continuing failure to conceptualize coherently and persuasively the profound manner in which the world was changing, and a related inability to engage in persuasive public explanation and exhortation. He was able to cope with crisis very effectively; he proved unable to orchestrate a long-term, diverse set of international relationships in the post-Cold War world. Arguably he handled the great foreign policy challenges effectively in terms of day-to-day business, but more is required for political survival in our age of democratic review and mandate.

Bush may ultimately go down in history as a President who was almost the reverse of Reagan in office in foreign policy terms. In a variety of circumstances, including major crises, he demonstrated considerable executive ability, especially but by no means exclusively in mobilizing people and institutions for the Gulf War. Yet he remained deficient at the most fundamental level of major political leadership; there was within him an inability to move the electorate emotionally, to identify with the concerns, fears and drives of the average person, or to exercise the rhetorical skill needed to transform voters in a democracy from observers into followers.

Bush won the White House in 1988 over Democratic nominee Michael Dukakis because of an ability to mount a campaign which was aggressive and persuasive, even if not uplifting or inspiring, and this dimension should not be underestimated in any major political campaign in the American democracy. 'Negative' campaigning is as old as American politics, contrary to current assumptions in the media and among politicians themselves. While Bush was not particularly inspiring in either the 1988 or the 1992 campaign, in the latter he failed as well to be politically effective. Had foreign policy accomplishments in his term in office been catalogued clearly and presented dramatically to the electorate, he might well have won. Such an appeal could have bridged the great emotional gap, never in fact spanned, between Bush and the people. Arguably Reagan's ability to generate a broad feeling of self-confidence and strength among a majority of Americans regarding US dealings with the world was a vital component in his re-election in 1984 following his first term. Bush was simply unable to do likewise.

Regarding Bush as President compared with Bush as candidate, there is an especially dramatic contrast between the actual record on foreign policy, including relations with allies in Europe and Asia, and the marked inability to translate tangible success in policy into reliable public support. At the end of the Gulf War, with the strikingly quick and easy victory in liberating Kuwait from occupation by Iraq, Bush's popularity in the opinion polls was at 84 per cent, higher than any modern President except for Truman in the period immediately after the death of FDR. Bush, like Truman, found that this enormous popularity dissipated, but with Truman the decline took years and the enervating ordeal of the Korean War, while Bush found his standing dropping precipitously between the Gulf War victory in early 1991 and the presidential election of November 1992.[2]

The difficulty the President experienced in articulating his foreign policy concepts was apparent, through omission, at the very start of his administration, with his inaugural address in early 1989. The speech was eminently ecumenical in theme. There was also an explicit moral flavour to his remarks, including such declarations as the following: 'We must act on what we know. I take as my guide the hope of a saint. In crucial things, unity – in important things, diversity – in all things, generosity.' On foreign policy, the President had almost nothing to say in this address, a curious development since his leadership credentials for the White House included primarily international experience, representing President Reagan and that administration abroad as Vice President, and earlier as head of the CIA, representative to China and Ambassador to the United Nations. He referred specifically to the Vietnam War, noting that 'surely the statute of limitations has been reached' on a war that began 'in earnest' a quarter century earlier, and that '. . . no great nation can afford to be sundered by a memory'. He also mentioned the Soviet Union very explicitly, stating 'we will continue the new closeness with the Soviet Union, consistent both with our security and with progress'.[3]

The President's inaugural address was businesslike, generally uninspiring, and more comparable to a report to a company board of directors than an effort to define the parameters of leadership of a great nation in a world of turbulent change. Later presentations, including discussion of momentous revolution in central and eastern Europe, were also characterized by attention to the detailed profit and loss dimensions of the nation's actions in the business of international relations, with no capacity to provide a comprehensive 'vision' of the international realm or our place therein.

President Bush generally did not project well over television, or for that matter over the media generally, in communicating with the electorate, yet in another sense he was very comfortable with the contemporary high-tech electronic communications environment. Cautious, perhaps too hesitant, concerning policy departures beyond the Gulf, Bush was quite daring in the mechanisms by which he did business. The President was especially inclined to simply pick up the telephone and call counterparts in other countries, to the frustration of normal diplomatic channels, procedures and techniques. The resulting anxiety of traditional foreign service officers was very appropriate, given the opportunity for misunderstanding and miscommunication that such an approach opens, especially in the absence of careful planning in advance, sometimes excluding aides. Yet Bush was also extremely successful, probably more than Reagan, at forging and maintaining good personal relationships among foreign policy leaders around the globe, and no doubt his personal approach had advantages as well as risks.

In late 1989, the *Wall Street Journal* addressed this dimension of his leadership in a front-page article, headlined 'Personal Touch – Bush Shapes His Policy By Often Telephoning Other World Leaders', with the sub-head: 'President Bonds With Likes of Mubarak and Kohl; Staff Can Be Left in Dark'. White House officials, privately edgy, put a positive public face on the practice:

White House officials acknowledge that managing the Bush penchant for spontaneous diplomacy is a problem. But they insist that Mr. Bush is aware that his personal diplomacy may leave even his top aides uncomfortably ignorant about agreements he has reached with other nations, and he takes steps to minimize the problem.[4]

In this sense, Bush was a very contemporary President, continuing a trend of using the telephone for top-level communication that was apparent as early as the beginning of the Kennedy administration. Professional diplomats worried about repercussions, staff members struggled to handle details of any follow-up, and media analysts were right to focus on the phenomenon. Reflective participants no doubt had occasion to ponder the flaps and human errors that the established customs of traditional diplomacy are designed to avoid. Bush, however, was never really deterred by such arguments, and did not change his preferred method of doing business during his White House tenure.

This dimension of the Bush leadership style was very much in line with evolving pervasive public and business communication technologies, which are changing everyday life as well as the international system. Eisenhower and Truman may have been inherently superior executives, with orderly meeting styles, but the point is also valid that they operated well before the modern electronic media had taken hold. The end of the familiar Cold War has taken place in a context which is also changing dramatically in the way business of all kinds is done. If all politics is truly local, increasingly the outside world impinges on everyday life through trade and commerce, travel and communications. Bush, in many ways the personification of the traditionalist, represented this change in ways different from but also congruent with Reagan's style.

COHESIVE, COLLEGIAL STYLE

One of the most notable positive features of the administration, in turn a direct result of good executive perception, analysis and decision-making, was the overall effectiveness of the cabinet. Perhaps more than any other presidential responsibility, this is a function of executive management above purely political leadership. President Bush was able to assemble a team of extremely strong-willed, ambitious individuals, an accomplishment hardly unique in Washington. Beyond this starting point, however, he was also able to persuade them to work together as a team over a four-year period in a sustained manner with a relative absence of the sorts of fundamental personality, ideological or policy differences that normally divide administrations.

The collegiality of the Bush cabinet is especially notable in light of the fact that the administration had to address truly momentous events during the term in office. The Soviet Union had provided the principal incentive for the formation of the post-Second World War set of security arrangements, beginning with Nato. Efforts to co-exist and reduce tensions with the other superpower had preoccupied administrations dating back to the Truman years. With the end of the Soviet Union, an international system which was dangerous but also familiar, and relatively predictable, came to an end. However limited Bush may have been in addressing the rhetorical and symbolic demands of office, keeping the Cabinet together as a team which pulled together, not separately, does great credit to him as a strong executive in a crucial time. Beyond his highly individualistic style and other personal idiosyncrasies, Bush also provided good lessons in the capability of the administration to pull together at the top. Professor Terry Deibel of the National War College wrote in the journal *Foreign Policy* in late 1991 that, 'This group emphasizes loyalty and quiet teamwork, in marked contrast to the public feuds . . . in previous administrations – the Shultz/Weinberger, Vance/Brzezinski, or Rogers/Kissinger battles.' He argued that 'Their harmony stems in part from an utter lack of ideology, an absence of passionate commitment . . . Instead, the President and his associates embrace pragmatism . . .'. Certainly no other recent president has done as well in this dimension of leadership. During the post-Second World War period, perhaps only Truman and Eisenhower have been able to equal this accomplishment; more recent presidents have not. Yet Professor Deibel, along with others, was also finally critical of the Bush administration for lack of comprehensive strategy and ready willingness to compromise.[5]

Beginning with the Kennedy administration, tension between the national security adviser and the secretary of state, and the broader White House national security staff and State Department bureaucracy, has served to frustrate smooth and effective policy definition and implementation. Tensions in the Kennedy period arguably were primarily a reflection of the President's desire to be directly engaged in the foreign policy process, heightened by frustration with the manner in which the State Department functioned. Meanwhile, Secretary of Defense Robert McNamara became assertive in foreign policy across the board in a way that tended to limit the role of the Secretary of State. In the Nixon administration, the President clearly distrusted the State Department and moved to concentrate power in foreign policy in the White House, a task in which he was aided by the impressive capabilities and congruent ambitions of his national security adviser, Henry Kissinger.[6]

With the Carter administration, interpersonal conflict emerged once again, this time in the conflict between Secretary of State Cyrus Vance and National Security Assistant Zbigniew Brzezinski. The variation on this theme provided by the Reagan administration was the conflict between Secretary of State George Shultz and Secretary of Defense Caspar Weinberger. Often turning on differences over whether or not to use force, the inevitable clashes of strong personalities fuelled such conflicts.[7] Differences of opinion and interpersonal tension are part of the human condition, and certainly are to be expected in high offices in Washington. Bush's skill was to control such differences, at the start by emphasizing teamwork and recruiting individuals who found that approach congenial, and during the course of his regime by exercising strong personal leadership.

THE GULF WAR

The greatest foreign policy challenge, and also the greatest success, of the Bush administration was the Gulf crisis and war. The events also had a strong bearing on alliance relations, in Asia as well as Europe. The takeover of Kuwait by Iraq was perhaps the most clear-cut case since the Second World War of one sovereign nation engaging in an invasion of another, and Iraqi leader Saddam Hussein's efforts at rationalization were singularly unpersuasive outside the borders of his police state. Whatever the exact relative importance of the oil factor in the ultimate decision to go to war, the undeniable reality that international aggression had occurred gave many nations, including but not only the industrial powers, a very persuasive incentive to react with force. President Bush was also quite effective at mobilizing public opinion and leadership sentiments in the USA and overseas, forging an impressive comprehensive coalition under the auspices of the United Nations. Bush secured the equivalent of a declaration of war from the US Congress in legislative confirmation of military intervention under UN mandate. This was by the early 1990s an unusual step that had not really taken place in the United States since the entry into the Second World War.

The Gulf War also revealed important characteristics of the use of the mass media, especially television. The capacity for instantaneous communication again brought the war home to living rooms in not only the United States but also other nations. At the same time, strict wartime censorship was imposed for the first time since the Second World War. There was a return to an earlier tradition of control of the flow of war information that is historically customary but had not been used by the USA during the

Vietnam War, when quite a different, open approach was employed, at least during the Johnson administration.

The war, in contrast to others of the past few decades which involved the United States, also served to encourage a sense of unity among the major powers, especially in Europe and Japan. The Vietnam War was an exercise in the USA operating virtually alone, at least regarding its European allies, although South Korea provided substantial assistance and Australia and New Zealand contributed some troops. Japan was a loyal ally in the less direct sense of providing a hospital and logistical base. The Korean War took place at a time when Germany and Japan were defeated and occupied nations. The Gulf War provided a genuine opportunity for co-operation among the major nations of the world, with no lingering legacy of the Second World War or complications resulting from the Cold War. This is more important than such matters as tension over Japan's contribution or the most appropriate form of any German participation.

The brevity of the war, and the comparatively low cost in lives for the allies, should not be permitted to minimize the success of the President in mobilizing a comprehensive international coalition, under the auspices of the United Nations, to implement first sanctions against Iraq, and then the liberation of Kuwait and the decisive defeat of Iraqi forces in the field. This international coalition building, plus institutional involvement of the Congress, demonstrated that the Bush administration possessed a capacity both to learn from history and to implement a clear and effective policy. The administration's success in working under the UN umbrella recalled the Korean intervention of 1950, when the Soviet walkout gave an opening to the USA and allies to resist the North Korean invasion of South Korea under the auspices of the world organization. Korea, however, involved really a purely executive branch decision in Washington to intervene. Through the public involvement of Congress, Bush was able to respect institutional balance within the US government even while asserting the sort of presidential authority which had been so badly undermined by the Vietnam War and aftermath.[8]

EUROPE: UNITY, DISUNITY AND 1992

Europe east and west provided a second area of significant challenge to the Bush administration. This was overall a more complex policy arena than the Persian Gulf, where diplomacy may be convoluted but the war had been an extremely straightforward exercise. The Europe that confronted the Bush administration included the promise of economic and perhaps political integration along with the threats of political instability and, in the Balkans, open warfare. There was no threat of international aggression comparable to that which Saddam Hussein had posed before the decisive allied military action against him. Yet the Balkan conflict would prove far more long-term and frustrating than the Gulf conflict, threatening the reputation and effectiveness of the United Nations, which had seemed invigorated and re-legitimized through the victory against Saddam Hussein.

'Europe 1992' might also be described as a diplomatic slogan of the Bush years, given the lack of catchy phrases emanating from Washington, a common shorthand reference not just for the specific plans for greater integration of the European Community but also the unending hopes that destructive nationalism in Europe could be overcome through the right sorts of regional economic and political mechanisms. In the words of Professor William James Adams of the University of Michigan, an expert on European integration and director of a very comprehensive research project and resulting volume on the subject:

> Nineteen ninety-two is not just a period of time; to many people it is a deadline for and symbol of European economic integration. It acquired this status on June 14, 1985, when the EC Commission transmitted to the European Council a white paper proposing elimination of some 300 specific impediments to the free flow of goods, services, workers, and capital within the Community.[9]

The task in total was anticipated to take two full terms of the Commission. This period would conclude on 31 December 1992, resulting in the title 'Project 1992'. In December 1990, member governments of the European Community established a conference to examine political union. This project was concluded at Maastricht in December 1991, and the Treaty on European Union was signed on 7 February 1992. The ambitious enterprise was designed not only to remove government barriers to trade and commerce, but also to achieve a form of actual political union.[10]

In practice, there was much more willingness to accept a common commercial market than a common currency, the second main dimension of Europe 1992. When the report of the Delors Committee on monetary union was made public in April 1989, the British Chancellor of the Exchequer, Nigel Lawson, had said that 'monetary union would require political union, which is not on the agenda'. He was stating, with the bluntness the British often reserve for Community matters, that supranational integration in fundamental political terms is 'not on' for the British. He was also on firm ground, for EU members have demonstrated over time that they will not sacrifice basic sovereignty, even if that position has been only occupied very explicitly in public by the British and, earlier, the French.[11]

GERMANY: UNIFICATION

The importance of Germany in European affairs generally, including European integration, leads naturally to a focus on the now-unified nation as the source of a singular foreign policy relationship in that region for the United States. During President Bush's first year in office, the Berlin Wall came down, reflecting the enormous popular political as well as economic pressures which had by then brought an exceptionally large number of refugees from East Germany, Hungary and other parts of Eastern Europe into Austria and West Germany. The wide flow of human traffic symbolized the decay, final failure and collapse of the communist regimes in the east.

The unification of Germany provided the Bush administration, and Europe generally, with a very great specific security as well as diplomatic challenge, though this momentous event was only one of a series to confront Washington, symptomatic of the revolutionary changes sweeping Europe. Again, the implications of unification were profound, and not necessarily positive for either Europe or the United States. Germany divided could not provide a decisive threat to the peace of Europe. Germany united, however, raised all the imagery of the aggressive, dominant military and economic power which had broken the otherwise effective peace among major powers in Europe in the nineteenth century, and brought on two cataclysms of destructive world wars in the twentieth century. The unification of Germany, like the collapse of the Soviet Union, showed the ultimate weakness of communism, at least in a European context. But a unified Germany also represents a great concentration of power, with a history of militarism that can only encourage worry when contemplating the future of European and wider Atlantic area relations. Washington therefore was confronted with a significant double challenge with the disintegration of one superpower and the unification of another great power. The Soviet Union had been generally cautious in using military force; Germany has given the world startling lessons in military adventurism – and effectiveness.

The Bush administration, populated with experienced, generally moderate government professionals, including the President himself, confronted a world in which extraordinary forces of revolutionary change had been unleashed. Not surprisingly, Washington generally opted for the status quo, trying to maintain the present rather than drive for the future. In the case of the unification of Germany, the United States was largely an observer, with some efforts to applaud publicly from the sidelines, combined with worried private speculation about what the Soviet Union might do in response to the breakup of the East European bloc. President Bush and his associates, like most of the world, did not foresee in any detail what was coming in Eastern Europe. The swelling tide of refugees from the east, followed by the crumbling of the East German regime along with the collapse of the Berlin Wall, was rightly greeted as a major, indeed historic, victory in the Cold War, while at the same time there was no real effort to define in detail the new international order.

President Bush, daring in the Persian Gulf, was cautious in seeing any major revolution as a result of the turmoil in Germany, and that attitude carried through his administration. The reticence of President Bush contrasted with the style of his predecessors. Kennedy, much criticized for inaction when the Berlin Wall was secretly and suddenly put in place in 1961, is remembered much more widely for his magnetic, gripping appearance at that wall in 1963, proclaiming defiantly in German that he was a 'Berliner'. Kennedy used the leverage and influence he gained, and the more sober international atmosphere regarding nuclear war that resulted from the Cuban Missile Crisis, to pursue the partial nuclear test ban treaty of 1963 with the Soviets. Ronald Reagan likewise used the drama inherent in this particular site of Cold War confrontation very effectively.[12]

Bush, by contrast, seemed to play the role of observer and analyst, not actor, and diplomatic efforts in arms and other fields failed to have a really significant impact. The *Wall Street Journal* noted the contrast in late 1989. After reference to both Kennedy and Reagan, the piece continued that

> George Bush, by contrast, presided over the most dramatic turn in East–West relations in more than 40 years sitting behind his desk last Thursday, looking at a map of Germany and saying to a group of reporters, 'We are handling it in a way where we are not trying to give anybody a hard time . . . I'm elated . . . I'm just not an emotional kind of guy.'

The American ambassador to West Germany, General Vernon Walters, predicted in December 1989 that reunification of Germany might occur within a five-year time period. Bush stated that 'I am not trying to accelerate that process.' That statement, more than the belligerent rhetoric of the President regarding Saddam, might be used to sum up his overall approach to foreign policy, and to the presidency in general.[13]

THE EASTERN BLOC

The revolution within and then collapse of the Soviet Union, ending both a communist political regime and a well-established nation-state, represented a distinctive fourth geopolitical challenge to the Bush administration. The extraordinary events which ended the Soviet Union and the communist regime there, as well as those in client states in Eastern Europe, is again properly seen in mixed terms. The victory for the West in the long Cold War with the Soviets was joined to uncertainty about the future of the region of Europe as a whole. The wider international system no longer had the stabilizing influence provided by the established, relatively predictable confrontation between the two superpowers, the United States and the Soviet Union.

President Mikhail Gorbachev of the Soviet Union, overshadowed since his departure from power by events and his successor in Russia, Boris Yeltsin, was an overshadowing presence during his time in power, a striking personal image combined with a remarkable capacity for surprise. President Bush, probably through a combination of loyalty and the perceived desirability of the status quo, remained committed to Mikhail Gorbachev long after that Soviet leader clearly was being swept away by the revolutionary forces within his country, and the Soviet Union was itself breaking apart.

At the beginning of the Bush administration Secretary of State James Baker made a trip to Europe. One unexpected reaction of the American visitor was startled surprise that the focus in capitals visited was not on the obvious failures of the communist system, but rather the exciting leadership of Gorbachev. Baker and others in the administration quickly determined that the United States was facing a strong challenge to regain national foreign policy initiative. The Secretary, returning to Europe for his first trip to Moscow on 10 May 1989, was prepared with his aides to be assertive in discussion of a broad agenda, including arms control and Central America. The Soviets, however, had initiatives of their own to pursue, especially in arms control, where Gorbachev announced a plan for dramatic deep cuts in conventional forces, to be made public the night Baker was departing for Brussels to reassure American allies concerned about caution in Washington. The *Wall Street Journal* observed:

> The secretary of state – politically astute and experienced in international negotiations – returned home convinced that the Soviet president was deeply serious about scaling back arms and reforming the

USSR. Mr. Baker was also convinced that Mr. Gorbachev was too good a politician to be treated lightly.[14]

The relationship was solidified at the presidential level with the summit meeting of Bush with Gorbachev at Malta in December 1989. Bush, ever cautious in policy, as usual was not so cautious personally. At a news conference just after the summit, Bush was questioned about putting himself at risk in boarding a small launch in 60-mile-an-hour winds to make the trip back to his own ship, the USS Belknap. More fundamentally, the summit encouraged speculation, which perhaps was more frequent in the case of Bush than some other American presidents, concerning the degree to which the incumbent was demonstrating leadership qualities that were persuasive and effective with the public.[15]

In the case of the breakup of the Soviet Union, the USA looked to the established order rather than opting for forces of radical change. Mikhail Gorbachev, in power since 1985, initiator of major reform at home and arms control agreements abroad, including significant accords with the Reagan administration, had strong practical claims on the loyalty of the Washington administration. Bush put personal loyalty above other considerations. Moreover, Gorbachev had strong claims from a practical tactical point of view as well. The communist turned reformer, he had guided the Soviet Union in comparatively liberal directions when confronted with a revolution that clearly could not be ignored or defeated. There were good reasons for thinking that any likely successor would be less desirable from the perspectives of the USA and Europe as well. The Bush administration, however, remained with Gorbachev long after it had become clear that the Soviet Union was disintegrating as an established unified state, and that their designated leader was becoming less and less consequential to the process. He had become a passenger on a revolutionary train with no engineer any longer at the controls, on a path to a future which was increasingly unpredictable.

Given this unfolding situation, a more daring President would have searched for viable alternatives to Gorbachev, who was by 1991 clearly a prisoner of events. Bush, essentially an establishment man from Connecticut (even if via entrepreneurship in Texas), was committed to the established order in the Soviet Union, albeit an order immersed in tides of fundamental change. The President was very explicit, unfortunately so in retrospect, in stating that Boris Yeltsin was not the man whom the United States would support. When Yeltsin appeared to be toppled by a military *coup* in 1992, the Bush administration, perhaps wisely, did not intervene, but only after that event did Washington grudgingly give the Russian leader unqualified support as the head of the government of his nation. Being ahead of events is a sign of rare genius, or at least insight and good luck; being so far behind events guarantees being controlled by them rather than the reverse.

JAPAN: FRUSTRATION

Japan and Japan–USA relations were the fifth main area of foreign policy challenge and conflict. In Asia, Japan, which had appeared ever more dominant in the 1980s, experienced sudden reversal with the collapse of the 'bubble economy', built up through real estate, financial market and associated speculation through the decade, encouraged by the peculiar economic – and psychological – isolation of the nation. The protected nature of the Japanese economic environment, and related lack of free flows of investment in and out of the country, meant that financial speculation was given unusually wide, untrammelled freedom, making the collapse which came all the greater, more dramatic and more costly. At the same time, China was emerging as an increasingly important domestic market for a growing array of investors, including a wide range of American companies.

Other media imagery aside, the Bush decision to take leaders of the US Big Three automobile manufacturers to Japan for a major summit meeting was an odd blunder. The automobile industry both highlights the trade difficulties at the governmental level between Japan and the USA, and symbolizes the high priority in the former country and the lower priority in the latter of coming to terms with foreign markets. Perhaps no contemporary industry more effectively illustrates the point that much of American industry remains heavily focused on the American market. At the same time, beyond specific trade conflicts, the automobile industries of both Japan and the USA have at this point successfully developed a number of important joint ventures. These relationships are further knitting together the two great economies, mitigating trade differences, and illustrating the robust capacities of market forces to overcome even very tangible policy differences between national political capitals.[16]

Little of this co-operative spirit was evident in a visit which quickly became a confrontation, with the usual American demands for more 'open' markets in Japan. Lee Iacocca of Chrysler was notably pugnacious, as usual. The President's failure to give equal billing to representatives of American companies which have been far more successful than the automobile dealers in Japan must remain one of the mysteries of White House political miscalculation. Certainly a diverse group including representatives of computer hardware and software manufacturers, food and other consumer goods, banking and other financial services, would have provided for more congenial interchange, more effective discussion, and a more satisfying television image no matter what problems might have occurred on the visit. Top executives of the Big Three US automobile makers reinforced images of conflict, while providing only one dimension of a picture of USA–Japan economic involvement which is really quite diverse.

Perhaps the most accurate overall assessment of the Bush administration is that he proved extremely adept at handling the tactics of big issues and large challenges, yet had difficulty in providing a general policy 'vision', meaning a framework of ideas and concepts that was both practical in terms of policy formulation and persuasive in terms of the political competition. Arguably significant presidents in the foreign policy field, including in particular Eisenhower, Kennedy, and Nixon, have been able to do both. Hans Binnendijk of Georgetown University made this point in an assessment of Bush's record in the fall of 1992, just before the election in which the President was defeated. On concrete, tactical aspects of his performance, the President received high marks:

> With Helmut Kohl, Mr. Bush earned an A by overcoming opposition in Western Europe and convincing Mikhail Gorbachev to accept German unification without a restructured Nato.
>
> Similarly, Mr. Bush and Boris Yeltsin agreed to trim strategic nuclear weapons to a third of the existing inventory, and together they convinced the other republics of the former Soviet Union to give up their nuclear weapons before the end of this decade.

The President was faulted, however, for lack of effective initiative in addressing the broad strategic problems presented by the end of the Cold War:

> Delays and lack of leadership earn Mr. Bush only a C for managing the new problems of the post-Cold War world. With the end of the ideological struggle and the rising U.S. budget deficit, he has lost his compass and his wallet.
>
> A good example is the Russian transition. A dangerous gap has emerged between the West's high stakes in the Russian transition and the West's limited effort to make that transition a success. Instead of seizing the opportunity and forming an early international consensus to

support democracy in Russia, Mr. Bush had to be prodded by allies and friends, including Richard Nixon, who rightly called the initial U.S. response 'pathetically inadequate'.[17]

Whether or not Richard Nixon should have been included among Bush 'friends', the more important point is that the President seemed to be operating at the hands of events rather than putting his hands effectively upon events. Lincoln could state that events had controlled him only because that so obviously was not true. The political leader can only afford an Olympian stance of reserve and dignity when he has struggled and driven himself to overcome barriers to his policy success and his political standing.

There is rarely just one factor in the defeat of a president in the large, diverse American political democracy. No doubt the state of the domestic economy was an important factor, and probably the most important single element, in the defeat of George Bush in 1992. A still more fundamental point, however, is that leadership is a broad quality that encompasses foreign as well as domestic policy, and perceived weakness or ineffectiveness in one area can encourage the same evaluation in others. Likewise, perceived strength can encourage a positive impression across the board. In 1992, the state of the economy and more general failure of communication on the part of the President proved fatal at the polls. 'I just don't think he has done anything,' said a Rockford Illinois resident about the performance of the President in the fall of that year. 'Not a lot went on while he was president [already referring to the leader in the past tense]. Not a lot of action, not a lot of results.' Another resident of the same city added: 'People always get scared when there's nobody to lead them. We've done as much as we can do. We have talked, we have planned. It's time that we got some direction from above, and I don't mean God.'[18]

Other presidents have used foreign policy to remarkably good effect in the electoral battles. In 1956, President Eisenhower's recognized strength in foreign policy, which he had recently demonstrated in the Suez crisis, permitted him to overcome the normally severe problem of an economic recession and return to the White House with a smashing second election victory. Richard Nixon, always under challenge at home because of the low comfort level many voters felt regarding him, was able skillfully and effectively to develop foreign policy themes and victories, including the SALT I treaties with the Soviet Union and a diplomatic breakthrough with China. These were important factors in his 1972 election victory, also a landslide. George Bush was simply not able to do likewise, a shortcoming essentially political rather than policy in nature.

CLINTON: FOREIGN POLICY UNFOLDING

In contrast to Bush, President Bill Clinton has proven to be more gifted rhetorically, able to provide clear and coherent explications of a wide range of policy matters, often with an impressive command of specific detail. This includes foreign policy when the occasion requires. Yet this President has suffered, at least up to 1996, from the reputation for lack of interest in the subject and the accusation of ineffectiveness in the actual implementation of policy. The 1992 presidential campaign did feature a heavy emphasis on domestic rather than foreign policy matters, including the economic recession then in progress. Clinton's tactical emphasis on this advantage in the electoral political debate reinforced the perception that he was more comfortable dealing with matters at home, so to speak, than abroad. Whatever the truth regarding Clinton's level of interest in international affairs, the world is very interested in any American president, and this reality has not changed with the end of the Cold War. Clinton has been confronted with no shortage of international crises, a number of which have involved the potential or actual use of military force. These include not only the Balkans but also involvements in Haiti, Rwanda, and Somalia. The fact that such major challenge areas were largely inherited from the Bush administration has not eased problems for Clinton.

The Clinton administration has been described as less successful than the previous one in implementation of foreign policy, though this may be changing, and neither has yet defined succinct and effective concepts and themes to flesh out the 'new world order'. Clinton managed an effective presidential campaign, in no small measure because of that capacity readily to employ large amounts of specific information persuasively with the various policy constituencies important to the party nomination process, along with an organizational structure that was considerably superior to the chaotic, ramshackle, disastrous Dukakis effort. Because of this success in the campaign arena, there was some expectation by many, encouraged by the President's representatives, that the Clinton administration would excel in management of the executive branch. This has not yet been the case, or at least critics have not yet been disarmed. Yet foreign policy has proven to present – as usual – a frustrating, complex array of problems. The President's rhetorical skills alone have not persuaded the public overall that the administration is successful in foreign policy. The temporary rise in presidential public approval ratings in late 1995 and early 1996 was notable, and was clearly at least indirectly linked to Clinton's more active foreign policy role, especially with progress in the Balkans. The region, scene of the violence, war and murder that have plagued the Bush and Clinton administrations, is the source also of the greatest Clinton foreign policy success to date.[19]

EUROPE: BALKAN QUAGMIRE

To some extent, Clinton – like all presidents – has been a victim of circumstances beyond his control, partly because events elsewhere in the world are often not directly manageable from Washington, partly because of the actions of predecessors. Nowhere is this more clearly apparent than in the enervating, frustrating arena of Southeast Europe, where the Bush administration made a commitment of US influence with no clear guidelines concerning the use of force. Clinton inherited this situation and found circumstances deteriorating. To be totally disengaged would undermine American credibility to allies in Western Europe who are more directly involved; to be engaged in the use of military forces on the ground risked a crisis of support from the US electorate. The Clinton administration was caught up in the difficulty both the UN and Nato faced in acting decisively in the region, which in turn provided opportunities for partisan political attacks by opponents at home.

The administration, in a major initiative, proposed the Partnership for Peace, designed to reconcile desires to maintain the strength and continuity of the Alliance with the opportunity and necessity to try to impose some diplomatic order and a regional security regime within eastern Europe generally. The declaration by the President provided a conceptual framework for association with the Nato Alliance of former Warsaw Pact members.[20] The Partnership for Peace only very indirectly and potentially addresses the problems of war in the Balkans. Washington was accused of indecisiveness, when in reality the international coalition struggling to manage the fighting had that problem. Historical lessons from both world wars taught that doing nothing has been disastrous in the past, yet there was no national consensus in the USA or Western European countries to pursue full-scale active military intervention. History also argues that Balkan wars have been both costly and at least to some extent unavoidable. The frustrations involved in getting two coalitions, the United Nations and the North Atlantic Treaty Organization, to take action were antithetical to the goal of pursuing a sustained, effective military policy. The *Financial Times* issue of 3/4 December 1994 seemed aptly to sum up the situation, in which crisis unresolved seemed to create even greater indecision:

Nato yesterday pledged to continue military flights over Bosnia, in spite of a request from the UN to scale them down, in the latest in a series of rows between the two international organizations.

The dispute erupted as foreign ministers from the US, Russia, Britain, France and Germany – the so-called contact group – met last night in Brussels in an attempt to revive the stalled peace process.[21]

Characteristics of the ongoing crisis made diplomatic and political life especially difficult for Clinton. The United States appeared very free with advice on how to manage the situation, yet had no troops directly involved on the ground, in contrast to European allies. Divisions between the Congress and the Executive Branch became severe over Bosnia, reflecting in part the manoeuvring for position in the presidential race of 1996.

Writing in September 1994, conservative American political columnist William Safire declared that the USA was giving in to appeasement-minded European allies. He refrained from acknowledging British and French courage in actually committing troops on the ground in harm's way in the Balkans:

> Taking advantage of a weak U.S. president, Britain and France – partners in appeasement in Bosnia – have seized leadership of the Atlantic Alliance. The American idea was to enforce a cease-fire with Nato air power, while lifting the one-sided arms embargo . . . But the British-French notion was to put peacekeeping troops in Bosnia that confirmed the Serbian gains . . . Prodded by Congress, Clinton prepared to go to the UN Security Council to lift the embargo. To prevent this, the Brits and French . . . warned Sarajevo . . . they would pull out their peace-keepers . . . Not since World War II has the world seen such a callous betrayal . . .[22]

One of the most serious reversals suffered by the administration *vis-à-vis* Congress took place on this matter. On 11 July 1995, the Bosnian Muslim stronghold of Srebrenica was taken by Bosnian Serb forces. Assaults continued against Zepa, another UN safe area. This Serb victory, involving the first of a series of 'safe' areas identified by the United Nations, and the attendant failure of the United Nations Protection Force (UNPROFOR) to provide adequate defense, generated considerable American legislative support for a change in US policy. Late in the month, the US Senate voted on and passed bill S.21, lifting the arms embargo against Serbia twelve weeks after UNPROFOR withdrew or was requested to do so by the Bosnian government. At the initiative of Senator Robert Dole, the front-runner for the Republican presidential nomination in 1996, the Senate and then the House in the summer of 1995 voted to lift the Bosnian arms embargo, an action vetoed by the White House yet sufficient further to rupture allied relations. Supporters of the Dole initiative argued that the maintenance of the arms embargo on Yugoslavia imposed by the UN in 1991 permitted the 80 000 man Serb Bosnian militia, supported by Serbia next door, to hold the approximately 70 per cent of Bosnia that had been taken in the fighting without effective challenge from domestic opposition, which was restricted by the embargo. The debate over Bosnia became more muted later in 1995 with the reversals suffered by Serb forces on the battlefield, and finally ceased at least for a time with the remarkable peace accord worked out among the warring factions by Assistant Secretary of State Richard Holbrooke, with some intervention by President Clinton directly.[23]

Armed conflict within the former Soviet Union has reinforced the picture of instability in this part of the world. On 1 November 1991, President Dzhokar Dudayev unilaterally declared the independence of his nation of Chechnya. There was initially very little response from the Russian government. But on 9 December 1994, President Boris Yeltsin issued a decree that the government of Russia had the duty 'to safeguard State security, legality, citizens' rights and freedoms, to maintain public order and the drive against crime, and to disarm illegal groups.' Within forty-eight hours, Russian troops were moving into Chechnya to quell the rebellion, and also provide some humanitarian relief. The adventure led to divisive debate in the Russian parliament as well as strong opposition in Chechnya, which initially was able to deliver embarrassing defeats to Russian forces. Again, as the 1996 US presidential election approached, there was no shortage of partisan criticism of the Clinton administration, but in this case no clear insights concerning what exactly Washington could do to end such problems.[24]

Yet this region also has demonstrated the dramatic shifts and ironies of diplomacy and the consequent impact on American domestic politics. As 1995 drew to a close, Assistant Secretary of State Richard Holbrooke orchestrated the dramatic reversal of fortunes for the Clinton administration in the Balkans, driving a process of negotiation that began with shuttle diplomacy in the region and ended with a successful peace conference in Ohio, a state by the way important to Democratic Party presidential fortunes in 1996 and an appropriately Middle-American scene for the culmination of yet another US effort to assist Europeans out of their propensity for armed strife.

NATO: DURABLE, EXPANDABLE

The frustrating, seemingly intractable problems of the Balkans, and the tenuous peace accord, have drawn attention to Alliance discord and the difficulties of getting a coalition to work together in any crisis short of general war directly threatening members' security. Concentration on the state of affairs in the Balkans has masked genuine accomplishments of the Clinton administration in the foreign policy field in Europe. The Partnership for Peace represents a comprehensive practical guidebook to handling alliance and regional affairs in Europe. To some extent, Nato expansion is congruent with a history of receptivity to broadening membership in the Alliance, in the early years primarily at American initiative. The primary decision to establish Nato included joining the United States and Canada with Britain, France, Belgium, Luxembourg and the Netherlands. The USA insisted that the new alliance include Denmark, Norway, Portugal, Italy despite the former Axis tie, Iceland for geographic reasons, and Greece and Turkey as the result of an impetus provided by the Korean War. The Federal Republic of Germany entered in 1955 with the following restrictions: force levels of no more than 495 000 and no weapons of mass destruction. Spain upon entry refused to participate in the integrated military command. Incentives for that nation to join included strengthening democracy and providing an opportunity to enter the European Economic Community.

Despite efforts of the Western European Union to play a more active and assertive role in Central and Eastern Europe, the Nato Alliance remains the main and most likely means for expansion of the regional security relationship. The most likely new candidates for Nato membership are to be found among states identified in the Partnership for Peace concept outlined in January 1994 at the initiative of President Clinton.[25]

ASIA: APEC, CHINA, JAPAN

Asia has represented a region of both rhetorical inspiration and trade controversy, but no current armed conflict of direct danger to the United States, perhaps ironically given the USA's history of involvement in wars there in this century. APEC, the Asia–Pacific Economic Co-operation association established by Secretary of State James Baker during the Bush administration, has continued to serve during the Clinton years as an effective mechanism for communication among trading nations of the Pacific region. Clinton made a persuasive speech in the fall of 1993 to the

APEC meeting in Seattle, Washington, underscoring the importance of the organization, which has grown steadily.

Unfortunately, deteriorating bilateral relations with both China and Japan have overshadowed such achievements. The relationship with Japan has been defined almost exclusively in terms of the trade frictions and disagreements. US Trade Representative Mickey Kantor's approach to difficult negotiations has been to take an outspoken, high-profile public stance, and the Japanese generally have responded in kind. In consequence, the flexibility which can be demonstrated in private diplomatic forums has not been available to either side, and public postures have at times masked fundamental discord on issues. For example, the 1995 trade agreement with Japan included a unilateral American declaration of understanding regarding the result of the negotiations which had just concluded, quite separate from the public bilateral document.[26]

In many ways the problems with China are at least equally worrisome, partly because there is no clear picture of what will emerge to succeed the long-term, unusually influential leadership of Deng Xiaoping. *Détente* – and confrontation – between the USA and the Soviet Union among other things provided opportunities for the two sides to become reasonably familiar with one another over time. In 1994 and 1995, USA–China relations steadily deteriorated. The administration, bowing to Congressional pressure, permitted the President of the Taiwan government to appear at Cornell University, a move defensible on free speech grounds but guaranteed to antagonize the Beijing government. In a scathing column in the *Wall Street Journal* in the summer of 1995, Karen Elliott House summed up much of the conventional criticism of the Clinton administration regarding China and Asia in general:

It's been the worst summer for Sino–U.S. relations since tanks rolled into Tiananmen Square in June 1989, and the outlook is only for worse. A combination of American ineptitude and Chinese paranoia are creating the fiction of a new U.S. containment strategy against China. And, however ironically, it could well become a self-fulfilling prophecy.

Far from reflecting any new-found strength or strategic purpose in Asia, Mr. Clinton's moves this summer are merely more of the reactions and reversals that have characterized his famously feckless foreign policy. These days that's compounded by congressional meddling that further underscores the void in White House leadership in world affairs.

Even this harsh critic, however, recognizes the importance of business and commercial activity, not surprising in the principal American capitalist newspaper, and grudgingly notes this situation is not all bad: 'Trade relations have continued to expand, and U.S. business has become increasingly active in China. But $48 billion in bilateral trade is no substitute for a broader strategic relationship.'[27]

Clinton was also confronted with a crisis over the threatened North Korean nuclear weapons programme, which his administration has handled so far effectively in terms of both avoiding war and achieving an agreement to dismantle the weapons-capable North Korean nuclear installations. The North agreed to abandon the installations over a period of ten years and to accept full international inspection of all nuclear facilities. In return, the United States agreed to organize an international effort, involving contributions from both Japan and South Korea, to substitute civilian use light-water nuclear reactors for North Korea. The replacement system will be expensive, costing approximately $4 billion. After initially balking at accepting reactors from South Korea, the understanding in late 1995 appeared to be continuing on track. The United States agreed to provide needed energy to North Korea in the interim until the new facility comes fully on line. United States Assistant Secretary of State Robert Gallucci conducted the sensitive negotiations, after an initial breakthrough was achieved by former President Jimmy Carter. Another Korean War has been averted, and at the same time the most pressing danger currently visible of nuclear weapons proliferation has been stopped. This did not result in much media praise for the administration, however. As usual, and as indicated just above and throughout this study, press evaluation of President Clinton was at best mixed. Clinton, like Carter and unlike Reagan, has received rather critical treatment by the press in his tenure, and such successes as this may have muted but not eliminated that attitude.[28]

At the time of writing, Clinton's tenure in the White House has still been too brief, with a record that is still unfolding, for any effective comprehensive analysis of administration performance. The President did initially appear to give a comparatively low priority to foreign policy as opposed to domestic concerns. Certainly public opinion poll evidence indicates that the American people have given the administration relatively low marks on the conduct of foreign policy. Whether fairly or not, the US media has been increasingly inclined during the life of the administration to express harsh criticism for alleged indecisiveness in action and lack of clarity in policy. The frustration regarding Bosnia, recently reversed, and also involvements in Rwanda and Somalia are cited as evidence for this proposition. A different sort of criticism holds that the administration often uses foreign policy for cynical, overly political purposes, notably in the decision to intervene with military force in Haiti, responding to complaints from the Congressional Black Caucus and –

allegedly – political campaign-style concern that the President was widely viewed as unwilling to exercise force in international affairs. Such a critical focus overlooks Clinton's considerable success in securing Congressional approval of both the North American Free Trade Agreement and the renewed General Agreement on Tariffs and Trade (GATT) accord, providing for a new World Trade Organization, as well as highly effective promotion of APEC as the central mechanism for co-ordination of national economic interests in Asia.[29]

CONCEPTUAL FRAMEWORKS PAST AND PRESENT

A basic frustration for policymakers as well as policy analysts is that there is no reliable intellectual structure for the international system which has emerged, no clarifying set of generally agreed upon concepts which highlight the main components of the international system. One of the most important characteristics of the Cold War period was that from the start there was an active effort to define the nature of the international system. From the very beginning of that era, George Kennan was elucidating the nature of the perceived threat represented by the Soviet Union. Kennan's contribution was fundamental given his influence with senior policymakers as well as the scholarly and journalistic communities.

Opinions do vary about whether his analysis was apt or overdone. The restraint he preached in addressing the perceived Soviet threat, with emphasis on containment rather than active opposition, designed to limit the opponent rather than risk war, was rightly seen at the time, in the midst of anti-communist hysteria, as prudent. In more recent years, academic evaluators in particular have focused more on his support for an automatic application of containment, in areas where vital interests were obvious (that is, Europe) as well as, implicitly, in areas where vital interests were extremely hard to identify (that is, Vietnam).

Yet at least there was a conceptual and policy roadmap. Currently, there is no such guidance for American leaders, partly because the world is extremely complex in the number of factors involved. The Cold War period may be frightening to contemplate, but also contained a division between two camps in ideological, military, even geographic terms, which was easy to understand in part because it was so stark. During the Cold War, America faced a perceived danger that resulted in broad consensus for containment. There is no such clarity of purpose today.

In the absence of conceptual guidance, the inevitable limitations of particular presidential leadership styles become more obvious. George Bush may have been competent in crisis decision-making, but he did not have the capacity to articulate the goals and purposes of his administration or the international context in which they operated. Clinton's reputation for pragmatic adjustment to circumstances is heightened and turned into a disadvantage when there is no clearly defined compass or course in foreign policy that has been made understandable to the public at large as well as leadership groups.

This point is reinforced by what each of these presidents has said about foreign policy and international relations concerns. Bush's inaugural address mentioned the need for an orderly and peaceful world, and a strong America, but as mentioned earlier he did not elaborate or emphasize foreign policy. There has been none of the rhetorical departure of a Kennedy, Nixon or Carter among these more recent presidents, promising in each case a new, more active rebirth of American foreign policy leadership. In this area as in others, the Bush administration was a regime that stressed the value and importance of continuity. President Clinton delivered an inaugural address which was probably more distinguished in pure rhetorical terms, yet he did not really discuss foreign policy at all in a presentation that included discussion of poverty, racial justice, the need for an inclusive American society and other matters on the Democratic Party agenda. Here he contrasts dramatically with his hero, John Kennedy.[30]

Nor have these two Presidents been operating in a context of much new thinking on international relations. At the start of the Cold War Kennan represented a vanguard of scholarly and policy efforts to come to grips with that new world order. In the 1950s, strategic studies blossomed, providing among other ideas mutual assured destruction, which for better or worse guided US nuclear weapons policies for years. Over two decades ago, noticeable proportions of academic political scientists began – finally – to include in-depth attention to economics in their research and analysis. With the end of the Cold War, there has been a spate of articles about the need to think in new terms in international relations, but nothing comparable to the previous conceptual framework has been developed. Perhaps such clarity is impossible in a world of multiple conflicts and alliances, with no clear overall bifurcation such as that between the two nuclear superpowers. Earlier analysts had an easier time with that international system.

THE EYE OF PRESIDENTIAL POLITICS

The argument is sometimes heard that foreign policy does not play a major role in American presidential elections, yet the evidence is quite the contrary.

Implicitly, the Republican commitment to isolationism after the First World War had a great deal to do with the success of the party in dominating the nation's politics. Lack of engagement in the world nevertheless involves some conscious policy choice. President Franklin Roosevelt persuasively made the case that the nation must stay out of the world war in the presidential campaign of 1940, and in 1944 argued that the leadership of the war effort should not be changed before victory was achieved. In 1952 and 1968, Presidents Harry Truman and Lyndon Johnson respectively decided not to seek re-election in the face of growing unpopularity linked to prosecution of unpopular wars in Korea and Vietnam, and in each case these wars contributed to Republican victory. Eisenhower's ability to keep the country out of war, and Nixon's capacity to achieve diplomatic breakthroughs with the Soviet Union and China, were each important in their respective re-election victories in 1956 and 1972.

Has the importance of foreign policy in the electoral success of presidents and presidential candidates waned in very recent years? There is no truly persuasive evidence that this is now the case. Bush's success in 1988 was related in part to his ability to link his standing with the great popularity of President Reagan, a public appeal that was to some extent a function of perceived strength on the world stage. Clinton's success in 1992 did involve a campaign which was heavily domestic in emphasis, but even this notably non-foreign policy candidate still made major serious statements on foreign policy during the course of the campaign. Bush's defeat despite decisive victory in the Gulf War does indicate that international dimensions of a president's job may be growing less significant for the public. This is by no means clear, however, thanks to the notable lack of success of this particular leader in the vital field of public communication and persuasion, and perhaps also to the fact that the Gulf War was not a 'real' war in terms of combat impact on the United States. Saddam Hussein's invasion of Kuwait may stand as one of the very few examples of outright aggression – invasion of one nation by another – since the Second World War, but the actual time spent in combat was very brief, and US casualties strikingly low. Bush's international leadership was not dramatized by circumstances on a continuing basis, or by the man himself.

THE STATE OF OPINION

Both George Bush and Bill Clinton have had to deal with a much more complex, uncertain international system. 'Why We Will Soon Miss the

Cold War' was the title of an essay by Professor John Mearsheimer of the University of Chicago in *The Atlantic* in the closing phase of the long-term conflict. Indeed he was right; there was a certainty to the rigid stand-off between the two superpowers that restrained each and kept the Europeans in check besides. With the collapse of the Soviet Union, that certainty was gone. Bush and Clinton have both had to deal with that environment without the advantages a new conceptual framework for the international system would have provided.[31]

Recent public opinion poll evidence indicates that the American people are not growing more isolationist overall, that rather complex mixed patterns are developing. Surveys and analyses carried out by the Chicago Council on Foreign Relations with the Gallup Organization provide useful snapshots, now on a long-term basis, of the evolution of public opinion. The most recent such survey in the fall of 1994 indicated a duality to opinion, with evidence of inward-turning but no movement toward isolationism in the traditional sense. The term 'pragmatic internationalism' is used in order to try to capture this mixed sentiment. To be sure, the public is generally reluctant to use military force overseas, but that has been a consistent sentiment over time. There was also a focus on largely domestic problems such as crime, drugs and unemployment, and a reluctance to become involved in the affairs of other nations. At the same time, a total of 65 per cent of Americans felt the United States should have 'an active role in world affairs', continuing an upward trend since the early 1980s. There was sophisticated awareness of the impact of events abroad on developments at home, support for the United Nations increased, and support for economic protectionism actually declined.

In the fall of 1994, Americans felt notably self-confident and influential in the world. An overwhelming 73 per cent of the public responded that the United States would play a more influential role in the world in ten years. Concerning the current role of the USA, 47 per cent of the public and 44 per cent of the leaders believed the USA was more powerful now than ten years ago (37 per cent of the public and 26 per cent of the leaders felt this way in 1990). Some evidence of uncertainty about the position and role of our nation, combined with growing hostility to Japan, apparent in the 1990 survey had dissipated by 1994. The percentage of the public seeing a 'vital interest' in Japan increased from 79 per cent in 1990 to 85 per cent in 1994. Leaders, though not the public, were less inclined to see Japan's economic competition as a 'critical threat'; this index went from 63 per cent in 1990 to 21 per cent in 1994.

Korea stands out in the 1994 and earlier surveys in several respects. The public and leaders gave relatively strong positive evaluations to the Clinton administration in handling the potential nuclear threat from North Korea. Large totals of 82 per cent of the leaders and 39 per cent of the public favoured using US troops to oppose a North Korean invasion of South Korea. Among leaders, only a Russian invasion of Western Europe and an Iraqi invasion of Saudi Arabia elicited a greater response in favour of use of ground forces.

American confidence and commitment to internationalism are both apparent in support for the Nato Alliance. Fifty-six per cent of the public wanted to keep the commitment to the Alliance, after a movement visible in 1990 for cutting back involvement. A separate leadership sample reflected the same shift; between 1990 and 1994, those who wanted to maintain the Nato commitment increased from 35 per cent to 57 per cent, while those who wanted to cut back went from 61 per cent to 37 per cent. Though Nato originally was created directly to counter the Soviet threat, perception of the value of the organization, like the institution itself, seems to be surviving the end of the Cold War. The general trend toward greater self-confidence and perception of American effectiveness has been apparent since the early 1980s, and is perhaps the greatest combined legacy of Presidents Reagan and Bush. There was more criticism of the Clinton administration's performance in foreign affairs, though relatively high marks were given for relations with Russia, Middle East policy, and trade policy.[32]

COMMUNICATION BEYOND POLLS

Mass communication, transportation and travel are becoming more and more important, while national boundaries are breaking down. This may be one reason why Bush and Clinton have not been very successful at defining the new world of international relations. A world more integrated in human terms, and therefore less divided, is harder to define in conventional foreign policy and international relations concepts and terminology – though not necessarily harder to manage.

The world of visual imagery and sound linked primarily to entertainment has become increasingly pervasive. In this dimension, political leaders such as Bush and Clinton are linked through having to try to come to terms with the media. Bush in this context appears to stand apart, not because he was a traditionalist unwilling to employ the modern tools and even tricks of media and public relations, but because his traditionalism came through in a lack of interest – and lack of talent – in employing these media. Ronald Reagan is rightly credited with mastering the medium far better than Bush, and, so far, better also than Clinton. In the visual world, imagery as manufactured in the context of public relations, and projected in the context of the political campaign, is unavoidable.

The importance of the visual image tends to drive out the reflective spoken word, representing a kind of Gresham's Law of politics. In currency, the less valuable drives out the more valuable. In public discourse, the quick undercuts the profound, the more superficial becomes relatively more influential. Lincoln and Stephen Douglas debating the issues of the day in contesting the 1858 Illinois Senate race was taxing and tiring in a way that exists on a different plane from cryptic recorded sound bites, posed images, endless plotting of media strategy and rushing to the next airplane flight to the next rally. Those debates were not typical of politics in the nineteenth century or any time: Lincoln was in many ways the most adept player of the nineteenth-century American version of media politics, and political campaigns in that era were often characterized by low invective and mean spirit. Negative campaigning is nothing new in American politics. Yet the pervasiveness of the media has without doubt diluted political discussion and debate in ways which are having negative effects on American politics. Coming to grips with American foreign policy after the Cold War therefore involves not just some new conceptualization, but dealing with an electronic world where the media is especially important to democratic politics, and therefore the foreign policies of democratic nations.

Part II
Foreign Policy after the Cold War

4 Soviet Collapse, World Disorder

COLD WAR AND AFTER

The phrase 'new world order' may prove to be an enduring rhetorical legacy of President George Bush. The answer to the question of whether there is in fact such a new international system is actually not entirely one-sided, or even two-sided. The Cold War is over and communism is waning. On the other side of the ledger, the nation-state remains the basic unit in international relations, national military force and economic power the main measuring sticks of influence in that world. Yet beyond these traditional fundamentals there has been an enormous transformation in the relations among and the factors bearing upon nation-states. The remainder of the discussion will attempt to address these great shifts, with some suggestions about useful analytic perspectives and future policies.

The Cold War ended very abruptly. Many in the intellectual community had staked out positions emphasizing the importance of the indefinite gradualism of *détente* and accommodation between the two sides, while experts on the Soviet Union and international relations generally did not foresee the fundamental weakness and ultimate collapse of the Soviet system. In fairness to the experts, very few others as well accurately predicted how the future would unfold.[1] The end of the Soviet Union immediately transformed the constellation of power in the world. This is true in part because of the stark and intense character of the confrontation between the two superpowers, but primarily because of the extensive range of capabilities included in the term 'superpower'. From a purely technical perspective, the two enormous nuclear arsenals of the United States and the Soviet Union were not the only ones capable of extraordinary destruction. Modernization of British and French nuclear forces has brought them on a strategic par with the superpowers in terms of ability to bring utter devastation to other nations. The USA and the Soviet Union also supported very substantial conventional military organizations. If the American reliance on air power over time roughly corresponds to traditional British sea power, a parallel can also be drawn with traditional Soviet, and Russian, emphasis on enormous ground capabilities. Yet, whatever the military arsenals of third powers, analysis of international relations in comprehensive terms was very understandably drawn to conceptions of 'bipolarity' as a result of the prominence – and dominance – of the Soviet–American conflict. The conflict in total involved a great deal more than sheer military power, conventional as well as nuclear.[2]

As mentioned earlier, a range of cleavages, ideological, diplomatic and geopolitical, significantly divided the two superpowers and set them against one another. There was the philosophical confrontation, in practical as well as conceptual terms, between communism and capitalism. There was the equally stark confrontation between two very different conceptions of the history of man; on the one hand the gospel according to Karl Marx, and on the other the diversity of a broad western commitment to liberal democracy and generally open economic markets. Each of the superpowers commanded a large economy. Each maintained general authority within two large alliance blocs, granted such notable exceptions and nonconformists as France and Yugoslavia during the Cold War. There was an appropriately stark division between the two camps bifurcating Europe, which was in turn an arena of the two vastly destructive world wars of the twentieth century. There was a self-reinforcing quality to not one but a series of divisions that characterized the Cold War competition.

Throughout the Cold War, continuing into the age of *détente* engineered by Nixon and Kissinger in the 1970s, there was constant fencing for position and advantage in seemingly endless conflicts and confrontations around the world. The Cuban Missile Crisis of 1962, the most direct and dangerous confrontation between the two superpowers, was one result of this contest. The victory of the Soviet Union in the formation of the communist Castro government in Cuba led directly to US efforts to destroy the regime, which in turn along with the general strategic arms race encouraged Moscow to place offensive nuclear missiles on the island. Certainly external revolution linked to Moscow was one important factor during the Cold War; yet too much was made by tense American analysts of the deviousness, effectiveness and reach of a communist movement which was viewed as seamlessly linked through strong political bonds to Moscow.

None the less communist ideology, in more limited and much more ambiguous ways, was an important dimension of the Cold War international competition. Communist parties tied together through an international association were important components in the Soviet conquest of Eastern Europe after the Second World War. Ho Chi Minh, the great leader of the Vietnamese revolution, did spend time in Moscow and was an active participant in the Communist International in the period between the two world wars. Communist party activity at some level was no doubt significant in the political and revolutionary education of Fidel Castro.

Moscow was an education centre, though not always a congenial one, for a range of representatives of emerging Third World nations during the Cold War, especially its earlier phases.[3]

SOVIET THEORY, SOVIET PRACTICE

Fortunately for world stability, Soviet ideological fervour was inevitably married to Soviet military caution. More than one student of international relations has remarked that Russians are not Germans, meaning that through their history they have generally not been anxious to risk or undertake war. This was true in the early stages of the Cold War, when the Soviet Union was aggressive only in establishing a buffer zone on the western borders, a traditional foreign policy goal, and in the latter stages of the Cold War, when the Soviets became more adventurous in sending military forces beyond their borders. They continued to operate in Cuba and entered such realms as Southwest Africa, but stopped short of undertaking any direct confrontation with the United States or our allies. There remained a traditional caution about use of force which in past and present times has served as a major drag on Soviet (and earlier Russian) adventurism.[4]

If German expansionism over the past hundred years can best be described as a series of bold, violent, at least initially successful military strikes, with a premium on use of new technologies and tactics to evoke victory, Russian expansionism has been almost the reverse – cautious, slow, usually directed at the most immediate territory. The wolf and the bear remain very appropriate, if now overused, imagery for Germany and Russia respectively and their two very different, contrasting styles. In an earlier period, the totalitarian nature of the regimes in both Nazi Germany and the Communist Soviet Union, and the apparent similarities in ruthlessness of Hitler and Stalin, masked differences which indeed appeared to be erased with the German–Soviet non-aggression pact and the carving up of Poland in 1939. Under surface appearances, however, those profound differences remained.

The genesis of the Cold War was not overt military attack by the Soviet Union as part of a vision of rapid world conquest, although analogy from immediate experience with Nazi Germany and Imperial Japan was commonly accepted in the West, even in sophisticated circles. Rather, the immediate source of the conflict between the Soviet Union and the West was the result of the fundamental incompatibility between territorial control in Eastern Europe essential for a Soviet sense of security against Germany, and the United States' commitment, from its origins, to self-

1960 presidential contest, his own campaign a testament to more activist government abroad as well as at home, the former dimension reflecting the tension and insecurities brought by the Cold War, the latter dimension considered progressive in part because of rejection of internal security emphases and the McCarthy witch hunts of the early 1950s.[8]

LEADERS AND GOALS

President Kennedy's famous 1961 inaugural address flowed directly from this desire for a positive alternative. Criticized by some in recent years for excessive rhetoric and a universal global commitment, with the sort of hubris that led into Vietnam, the speech was an effort above all to articulate a positive direction for American foreign policy, show that the USA could take the offensive in the global competition, spark a new faith in government efforts, and spur the citizens with something beyond pure anti-communism. The notion of America as a special place, with a special doctrine of freedom, after all resonates through our history from the beginning. Given this characteristic American vision, self-important but also sincere, no one should be surprised that there were efforts to define US national purpose in the world in ways that meant more than just anti-communism.[9]

The problem is that there was never clear agreement on the best way to implement an assertive American vision in foreign policy terms. Ideals of freedom and equality kept colliding with the realities of dictatorships, corruption and the impenetrability of foreign cultures. The clearest and most important demonstration of the limitations of 1960s activist foreign policy in global terms was the Vietnam War. American leaders of the 1970s and 1980s were variously committed to defending a United States in retreat (apparently Henry Kissinger's view, at least from time to time) or rebuilding the confidence of an American people still capable of great achievements (clearly Ronald Reagan's fundamental perspective), but there were no further major public efforts to undertake a sweeping international mission beyond anti-communism and containment.

The Reagan administration encapsulated these differences. President Reagan had great capacity to inspire the American people, and his high popularity ratings in office would have permitted departures in foreign policy, yet most of the time his political priority was emphasis on hard-line anti-communism reminiscent of the height of the Cold War. Only in the President's second term were there priority efforts to undertake new arms and related understandings with the Soviets. In this environment, the role of Secretary of State George Shultz became pivotal. Raymond Garthoff of the Brookings Institution has analysed in detail the divisions in the Reagan administration between those committed to the traditional hard line, and Secretary of State Shultz and others anxious to maintain communication and the possibility of agreement between the two sides. Moreover, the relative international decline of American economic dominance, undeniable from the late 1960s as other industrial nations fully recovered from the Second World War, meant that policy attention high and low within the government was devoted to nitty gritty details of technical issues, forcing out grand designs of all sorts.[10] In consequence, the victory in the Cold War has been far from hollow but not fully satisfying.

The most successful American political leaders, in the past as well as contemporary times, have provided a doctrinal or thematic base to their policies. The greatest have had the challenge, and ultimate historic opportunity, of tremendous threats to the nation. Those threats provided context of both high drama and high-stakes decisions. Abraham Lincoln was remarkably consistent in his goal of preservation of the Union, was rightly viewed as firmly and unswervingly committed to that purpose, yet used an amazing variety of tactics – including arbitrary search and seizure – to pursue his end. Franklin Roosevelt proved remarkably consistent after achieving the presidency in pursuing the goal of transformation of the social and economic dimensions of national policy, was viewed by many as opportunistic and inconsistent in his policy course, and also used a wide range of tactics – including an abortive initiative to change the Supreme Court – to pursue his policy end. Consistency in fundamental goals united both leaders, and rhetorical and other persuasive skills were obviously essential. Both aggressively used the main communication mechanisms available, in Lincoln's case the newspaper and photograph, in Roosevelt's the radio and newsreel. Both were also great speakers, and the content as well as the means of delivery solidified their political constituencies, reconfirming the importance of rhetoric to democratic political leadership.[11]

In more recent times, the Americans have experienced a diverse list of leaders over the very long term of the Cold War, and perhaps that has been another reason why positive themes to encourage the competition with the Soviet Union were hard to define and to develop. Ronald Reagan was a gifted television performer, obviously effective in direct communication with the electorate, yet his twin themes of less domestic government and ardent *anti*-communism did not provide comprehensive popular satisfaction or success once the Cold War concluded.

The absence of a clear positive theme undergirding the American effort during the Cold War might have resulted in considerable instability in the domestic political debate over foreign policy once the conflict ended, but this also has not been the case. Uncertainty, not instability, is the most that can be said about the atmosphere in the United States. Patrick Buchanan's challenge from the far right in the Republican Party, with the siren song of nationalism, nativism and neo-isolationism – the 'three n's', was sufficient to undercut President George Bush to a degree in the presidential primary elections of 1992 but did not go on to secure a genuine national political victory. Likewise, there has been no embrace of the ardent communal internationalism, including emphasis on international organizations rather than national sovereignty, that traditionally has attracted many on the American political left.

This in turn may be related to one further reason why the end of the Cold War has not had a more pronounced popular impact in the United States. The conflict was long, and during the 1950s and early 1960s very intense, but in later years did not appear to threaten our national, institutional or personal survival. The danger of nuclear war, at least after the Cuban Missile Crisis, was apparent but not immediate. For the majority of the American people, the challenge of earning a living and the opportunities of consumer society have far outweighed the concerns and any allures of international relations, which remain the preoccupation mainly of professionals in government and intellectuals in academic and research institutions.

In earlier times, Lincoln and Roosevelt provided superb leadership, but in the context of enormous crisis which represented a fundamental threat to the nation. No such danger has been perceived by Americans in recent years, with the waning of fears about communist expansion and nuclear war. Great leaders possess fundamental qualities of character, intellect and personality, but circumstances of great crisis facilitate the emergence and demonstration of their strengths and skills. In the Cold War period, American leaders coped in ambiguous circumstances with varying degrees of effectiveness. In the post-Cold War world, the challenge for our political leaders is even greater, for the danger is complacency, drift, letting events assume control precisely because there is no imminent fundamental threat.

STRUCTURES OF ALLIANCE

The end of the Cold War might also have ended the North Atlantic Treaty Organization, but rather surprisingly that has proven not to be the case. The Alliance has survived both the collapse of the great power which it was formed to oppose, and a series of disruptive, depressing and generally frustrating crises which also might reasonably have been expected to lead to demise. The Nato treaty ironically nowhere mentions the Soviet Union, though perceptions of Soviet expansionism and threat to Western Europe after the Second World War were what led to the formation of the Alliance. The treaty simply states that an attack against one member will be interpreted as an attack against all. Yet the Soviet Union's perceived goals of domination and expansion were the reasons for the very existence of Nato. Habits of co-operation have apparently become so firmly established that the perimeter is maintained, albeit with reduced forces, even though the enemy is gone.

The secret of Nato's durability has little to do with the specific treaty document. Henry Kissinger was notable during his scholarly career for criticizing the impractical influence of legalism on the American foreign policy process. Once in office himself, he never confused paper with power. Certainly American behaviour during the early phase of the Cold War, and to some extent later, provides evidence for Kissinger's thesis, and Nato as a 'contract' among partners engaged in the 'business' of opposing communism became a document of central importance to those disposed to such attitudes. Faced with the success of Nato in providing cohesion and strength against the Soviet bloc, Secretary of State John Foster Dulles spent a great deal of time during the Eisenhower administration in a singular effort to reproduce Nato around the world, literally 'ringing' the Communist camp with a variety of similar treaty arrangements. Relentless in purpose, endlessly energetic, driven as only the righteous can be, Dulles was effective in achieving accords on paper, the lawyer's tangible measure of success in the commercial world, but these understandings did not have a lasting impact on the structures or practices of international relations, the diplomat's measure of ultimate success in the political world. The result was treaties – Cento (the Central Treaty Organization) in the Middle East, Seato (the Southeast Asia Treaty Organization) in Asia – which had no meaning or impact outside the files containing them, joined no genuine interests in the real world, and are today justifiably forgotten. Dulles' efforts may have been one factor encouraging the USA to use force outside of Europe, in particular in Vietnam, though even this is highly uncertain; during the Eisenhower years, the Secretary of State's personal activism co-existed with the President's notable caution and particular reluctance to undertake armed combat.[12]

Early in the existence of Nato, an elaborate organizational structure was created. Justified no doubt by the large size of the Alliance and the challenge of maintaining cohesion among so many different national cultures, the approach also was very characteristic of the American disposition to handling military affairs. In modern times, an exceptionally large percentage of US forces has been devoted to non-combat, administrative functions. The influential French strategist General André Beaufre addressed this feature, probably too sarcastically, and Eisenhower's selection as the first Nato commander in a book which appeared in 1966, the same year that his nation withdrew from the Nato integrated command and forced Alliance headquarters to move from Paris to Brussels. 'In view of Eisenhower's prestige . . . ,' he wrote, 'it was the best choice that could have been made, but it also meant submitting to the cumbersome American administrative machinery, which perceives organization only in the form of highly complex diagrams.'[13]

The main source of strength of Nato is not specific documentary language, or even an ongoing bureaucracy, but the broad identity of national interests and purposes of the participants. Early on, Nato also had the good fortune to become defined in narrow terms, making the Alliance less likely to be undercut by members finding themselves at cross purposes in third areas of the globe. In 1954, the French found their colonial position in Indochina becoming untenable. A range of relatively isolated forts had been gradually but steadily surrounded and overcome by the enormously determined, numerous Vietnamese revolutionary army, the Viet Minh. The largest and most substantial such outpost, Dien Bien Phu, was under siege and increasingly at risk. Paris made a desperate appeal to Washington as a Nato ally for assistance.

President Eisenhower, very reluctant to intervene, characteristically anxious to avoid head-on confrontation, responded in constitutional and institutional terms. He argued that he could accept the French plea for military action only if Congressional leaders concurred and at least one other major Nato partner, meaning Britain, would co-operate. House Speaker Sam Rayburn and, ironically in light of later events, Senate Majority Leader Lyndon Johnson were against using force. The British wanted no part of the French disaster. Direct American military intervention was not forthcoming. Not many noted at the time or afterward that President Eisenhower had imposed a narrow 'strict constructionist' interpretation on the Nato treaty. In future Nato would be explicitly invoked on behalf of European territory of the partners, not their colonies or clients elsewhere in the world. Thanks to Eisenhower's restraint, and the manner in which the decision was made, European allies had a comparatively easy time rejecting efforts by President Lyndon Johnson and his Secretary of State to enlist their direct assistance in the Americans' Vietnam War of the 1960s. The end of the Cold War opens the new question of the degree to which the Alliance can and should become involved in European disputes beyond such immediate defence of members' real estate.[14]

Thanks to restraint as well as fundamental congruence of interests, Nato was still firmly in existence when the Cold War ended, and had even been able to undertake some expansion without apparent dilution. The structure has been able to survive the fratricidal hatred and occasional war between Greece and Turkey. The expansion of Nato is above all tangible testimony to the durability of the Alliance and the very long-term appeal of participation among the members.[15]

The United States has provided Alliance leadership of a very visible sort with the Partnership for Peace proposal of the Clinton administration, an effort to reaffirm the basic commitment to Nato while undertaking to expand the Alliance. The Partnership, eminently pragmatic, attempts to provide both a reaffirmation of the importance of the Nato Alliance while opening the door to partial and more informal co-operation by selected East European states that are both capable of and comfortable with such involvement. The Russian government, amidst the enormous political and economic uncertainties confronting that nation, and following threats and complaints about the expansion of the Alliance through 1994, has nevertheless recently agreed to closer co-operation with Nato as well, a step which must be viewed as a major concession given endemic suspicion of any East European involvement in what is fundamentally a West European, and North American, military organization. The Czech Republic, Hungary and Poland especially all have strong ties to the West, and have governments and histories that should be relatively congenial to continued democracy and the related requisite civilian control of the military, a statement that can hardly be made about other parts of Eastern Europe.[16]

Much less encouraging until recently has been Nato experience in promoting humanitarian assistance and peacekeeping in Southeastern Europe. Here the Nato relationships have been strained, though not yet broken, as a result of actual involvement in a war zone, occasional combat, and the cleavages between Alliance partners on how best to manage the challenge. There is no easy way to see how the Alliance could realistically have avoided the morass of the Balkans or disagreement and tension among the partners once involved. Given the very long history of bitter conflict in the area, with religious cleavages reinforcing ethnic divisions and profound historical memories of violence, the surprising fact is not that war broke out after the Cold War, but that reasonable stability among such divided populations was maintained for a time after the Second World War. Nato provides an obvious and proximate regional military instrument. History teaches that instability in the Balkans threatens to expand into wider conflict in Europe, which would probably have been sufficient incentive for intervention. Atrocities and more general human suffering provided a spur that Western nations could not ignore.

The strongest criticism that can be made of the intervention is that the 'rules of engagement', meaning really the purpose of the employment of military forces, were not laid out clearly at the outset. Perhaps this was not a practical goal, given the complexities of the conflict and the strength of pressures to intervene. Much of the criticism of the exercise reflects the comfort of not having to engage directly in pressured decisions involving considerable lack of information. However, there is a difference between protecting supply columns providing humanitarian relief, and trying very actively to separate the combatants; the fact remains that what was initially an effort to undertake the former expanded step by step to include the latter. Explicitly opposing Serbian military advances meant effectively taking sides in the war. Critics on the sidelines have argued that there should have been a strictly limited goal of protecting a few identified safe havens from Serbian attack, thereby providing cover for and assistance to refugees. This became the *de facto* policy of the United Nations forces in the area, only to find the Serb forces easily overcame such 'safe' areas when they chose. The UN effort was saved to some extent by the capacity of the Croats to mount effective counterattacks in the summer of 1995, though the credibility of the world organization for even limited humanitarian interventions in future has been eroded.[17]

In retrospect – always very clear – the United Nations would have been well advised to limit intervention efforts only to humanitarian relief assistance. Lack of commitment to combat for protection of the existing safe havens means that approach would have been better avoided entirely. Above all, the experience demonstrates that the United Nations is not an appropriate organization for detailed management of any war or for active intervention except in cases of clear-cut aggression, such as Iraq's invasion of Kuwait, or peacekeeping where all parties are agreed on the presence and legitimacy of the UN.

Yet the Balkan experience so far has also demonstrated that the Nato Alliance can survive armed conflict, including differences of opinion among the participants, even in the region of Europe, and provide the means to police an agreement reached with American leadership. The fact that the organization persists, and East European nations want to join, demonstrates a viable future. The fact that the Balkan war created such tensions within Nato, despite the consensus on the need for humanitarian relief, indicates that the Alliance should be cautious about undertaking any formal commitment to intervene in conflicts elsewhere. Nevertheless Nato survives and there is no practical organizational alternative available. The UN, EU, Western European Union, Conference on Security and Co-operation in Europe (CSCE) – renamed the Organization for Security and Cooperation in Europe (OSCE) as of January 1995 and other possible institutional mechanisms have either been too cautious and bureaucratic to succeed, or too marginal and abstract even to be employed. Professor Charles Glaser of the University of Chicago provided in a 1993 essay in the journal *International Security* a comprehensive, crisp summary of security alternatives in Europe, with a realistic appreciation for the importance of Nato that appears to be confirmed by events since:

> I find that Nato is likely to provide a better hedge than any of the alternatives. Nato can meet Western requirements in all three types of war – hedging against a resurgent Russia, providing the means to extend security guarantees to Central European countries, and reducing the already low probability of future tensions within Western Europe – both by preserving America's role in Europe as a defensive balancer and by maintaining institutions for concert-like coordination within the West.[18]

Much less practical than struggling with the status quo are suggestions to replace Nato entirely with some form of new 'Concert of Europe', harking back to the mechanism for stability in the nineteenth century. Professor Richard Rosecrance of UCLA has been notable for promoting this approach, building in a relatively recent article in *Foreign Affairs* on a theme and approach that have been of great interest to him throughout his career. References to history are both instructive and potentially misleading. In the case of the Concert of Europe, several different factors must be considered. First, the mechanism was the creature of a nineteenth-century world of diplomacy in which national elites by and large had considerable freedom to operate without democratic oversight or veto. This in turn facilitated flexibility that is more difficult to achieve when the diplomatic equation includes broad public involvement and debate over major decisions.

Second, Britain historically played a special role of balancer and independent influence within the Concert and in European affairs more generally, thanks to a combination of diplomatic skill, military and economic power, psychological distance, and the resources of an enormous global empire. The United States maintains some troops in Europe in Nato and now is putting forces at risk directly on the ground in combat areas in Southeastern Europe. The USA remains tied to Europe through institutional arrangements and the psychology of alliance, yet separate from Europe thanks to a very different national history and political culture. We are not inclined by temperament to reproduce the sort of dispassionate, finely tuned and constantly calculating diplomacy practised by London in an earlier age. The geopolitical map of Europe has also changed, with economic integration and commercial competition overshadowing national divisions, reinforcing the influence of multinational corporations.

Britain's history and diplomatic style are broadly instructive for Americans, but the geographic, technological, psychological – and political – positions of the older great power in the 1700s and 1800s were very different from our own. Modern nationalism had not yet emerged in colonial areas during the height of the British empire. Americans do not desire to reproduce the imperial role which gave Britain such influence in the nineteenth century. Even if they did, the international system is no longer so malleable to traditional military and economic power; this is the most important lesson of the tragedy of the Vietnam War.

Third, the most pressing issues for Europe currently include encouragement of economic integration as well as military stability. In this context, the comparatively specialized institutional arrangements of the European Union and Nato seem more likely to succeed on particular issues and disputes than a broad, traditional Concert sort of arrangement. The original Concert was very largely a reaction against the dangers of nationalism; the success of the European Union in limiting virulent modern nationalism provides a strong if implicit argument for continuing to try to work within this framework. Also, Germany's history places special restraints, which may be gradually fading, on use of military forces for any purpose beyond national borders.

Finally, any new Concert of European powers, with or without the United States, would run the risk that the first failure would destroy the new organization. Nato and the European Union, by contrast, have relatively long histories of existence through both successes and failures; the capacity to survive failure may in fact be the most fundamental test of such an organization. Previous association makes continued co-operation relatively easy and comfortable. As Professor Glaser notes, 'Good relations reduce the risks of attempting to co-ordinate.' Any new structure would have to overcome the barrier of lack of previous co-operation, plus the practical question of what a new Concert adds to existing arrangements beyond nostalgic satisfaction.[19]

EUROPEAN UNION AND DISUNION

Much of the history of the European Union has been defined in terms of attempting to resolve, or resolving to live with, a fundamental tension between those who wish to see the nation-state subsumed in a larger supranational order, and those who do not. Even individuals who agree in general on the goal of greater integration of Europe are divided over particular policies and approaches. The movement for European unification over time has been curious and deceptive because so indirect, like a flirtation or complicated dance, in which both partners engage in elaborate ritual, with some moves apparent only to the participants and not to the wider audience.

Europe after the Second World War was devastated spiritually and emotionally, as well as economically and physically, and the United States was both enormously self-confident with new-found global power and enormously troubled by the great ordeal just ended. By the latter part of the nineteenth century, Germany had begun to overshadow Great Britain as the capital of scientific and technical research, to rival the other nation in more general scholarly and educational activity, and had become the principal industrial power of Europe in terms of productive growth. Germany, a nation of extraordinary positive accomplishment, had by 1945 been reduced to a devastated pariah remnant of a state, the horrors inflicted on the region of Europe only becoming fully apparent after the unconditional surrender of the Nazi regime.

For thoughtful people, especially Europeans who had suffered from the world wars at first hand, the incentives for some sort of basic political reform to prevent a third cataclysm were obvious. This, far more than any positive visionary notions of human unity, provided the very practical incentive to try to reduce the likelihood of war between nations by combining them in a web of self-reinforcing economic interests. Nationalism had been fed by the Nazis, providing both fuel and justification for their initial territorial grabs and later genocidal crimes. Nationalism had been a principal cause of the First World War. Nationalism was the bane of modern diplomacy and international stability, and reducing the importance of national identity could reasonably be defended as a goal which would in turn reduce the likelihood of general war. After all, the establishment of the United Nations, generally accepted by major Allied nations even before the end of the Second World War, was motivated by these sorts of sentiment.

The nation-state, however, has been a tough, enduring entity. Hence Jean Monnet and the other planners of European supranationalism decided on the indirect approach to achieve their goal. The legitimacy of the state would not be attacked head-on; rather, a set of technical goals would be outlined, economic incentives would be used to open the regional market and encourage nation-states to band together for the sake of growth and prosperity, in the process diluting the importance, and ultimately the meaning, of national boundaries. The process began with the European

in the end rather limited though in this case also important practical gains. The treaty was extremely successful in providing the impetus for dissolving the remaining barriers to commerce across borders in Europe, a considerable achievement given delays of transport at national checkpoints and other such practical impediments to the smooth flow of commerce. The cumulative effect of this full market integration will be in these terms, allowing economies of scale virtually free rein, making life easier in particular for very large multinational corporations, which are as a result further enabled to place plants in and direct other investment to locations of maximum economic advantage, without much attention being required for remaining national distortions of and limitations on markets.[23]

The second part of Europe 1992 was to be a common European currency, though here integration efforts have been so far largely unsuccessful. A sophisticated formula was worked out for currency values to be maintained and co-ordinated in advance of creating the single currency. Britain and Italy both had problems remaining within the agreed values and eventually dropped out of the system. Aside from the problems of maintaining agreed smoothly co-ordinated values in an age of floating exchange rates, the concept of a single currency ran into the reality of the growing power of the German economy and the German central bank, the Bundesbank. Germany had become the dominant economic power in Europe by a steadily increasing margin; a single currency would without doubt be one that was managed primarily by German central bankers. Other Europeans simply would not accept this proposition, and a single European currency was postponed.[24]

ASIA

If European and wider Atlantic area relations are tied together in myriad ways by a complex set of regional relationships and institutions, the situation in Asia seems very different, both far more open and far more closed. Arguably the importance of economic and trade considerations alone is greater, but the security challenges for the United States probably less, in Asia than in Europe in the wake of the Cold War. To what extent does European experience provide suggestions for the policy guidance of Asia in the future? The environment is more open in the sense that the absence of long-standing alliances and other relationships of the Atlantic variety provides, at least in theory, the opportunity to construct entirely new institutions, reflecting post-Second World War experience and anticipation of what international relations will require in the twenty-first century. Economic collaboration, for example, can be pursued without the baggage of a Cold War military alliance structure.[25]

The environment is also more closed in that social, cultural and perceptual gaps between different nations are inevitably greater. Because there is not the same sort of history of regional co-operation, national cultural differences and economic protectionism are much more important as divisive, isolating factors. Racial diversity is also much more pronounced than in Europe. The Pacific region requires integrating and co-ordinating Eastern and Western perspectives; the Atlantic community of nations involves simply Western outlooks, and co-operation has been challenging and vexing nevertheless over the past half-century.

Regarding institutional networks and webs, one senior American expert on Asia remarked that the Northeast Asia region is 'under-alphabetized' compared with Europe and the Atlantic area. A working group of the Asia Foundation, after a series of meetings in 1992, concluded that,

> A central question now is how Asia will organize itself. Regional stability could be undermined by leadership succession struggles in Vietnam, China, North Korea, and Indonesia . . . Government institutions in much of the region are weak. Official economic cooperation in Asia has only recently begun to develop, with the formation of Asia Pacific Economic Cooperation (APEC).

In the security field, there is a set of bilateral and some very modest multilateral relationships, but nothing comparable to the Nato alliance, related organizations and the long history of military co-operation. In the economic field, they exist but are comparatively new, and again do not benefit – but quite the reverse – from the fact that the established major industrial nations most involved in the long history of major trade negotiations are concentrated in the Atlantic region.[26]

Contrasting experiences immediately after the Second World War highlight this point. There were efforts on both sides of the Atlantic, beginning almost immediately after the surrender of Germany, to integrate the devastated nation into the wider European and Atlantic area societies. The vision of Jean Monnet and his collaborators in the European union movement was of central importance, but there were other factors as well. The Marshall Plan was designed to foster political stability and an environment conducive to democracy along with immediate humanitarian relief. Dwight Eisenhower, as both general and President, took important steps to encourage human exchange programmes, especially between the younger generations of Germans and Americans. The Nato Alliance was generated by fear of the Soviet Union, but inclusion of the Federal Republic of Germany in membership in 1955 was not only an appropriate step toward recognition of the progress in building democracy and stability, but also very defensible on the grounds of deterrence of the Soviet Union and associated Eastern bloc allies. At least as important was the very good personal chemistry among President Eisenhower, Secretary of State John Foster Dulles and West German Chancellor Konrad Adenauer.[27]

A comparable combination of economic, military and political factors was not to be found in Asia. General Douglas MacArthur excelled as a radical reformer of Japan's lingering structure of commercial and industrial interests, providing as well a written constitution committed to democratic government, but his ruling style was aloof and autocratic, in keeping with the man. There was no effort to develop the sort of close collaborative relationships, including exchange programmes, that characterized the American approach to Germany after the war. The Japanese probably found this MacArthur approach easier to handle than would have been the case with a more open, typically American governor. One result of the MacArthur strategy of combining radical institutional reform with considerable distance from the culture and society was to maintain Japan's sense of separation from other nations, including the United States. Moreover, the eruption of the Korean War in 1950 meant that attention was urgently distracted from what might have been more thorough efforts to change the domestic environment in Japan.[28]

For this reason, the notion of simply transplanting Nato as a structural model to the Asian environment is misguided, impractical to a degree that simply reproducing the same structure in an alien environment would be guaranteed to fail. Germany's situation was very different from Japan's. The Federal Republic was integrated culturally into the wider Europe, aided by a largely benign occupation and contiguity with other states, before formal association with Nato was approved in 1955. Even so, the argument at the time about rearming Germany and allowing the former enemy into the Alliance structure caused extensive, at times bitter debate, with the proposal for German participation in a European army sufficiently explosive to bring down the government in France. The fact that Germany was safely divided no doubt made military co-operation appear less threatening than would otherwise have been the case, but the step to involve the Federal Republic was nevertheless a very great, controversial change.

Japan's distance from other nations in Asia is a function of history, economic development, psychology, harsh wartime experiences and memories, and the American approach to occupation. This makes Japanese military participation in a regional security pact hard to envision in realistic terms.

Moreover, trade is the very dominant secular religion of the region of Asia, clearly now more important than communism even in China and Vietnam. A security pact would tend to highlight divisions along national lines, drawing fresh attention to ideological gaps between communist and non-communist states, in particular China and the United States. Such an effort would also be unlikely to generate much enthusiasm among Asian nations which do not have a commonly agreed enemy, and have myriad particular tensions and conflicts dividing them. Any regional security initiative, which would have to be primarily an American effort in order to have any chance of success, would create more antagonism than concord. At a time when US relations with both China and Japan have been tense and deteriorating, any effort to recreate Nato in Asia would rightly be seen as crude, awkward, perhaps patronizing, and certainly impractical.[29]

More likely is an evolution of major-power partnership in the region. Here, the precedent of the Concert of Europe, the collaborative institution of the great powers of that region in the nineteenth century, is useful as a guide to thinking about how regional stability in Asia might be encouraged and maintained. Richard Solomon, former Assistant Secretary of State for East Asia, has been among the senior experts trying to come to grips with the changing constellation of forces in the region. He has emphasized the importance of at least informal co-operation among China, Japan, Russia and the United States. While the truly active participation of Russia remains problematical, given the abysmal state of the economy and the uncertain state of the domestic political regime, the other three powers will remain unavoidably involved in the region, standing apart from others by virtue of their scale and international impact.[30]

Given this construction, the United States would be well advised to think in terms of sources of leverage, partnership and persuasion on the other major powers in the region. Even if economic relations with Japan and diplomatic relations with China were less troubled, only a utopian would argue that good intentions would alone guarantee stability, only a caricature version of a business executive would argue that growing profits and shared markets would guarantee peace between such contrasting national interests and cultures. The fundamental dilemma, perhaps the greatest now confronting Washington, is that the US is relatively distant from both of the other major Pacific powers. This separation in turn creates problems in trying to exercise influence, which is increased to the degree that the US is able to use the relationship with one power for leverage on the other, decreased to the degree that we are isolated from both. The absence of substantial regional organizations in Asia gives much greater importance to such interplay among the great powers and heightens the problems of disagreement with no leavening institutional structure. Henry Kissinger has insightfully described this particular triangle:

> In a curious way, the firmness of Japanese–American relations will be the reverse side of the Sino-American relationship. Despite a considerable affinity for Chinese culture, Japan has been torn between admiration and fear, between the desire for friendship and the urge to dominate. Sino-American tension tempts Japan to disassociate from the United States in an effort, if not to enhance its influence in China, at least not to diminish it by following the American lead too closely. At the same time, a purely national Japanese approach runs the risk of being interpreted in Beijing as an expression of the Japanese appetite for domination. Good American relations with China are therefore the prerequisite for good long-term relations with Japan, as well as for good Sino-Japanese relations. It is a triangle which each of the parties can abandon only at great risk. It is also an ambiguity with which the United States is not totally comfortable.[31]

Public bashing of the Japanese over trade practices, and of the Chinese over human rights, risks drastic isolation and diminution of the influence of the United States throughout the enormous Pacific region, but such trends will probably become even harder to resist in the future. Uncertainty over leadership succession, and the very existence of a centralized state controlled by Beijing, will almost certainly grow in China, unless there is a right-wing reaction following the passing of Deng Xiaoping. In Japan, the reality is clear that no single political party or other institution is in control and that this state of affairs is not likely to change soon.

Consequently, for the United States neither human rights problems with China nor trade balance problems with Japan are likely to diminish. There are also in America the unavoidable political constraints imposed by the requirement that political leaders have to achieve election and re-election, which means that very public complaints about both China and Japan will inevitably be part of the domestic political debate. The challenge for American foreign policy leadership is not to transform this situation, but to navigate among interests and passions in a way that furthers the interests of the United States. This is probably going to be easier to achieve in the Atlantic than in the Pacific region. Expecting public criticism of both Chinese and Japanese policies to disappear from the American political debate is no doubt utopian; however, more muted comments, especially from prominent personalities in both parties in Washington, would be highly desirable and should be possible.

Frequent reference to possible Asian 'loss of face' by Westerners who vary widely in their actual expertise probably tends to undermine the very important point that public argument over trade and related issues taken for granted in Europe can carry very large political costs in Asia. The Clinton administration approach of public threats to take very extreme action, for instance a 100 per cent tax on Japanese automobile imports, therefore may appear in the short term to provide useful pressure in a specific trade negotiation but will almost certainly have long-term negative effects. Private pressure is preferable to such a public approach. President Bush, for example, used such effective leverage on China not to sell missile components to Iran. Technical satellite assistance over which the USA had control was the source of persuasive pressure on the Chinese. This worked very directly in securing the interests of the United States in the matter, with very little painful public debate.[32]

In this environment, the association for Asia Pacific Economic Co-operation provides a comprehensive mechanism for co-operation and co-ordination. Much criticized as only a talking forum, APEC nevertheless has done some important talking, including maintaining a commitment to free trade in principle at a time when the Uruguay Round trade negotiation on GATT was faltering. *The Economist* observed in 1994:

> The Chairman of the APEC eminent persons group, Fred Bergsten, who is also head of the Institute for International Economics, a think-tank in Washington, DC, believes that if APEC were now to act boldly, not merely by lowering some of the big barriers that still impede its economic growth, but going so far as to make its trade and investment rules more liberal than those required by the GATT, then it could serve as the catalyst for a whole new phase of global trade liberalization from which the APEC countries themselves would be among the biggest gainers.[33]

CHANGE IN INTERNATIONAL RELATIONS

The components of the emerging international system are diverse and complex, a strikingly dramatic combination of the old and the new. The nation-state remains durable, permeable but solid, utterly unwilling to disappear. Supranationalism nevertheless has been growing and will continue to grow, driven by technology as well as trade. Yet while regional and international organizations of an intergovernmental and even popular sort can restrict and dilute nationalism, such associations seem still very separate from the personal and emotional commitments that comprise very intense nationalism. The political threat to the nation-state from subnational regional movements of various kinds for this reason probably remains more significant, and explosive, than the influence of integrative organizations operating above the level of the state.

But if the nation-state is durable, the international environment continues to grow more complex, with a range of other organizations on the scene beyond the governmental and intergovernmental institutions emphasized above. Opportunities for a more stable international system therefore will have to be constructed on a combination of institutional mechanisms that already exist and others that do not. Among the panoply of organizations that have appeared or grown more important in recent decades is the multinational corporation, which represents a very powerful factor in international relations, explicitly in economic matters, implicitly in others. Multinational corporations are nothing new; indeed as long as international commerce has taken place there have been commercial entities which have transcended national boundaries. The great age of exploration and commerce in the sixteenth to eighteenth centuries witnessed the steady expansion of ocean-based trading. The industrial age in the nineteenth century saw very substantial growth of the volume and diversity of trade. The trading corporation was the product as well as implement of this global outreach, often in the past a very direct, explicit instrument of national policy.

The modern multinational corporation, however, seems different in kind as well as in scale. Contemporary industrial and commercial firms that are global in size have unprecedented capacity to mobilize and move human and financial capital very long distances. The modern firm is frequently characterized by very substantial operations located far from what is technically identified as the home base, and indeed sometimes no clear national 'home' really exists in a firm with great global reach and an executive staff that is highly diverse in national origins and identities. Financial transactions have grown enormously in velocity as well as volume, with very large amounts of funds transferable thousands of miles with the ease of a few computer key strokes.

The revolutions in transportation, communication and – relatedly – commerce have created a wholly new environment for business activity. The modern corporation really has the capacity for the first time in history to operate as a genuinely independent factor in international relations. Firms make decisions affecting huge numbers of people concerning allocation of investment and production resources in different parts of the world. Such companies often do not answer to any single particular government, and some indeed have total annual revenues greater than the budgets of some national governments. The modern international business executive, like the diplomat or military officer in eighteenth-century Europe, has expertise for sale and will often work for a corporation based in a country quite different from his or her own national point of origin.

This is significantly different from earlier periods in international relations, and is not necessarily undesirable for system stability or the interests of particular governments. The corporation is an enormous force for transnational cultural integration. Capital investment can lead to national development as well as expansion of profits and market shares for the firm. A broad acculturation can help introduce people in the Third World to international opportunities previously unforeseen. Clearly the firm is not a force for the automatic extraction of resources and concentration of wealth in any pure Marxist terms. The need for broad and diverse investment in more than one market means that the multinational corporation can bring people together in productive activity and does not automatically drive classes further apart.[34]

The most significant single feature of the modern multinational corporation perhaps is the fact that the political debates in both the US and Europe have not undertaken to include the firm in imaginative ways. To some extent this is not surprising, given the traditional role of big business as target and whipping boy in American partisan politics. Moreover, business is not a unique human institution; in reality virtues and vices, advantages and shortcomings are combined. If the Marxist conception of surplus value and exploitation is fundamentally misleading as a general set of principles, and the history of industrial development does seem to confirm this point, the fact remains that corporations can be exploitative as well as productive, and in any case there is an understandable desire by business executives to stay aloof from government involvement that might complicate or compromise the search for markets and profits.

At the same time, however, the continued significant distance between business and government in the United States is surprising, given the generally conservative political climate of American politics in recent times, the long period of Republican dominance in the executive branch, and Republican majorities now in both houses of Congress as well. A generally pro-business climate has not resulted in much discussion of business as a vehicle for either economic growth and development or furthering US foreign policy.

This state of affairs may reflect the continuing influence of significant domestic political considerations as well as chance and circumstance. Marx may have been wrong in conceptions of the relentless concentration of capital, but he was certainly right in focusing on the importance of 'alienation' from work as a fundamental component of the human condition.

Republicans as well as Democrats depend primarily on the votes of working people, not relatively highly paid business executives or other professionals, if elections are to be won. Too heavy an emphasis on opportunities for business–government co-operation, especially by Republicans, is probably still a recipe for political defeat at the polls.

GERMANY AND JAPAN

Analysis of United States foreign policy in the wider international system has generally focused on interplay with adversaries, especially though not exclusively the Soviet Union and China during the Cold War, particularly irritating smaller opponents such as Iraq, Iran, North Vietnam and – in an earlier period – Cuba, and potential and perhaps actual rivals for leadership in Europe and Asia, Germany and Japan.

The effective, benign integration of Germany and Japan within the wider world community is essential for stability; both nations in the relatively recent past have initiated disastrous world war. Both have great capacity for leadership and demonstrated capacities for economic productivity and growth as well as military destruction. Various studies have addressed the changing present and future roles of these nations, at times in tandem. One of the most thoughtful and – beginning with the title – provocatively argued of recent years is *The New Superpowers – Germany, Japan, the U.S., and the New World Order* by Jeffrey T. Bergner. This volume aptly reflects the sense of vindication and also uncertainty that has characterized American attitudes toward the two former opponents in world war: 'Germany and Japan will grow stronger and more competitive, that much seems clear. We have no way to prevent that, even if we wished to do so. But there is no reason to wish to do so.' He rightly points to the vital American role, noting that 'Germany and Japan have been the greatest success stories of postwar American foreign policy. Nowhere else has American guidance and American assistance so fully succeeded . . .' That comment is perhaps an exaggeration, especially given the political as well as economic frustrations afflicting Japan since the book was published in 1991.[35]

This last point introduces the tendency, especially in the 1980s, to emphasize and regard as unchanging the trend toward greater power of Germany and, in particular, Japan. Both nations have enjoyed exceptional economic success. Japan, however, has struggled with a very long-term, enervating recession that has been compounded by a crisis of political authority in the system. Germany has done a remarkable job of integrating the eastern section of the country following the collapse of the Berlin wall and the Communist German Democratic Republic in 1989. However, German labour costs are high, many commercial practices are rigid to the point of hurting productivity, and the industrial and banking power of the nation has not been matched by innovative political leadership in Europe or more generally. Both nations have remained very cautious on the world stage, for understandable reasons shadowed by their histories of military aggression in this century, and extremely reluctant to undertake political or military roles comparable to their economic influence. Finally, arguably they are very distinctive national cultures, a perspective each embraced in the most malign possible way in the years before and during the Second World War.

In looking to nations which can undertake comparatively unrestricted and imaginative leadership roles in the post-Cold War international system, a premium should be placed on those with demonstrated capacity for co-operation, where national distinctiveness has not precluded flexible alliance. These considerations lead attention elsewhere, not in rejection of greater regional or even international roles for Germany or Japan, but to look for nations with past and current experience that may be more broadly applicable to American foreign policy and international partnerships in the post-Cold War world.[36]

BRITAIN AND KOREA: DIPLOMATS, TRADERS, WARRIORS

Some combinations of nation-states are more easily conceived than others. Linking Germany and Japan is readily done. Linking Britain and South Korea at first glance seems a marriage of opposite, or at least contrasting, national cultures and experience. Great Britain until the Second World War arguably was the only truly global military and economic power, as well as possessing overall – with Commonwealth and Empire – the most important economy. Britain possessed in London a financial and banking centre of comprehensive international importance, very extensive if declining manufacturing capabilities, a long record of diplomatic as well as military success. The nation was sufficiently powerful to intimidate Hitler in his drive for total European conquest. Korea, by contrast, spent most of the first half of the twentieth century under the heel of Japanese occupation, and over the longer sweep of history has been overshadowed by two much larger Asian powers, China and Japan. Britain was for centuries the central element in the European balance of power system; Korea was for centuries preoccupied with maintaining an independent existence, sandwiched between two giants.

One basic similarity is that both nations, one an island, the other a peninsula, have histories of long-term distinctive national independence. Korea until very recent times was both unconquered and unified. From 1392 until the final takeover by Japan in 1910, Korea was ruled by a succession of twenty-seven kings of the Yi clan. During the period 1592 to 1598, the Japanese warlord Hideyoshi, after unifying his own nation, invaded Korea to develop a base for an attack on China. War continued for years, the Koreans effectively resisted and finally the Japanese gave up and departed. Korea had confirmed national strength, and a powerful warrior tradition, in maintaining national independence.

During this time, Korean Admiral Yi Sun-sin developed an iron-clad warship which proved very effective in destroying conventional Japanese wooden ships. The curved iron plates on the top of the hull, along with a distinctive raised beak-like ram on the front, gave the ships an odd turtle appearance, and they were dubbed 'turtle ships'. A statue of Admiral Yi, dignified and defiant, is prominently featured in Seoul on the main thoroughfare leading up from the city hall to the foreign ministry. The turtle ship is a popular current symbol, and Koreans note with pride that they invented iron-clad warships several hundred years before the *Monitor* and the *Merrimac*, American ironclad ships, battled one another indecisively in 1862 during the US civil war.[37]

Korean independence came to an end with the conclusion of the nineteenth century, when Japan consolidated control over the nation which had been growing since the Sino-Japanese War. In 1895, the Japanese killed Queen Min of Korea. By 1910, the invaders were strong enough to impose a police state system. There followed a period of harsh occupation until liberation in 1945. Even then, however, there was not an end of suffering in Korea, since two states were established following Soviet occupation of the northern part of the country. The Korean War of 1950 to 1953 was extraordinarily costly and destructive, ended in stalemate at approximately the pre-existing dividing line between North and South, and seemed to confirm the painful division of the nation. The war was also a defining experience of the Cold War, setting the stage for America's much more frustrating and ultimately failed intervention in Vietnam in the 1960s. The invasion of South Korea by the communist North seemed to confirm Soviet aggressiveness and the danger of communism in worldwide terms. South Korea, half of a nation which had maintained independence against both China and Japan for centuries, faced the trauma of division and war in ways that created special ties with the United States.[38]

If Britain and South Korea were two ships, the former would be best described as durable, with an unusually experienced crew, reliable in crisis, but slow in the ongoing commerce of the sea and use of new technology, stately but in many ways a relic of the past; the latter could be aptly summed up as fast-moving, indeed coming up on the British ship very rapidly from behind, angry in crisis, ferocious in combat, and constantly adding the latest in advanced-technology navigation and propulsion equipment. The sea, in both war and commerce, has been a vital, central dimension in the history of each nation, so this imagery is not as trite as some might imagine.

Britain in Europe like Korea in Asia has been a distinctive, separate culture, unique in its capacity to influence and guide developments in Europe in the past. 'Balance of power' is used in a variety of senses and contexts by those who study international relations. The term can be applied very literally to British foreign policy, thanks to the continuing national priority of seeking security through encouraging competing centres of power on the Continent. This general approach can be traced back to the reign of Henry VIII. In Hans Morgenthau's words, 'The classic example of the balance . . . has been provided by Great Britain. To Henry VIII is attributed the maxim: *cui adhaero praeest* (he whom I support will prevail).' According to one applicable story of the time, Henry had a portrait painted in which he held in one hand a pair of scales, labelled respectively Austria and France. In his other hand was a weight capable of tipping the balance toward one or the other nation. This image is a useful symbol for British attitudes toward Europe in the centuries that followed. Particular European nations were a source of special concern and danger. Historically, France was a continuing threat. More recently, Germany was the focus of attention. The British approach, however, remained constant even though the diplomatic tapestry changed. With Europe divided, Britain could feel secure.[39]

Britain employed various specific tools to gain foreign policy ends. The most direct and obvious was military intervention on the side of one nation or the other. While Britain did not have a very large army, the navy was able to provide a powerful complement to the various land forces to which the nation was coupled by alliance. Additionally, Britain at times used substantial economic resources to assist one side or another in European conflicts, through providing equipment and supplies or direct money grants and loans. Balance of power politics required alliances, and British economic and naval strength were persuasive incentives for Continental nations.

A necessary corollary of this general British strategy was lack of territorial ambitions within Europe. The nation was neutral in the sense of being in a position to intervene on any side to oppose another which was becoming too powerful. This required that Britain avoid the creation of a continuing coalition of opponents, which in turn dictated restraint of any desires to expand within Europe. As an alternative, the British conquered and colonized large parts of the rest of the globe. This was a game popular with all the great powers of Europe, but the British played with particular skill and drive. The British Empire provided a number of satisfactions, including formal control over large foreign populations, inexpensive raw materials important to manufacturing industries at home, and the symbolism of power and conquest for use on the European stage.

The flexibility of British policy reflected an approach which was moderate and dispassionate. The British avoided precise theoretical formulations or conscious general policy evaluations. Rather, they were supremely empirical, moving with events rather than trying to anticipate them in detail. The British method was to mitigate and dilute conflict, rather than sharpening and heightening differences, and to search for possible compromises rather than seeking total victory. Britain pursued shifting alliances in order to address changing situations. Policy was therefore reactive, attempting to limit concentrations of power, undercut tendencies toward rigidity by any power, and remain alert to development of instability. Among other things, the British were required by these goals to live with inconsistency and to prevent lines of conflict from being drawn too starkly. Kenneth Waltz has insightfully described the style:

> To proceed by a sidling movement rather than move directly toward an objective, to underplay one's hand, to dampen conflicts and depreciate dangers, to balance parties off against one another, to compromise rather than fight, to postpone decisions, to obscure issues rather than confront them, to move as it were by elision from one position in policy to another . . .[40]

This tradition retains a strong hold on British foreign policy style, but at the same time the nation's freedom of manoeuvre has been restricted. Since the last part of the nineteenth century, a variety of factors has limited and reduced Britain's old balancing role. The nation's decline since the Second World War has been dramatic, but the roots go much farther back in time. Political changes in Europe began to limit Britain's room for manoeuvre in the closing decades of the nineteenth century. Otto von Bismarck's skill in uniting Germany and then creating security through a variety of competing alliances was not matched by his successors, and the twentieth century began with Europe clearly divided into two blocs locked in arms competition. After one hundred years of limited and infrequent wars in Europe following the defeat of Napoleon, the new century brought total war, and total shock, to the political and diplomatic systems of Europe. The extraordinary devastation of the First World War, combined with the failure to foresee the impact modern technology would have on warfare, shattered the complacency along with stability that had characterized European diplomacy. Sir Edward Grey, the British foreign secretary, had provided a very characteristic conception of the national approach to diplomacy: 'British Foreign Ministers have been guided by what seemed to be the immediate interest of this country, without making elaborate calculations for the future.' He was the same senior leader who declared woefully as war commenced in 1914 that the lights were going out all over Europe, and one was at a loss to know when they would reappear.[41]

During the period after the First World War, Britain remained true to traditional balance of power approaches, but without positive effect. European politics had become extremely unstable. The punitive settlement of the war, without effective restraints on the defeated, fed German bitterness, which in turn led to support for the uncompromising messianic Hitler regime. The 1938 Munich conference was a characteristic British effort to avoid war through accommodation, but only encouraged German adventurism. Growth of ideologically driven politics had implications for the European international system which were not fully appreciated by Britain. Winston Churchill was different, but he was fixed on the menace of Hitler rather than the possibility of a much different international role for his nation.[42]

As discussed earlier, the system after the Second World War represented a great departure from the old European structure of international affairs, accustomed to variations on balance of power politics, with the precedent of a formal Concert of nations to manage relations. In the new system of nation-states which had emerged, there was no consensus. The expanding size and diversity of the international system also drew attention to the decline of the British Empire.[43]

Britain since the Second World War has been preoccupied with issues of retreat from empire and related international commitments and, more recently, economic decline but remains a centre of international banking and financial services. While London retains great importance in this world, British firms themselves have been increasingly overshadowed by competitors from other nations. As the *Wall Street Journal* described the development in 1995,

Lacking the financial muscle of their giant foreign rivals . . . many British investment banks could be forced to seek partners if they want to compete globally, even in businesses such as foreign exchange, international equity trading and bond underwriting. Those are the very businesses for which London itself is the undisputed leading center.

The article went on to note the changing financial services environment in the context of Britain's general decline:

In some ways, the decline of independent British investment banking isn't that unusual. The UK auto, steel and ship-building industriès were once world leaders but have been in steady decline.

But London as a financial center is getting stronger. Only a few years ago, many were predicting Frankfurt or Paris might challenge London's lead. That hasn't happened, in part because of the City's built-in advantages of being English-speaking and a convenient time zone between the U.S. and Asia. Top investment bankers, many of them American and British, have refused for cultural reasons to relocate to Frankfurt or Paris.[44]

In the period since the Second World War, some have argued that the United States has replaced Britain as the dominant power in international relations. Among these is Henry Kissinger, who in his recent book *Diplomacy* at least implicitly seemed to draw the analogy, describing the United States as 'an island off the shores of the large landmass of Eurasia'. Jonathan Clarke, former diplomat, emphasizes this quote in an article in the Spring 1995 issue of *The National Interest*. He develops the theme that the Americans run the risk that Britain failed to address in an earlier period: 'the central British failure to bring resources and aspirations into sustainable equilibrium'. He notes the obvious physical differences between the two nations. 'In terms of raw statistics of military power, wealth, size, and population . . . any comparison between Britain and the United States seems risible.' Then he goes on to argue that 'the parallels are striking' in the attitudes of foreign policy elites in Britain immediately after the Second World War and the United States after the Cold War.[45]

Considered in detail, the two states actually have differed significantly in outlook and approach. Britain as a great power was operating in a geographically and culturally limited system of states, with the opportunity to work to prevent rigid blocs from developing or another nation from becoming dominant. The British goal was to lighten national burdens and maintain diversity of power within Europe. During the Cold War, on the other hand, the United States was anxious to assume significant military obligations in order to surround and eventually overcome the communist bloc. Rigid confrontation was accepted as a given of the international system. A direct, straightforward approach might be described as archetypically American and certainly characterized the broad thrust of national diplomacy after 1945. The American preference has been to meet threats head-on rather than through a British combination of ambiguous moves. The Munich conference and the Vietnam War might be described as representing respectively characteristically British and American weaknesses. The British at their worst have been guilty of complacency, excessive flexibility and a tendency to view national leaders as sharing common traditional outlooks. Prime Minister Neville Chamberlain and the British governmental establishment were guilty of all of this in dealing with Hitler. The Americans at their worst have been guilty of an almost frantic crisis mentality, excessive rigidity in seeing communism as monolithic, and a tendency to view all peoples as fundamentally American in outlook. President Lyndon Johnson and many other US policymakers over a long period of time were guilty of all this in dealing with the Vietnam revolution.

From other perspectives, however, there are considerable similarities in the contexts or roles in which Britain in the past and the United States today are immersed. Both countries have possessed great economic power during their periods of dominance, and willingness to employ that capacity to assist and intimidate others. Both have rightly considered themselves to be of central importance in the international system, with power and influence decisive in character. Both states have had particular military advantages. The total panoply of American strategic air power has not been equalled by the Soviets or any other single power during the years since the Second World War. With the end of the Cold War, the Americans remain unequalled in their capability to move large amounts of military force virtually anywhere on the globe very quickly. In the eighteenth and nineteenth centuries, British naval firepower overshadowed that of other nations.

Finally, such discussion has been encouraged because British decline has taken place in correlation with the rise of the USA. Endlessly courting Franklin Roosevelt, and through him the American people, Winston Churchill demonstrated Britain's need for the United States. Symbolic of the close relationship, Churchill made a point when visiting the White House after Pearl Harbor of pushing the President in his wheelchair to the elevator to the private quarters, combining a gesture of affection and respect that recognized the great national strength Roosevelt represented, whatever his personal physical handicap. At this time, the British Prime Minister wrote his wife that 'The Americans are magnificent in their breadth of view.'[46]

SOUTH KOREA: ECONOMIC AND POLITICAL MIRACLES

South Korea's success story has two integrated parts, combining extraordinary economic development and growth with transformation of an autocratic military dictatorship into an open political democracy. If Britain played a vital role in the preservation of democracy and liberty when threatened by what Churchill rightly likened to a new Dark Age, South Korea represents the promise that the fundamental cultural gulf between East and West is not too great to bridge with democracy and liberty. Korean industrial and commercial successes are resulting in an increasingly visible, diverse and influential economy, with an impact in the USA and Europe as well as Asia. The nation has achieved genuinely peaceful and successful progress from military rule to civilian democratic government with open bidding for votes by separate political parties in the context of reasonably free, reasonably honest elections. While South Korea still receives criticism on human rights grounds, the political system overall has been successful in moving to democracy, a difficult course which has included the investigation and prosecution of senior government officials for corruption.

South Korea's economic growth has been nothing short of spectacular, in a scant three decades moving from third world to industrial world status. The country has been aptly described as 'the fastest growing developing country during the decade of the 1980s'. The government has encouraged growth with tax, loan and other incentives, by so doing effectively opening the door for the enormous productive capacity of the people. Land reform and government aid in the 1960s and 1970s helped make South Korea number one among nations in terms of rice yield per acre. After the 1960s attention was focused on heavy industry, and manufacturing leaped from 12 per cent of total national output in 1967 to one-third by 1979.[47]

In the 1990s, Korea is joining the ranks of major industrial nations. The per capita income is now estimated at $10 000 and may well reach $20 000 early in the twenty-first century. Forward projections regarding South Korea's growth are regularly revised upward. Korea is now the fifth largest producer of automobiles in the world, and the Samsung group is joining industrial giants Daewoo, Hyundai and Kia in this market. The nation's firms hold a commanding position in manufacture of DRAM 4-megabite semiconductors and are expected to do well with successor generation 16-megabit and 64-megabit semiconductors. South Korea is ranked with France and Japan as one of the world's top three producers of civilian nuclear energy. A recent comprehensive article in *Business Week* on the advanced technology drive in Korea stated: 'Korea is revving up. Having moved years ago from a low-wage economy where workers churned out shoes, textiles, small TVs, and cheap cars, Korea is bidding to become one of the world's leading producers of high-tech goods.' The piece declares without qualification that, 'Korea could become the first nation to truly establish itself as an advanced industrial power since the emergence of Japan.' John M. Beeman, representing Citibank in Korea, stated flatly that, 'This country has achieved more economically in a shorter period of time than any other country in modern history.'[48]

A variety of factors have contributed to South Korea's success. The labour force is exceptionally productive, reflecting a powerful work ethic and virtually universal literacy. Commitment to education within the population is very strong, a reality confirmed not only in statistics but for Americans in the increasingly visible outstanding performance of Korean immigrant young people in our educational system. The Korean saving rate is very high, by one estimate approximately 35 per cent in the early 1990s.[49]

David Steinberg, an experienced and knowledgeable observer of the evolution of South Korea, provided testimony from 1993 concerning the dramatic success of the nation: He suggested the following outlook of those evaluating the future of Korea from the perspective of the 1950s:

> If observers at that time had attempted to predict long-term economic growth in Asia by comparing Burma, Thailand, and South Korea, all of which had per capita incomes in the $60–80 range and populations within about 10 per cent of each other, Burma would likely have been their first choice and South Korea their last. Yet today South Korea's per capita income is some 6 times that of Thailand and some 32 times that of Burma, while its GDP is 3 times that of Thailand. In 1962, Burma's exports were 6 times greater than South Korea's; in 1990 South Korea's were 85 times those of Burma. South Korea's total annual exports in 1962 would have equaled about eight hours of its exports in 1990 . . .[50]

The importance of relatively new, very large firms, often dominated by a single individual or family, provides broader insights into the development of the South Korean economy. This structure appears to be fundamentally different from that of Japan, where there is a far longer industrial tradition, and corporate culture seems to be far more collegial, indeed collectivist, with fewer examples of individual or family dominance. Where a family is paramount in a very large firm, such as Toyota, their profile is generally lower and corporate decision-making far more bureaucratic and regularized in nature. The Korean approach is much more reminiscent of early capitalism in the United States, where individual entrepreneurs were able to accumulate great wealth, often in close partnership with major departments of government.[51]

Though complaints about Korea's domestic protectionism are common, especially from the United States, there has been some effort to open the economy. Since 1992, the domestic stock market in South Korea has been liberalized. Initially, foreigners were permitted to purchase up to 10 per cent of the total value of a listed stock, and this was increased in stages to 15 per cent in 1995. Investment in government bonds, certain private bonds and fixed income securities is also being liberalized. The government has been trying to open up the iron grip of the giant, family-dominated corporations by providing incentives to diversify equity holdings.[52]

Economic success is being recognized in the changing nature of Korean involvement with international organizations. When South Korea first joined the World Bank in 1955, per capita income was less than $200, one of the lowest in the world. In 1995, the Republic of Korea became one of the star 'graduates' of the global institution, completing thirty-three years of active loan involvement, having achieved a per capita economic product more than twice the combined per capita GNP of China, Indonesia and Thailand. Korea graduated to lending from the International Bank for Reconstruction and Development (IBRD) following completion of support from the International Development Association (IDA or 'soft loan' agency) in 1973. The Koreans are now poised to join the Organization for Economic Co-operation and Development, the association of the most advanced industrial nations, once a European and Atlantic area preserve, but no longer. Efforts to join the UN Security Council represent a different dimension of fundamentally the same process of pursuing recognition for dramatic achievement.[53]

Economic development along with political democracy has brought interest group politics to the forefront. This issue was raised, for instance, at a conference of the Asia Society and the Seoul Forum for International Affairs in the spring of 1988. The report of the conference included this point: 'The trade friction created by Korea's $10 billion trade surplus with the United States in 1987 is expected to be complicated by the process of democratization in Korea, where interest groups, emboldened by political liberalization, are calling for protection against foreign competition.'[54] Economic growth at a ferocious pace has been complemented by political development away from military autocracy to genuine party-competitive democracy. The last military general in a succession which ruled South Korea from the 1960s, Roh Tae Woo, instituted fundamental reforms which transformed the constitution and opened the door to civilian leadership.

His successor as President, Kim Young Sam, had a long history as a political dissident, far removed from the ruling military establishment, and no direct participation in the military himself. Kim's victory in the presidential elections ushered in a new era of competitive democracy as well as military eclipse.

President Roh Tae Woo took the initiative for reform, responding to public pressure concentrated in the middle class. On 29 June 1987, then-candidate Roh issued a comprehensive statement acceding to virtually all major demands made by the opposition to the regime. This meant accepting direct election of the president, a new constitution based on an inclusive referendum, and release of all political prisoners, including dissident leaders Kim Dae Jung and Kim Young Sam. He threatened to resign from all his positions, including that of recently selected presidential candidate of the ruling Democratic Justice Party, if these conditions were not met. Thus one man from an unlikely background served, not for the first time in the history of democracy, as a source of a fundamental shift to freedom.[55] Ironically, Roh was one of the principal victims of the reform process he had led. In 1995, both he and former President Chun Doo Hwan were arrested for corruption. Earlier in Korea's evolution, democratic reform pressures had toppled President Syngman Rhee in 1960, which in turn sparked a military *coup* in 1961. This time, freedom has so far survived, and immediate informal impressions are that knowledgeable observers believe this is a fundamentally reassuring process of South Korea's evolution to genuine democracy.

By the mid-1990s, government officials announced intentions of joining the ranks of the very top industrial nations by the early part of the new century, with the goal of membership in the Group of Seven. If Britain has provided reliable support from a very traditional and free nation, especially though not only in the enormous trial of the Second World War, South Korea has provided equally reliable alliance on the part of a nation at the forefront of the ideological tumult and quest for economic development that have characterized so much of the world since that war.

PARTNERS IN WAR

Britain and South Korea each has a strong military tradition. In a period removed from the experience of total war, we can easily overlook the importance of the warrior tradition to the success of a culture. This is a serious mistake. The military prowess of British and Koreans is directly related to their international and domestic success in general, the British in the diplomacy of the nineteenth century, the Koreans in the industrial growth of the twentieth century. In the past century, the British navy was an unequalled source of national power and international influence, the necessary condition for the development and maintenance of the global empire that was in turn the basis of national wealth. British combat proficiency has been demonstrated in various ways in this century, not just in world wars but in a variety of small conflicts in distant sections of the globe, including the Falklands war of 1982. In this century also, the South Korean army has been the necessary instrument for maintaining national survival and independence and, given the Cold War and division of the Korean Peninsula, provided the necessary conditions for the development of economic and political miracles. South Korea kept a substantial number of combat troops, approximately 50 000, in Vietnam throughout the period of direct American military involvement there.

There has been a regular debate over South Korean support and maintenance of US military forces on the Korean Peninsula, not unlike the more general burden-sharing debate that has animated Atlantic area security relations almost from the beginning of the Nato Alliance. A South Korean newspaper, the *Hankook Ilbo*, editorialized in early 1995: 'If we determine that stationing U.S. forces here is necessary . . . , the two per cent of the South Korean military budget allotted to pay for the stationing of U.S. forces, which at present amounts to some $300 million per year, is not such a large sum of money.' Then, tellingly, the commentary went on to focus on the need for national independence and national identity: 'The important thing is to make our own decision. The same applies to deciding whether or not U.S. forces help reduce the North Korean threat.'[56]

The military co-operation involving the United States with both Britain and South Korea was especially important in the earlier phases of the Cold War, when tensions were very high and the possibility of general war seemed genuine, at times acutely likely. Britain provided a catalyst to bring North America and Western Europe together in alliance, and also not least an effective partner of both the USA and South Korea in the Korean War. Our wartime ally Britain provided a steady and reliable partnership that continued after the war, often defined in close personal terms, in particular by Dwight Eisenhower and Winston Churchill, John F. Kennedy and Harold Macmillan, and Ronald Reagan and Margaret Thatcher. Britain, in the words of McGeorge Bundy, Kennedy's national security adviser, has been 'someone to talk to'. The British ally has been someone to listen to as well, including important conversations between Kennedy and Macmillan during the Cuban Missile Crisis and otherwise.

The nuclear dimension has been important in these alliance relationships as well. During the Second World War, President Roosevelt and Prime Minister Churchill agreed to share information and work together on the effort to develop the atomic bomb. The USA amended nuclear weapons policy to permit an exception in order to share information with Britain. South Korea has also emerged as a special partner not just in military terms but in nuclear matters. The 21 October 1994 accord to resolve the nuclear crisis with North Korea also means that Seoul and Washington have become very close collaborators in nuclear diplomacy. The agreement requires North Korea's government to dismantle the nuclear weapons programme over a ten-year period and accept full-scale inspection of all nuclear facilities. In exchange, North Korea is to receive technical and financial assistance from the international community to develop an alternative peaceful nuclear capacity.[57]

If Britain was the most influential and skilful practitioner of balance of power diplomacy in an earlier age, South Korea has applied a similar approach to further national recognition and best the North Korean regime. In recent years, South Korea's trade became far larger than North Korea's with both China and the Soviet Union. Seoul was in turn able to use the resulting leverage to secure diplomatic recognition from both communist powers, in effect isolating Pyongyang. South Korea has continued to employ economic diplomacy, especially in the case of Russia, to very good national effect. Willingness to invest in Russia, despite great economic and political uncertainties, has provided a dramatic contrast with the extreme caution of Japan. There has also been expansion of trade between South and North Korea. Imaginative diplomatic calculation links both the earlier great power of Europe and the emerging great power of Asia, undercutting any argument that no parallels can be drawn between cultures of East and West.[58]

AFTER COMMUNISM AND FASCISM

Britain and South Korea are now joined with the United States as democracies, the former with a very old tradition of representative government, the latter very new in embracing this system. How likely is the general current popularity of democracy to prove durable, and how directly can the United States pursue this goal for other people? If this question is considered too broad or visionary, consider that failure adequately to address the matter could result in an international system without American leadership, with all the opportunity for war and instability that implies. In the age of terrorism and nuclear proliferation, that is a danger that could 'strike home' literally in an enormously destructive manner.

One of the most visible answers has been provided by Francis Fukuyama in his popular 1992 book, *The End of History and the Last Man*. Fukuyama believes that liberal democracy may constitute a final level of political evolution, one in which earlier conflicts over class are abandoned in principle in favour of a fundamental commitment to liberty and equality. The author argues at length that democracy is more durable than most critics realize:

> while earlier forms of government were characterized by grave defects and irrationalities that led to their eventual collapse, liberal democracy was arguably free from such fundamental internal contradictions. This was not to say that today's stable democracies, like the United States, France, or Switzerland, were not without injustice or serious social problems. But these problems were ones of incomplete implementation of the twin principles of liberty and equality on which modern democracy is founded, rather than of flaws in the principles themselves.[59]

President Bush seemed to echo this point of view in his inaugural address in early 1989, and he demonstrated some eloquence in so doing. As noted, he did not spend much time on foreign policy, but he did address freedom: 'We know what works', said the new President. 'Freedom works. We know what's right. Freedom is right. We know how to secure a more just and prosperous life for man on earth: through free markets, free speech, free elections and the exercise of free will unhampered by the state.' Bush then went on to stress the same theme Fukuyama developed at length, that the divisions and clashes that from ancient times had caused political conflict seemed to have come to an end.

> For the first time in this century – for the first time perhaps in all history – man does not have to invent a system by which to live. We don't have to talk late into the night about which form of government is better. We don't have to wrest justice from the kings – we only have to summon it from within ourselves.[60]

President Clinton's 1993 inaugural address is also revealing concerning what is stated, and what is omitted, about the emerging international system. As discussed earlier, Clinton, in contrast to John Kennedy, said very little about foreign policy, but the one such point he made was crucial, concerning both Washington and the wider post-Cold War world: 'To renew America, we must meet challenges abroad as well as at home. There is no longer a clear division between what is foreign and what is domestic.'[61]

Political leadership in a democracy is always challenging, given the plethora of competing interests and perspectives which must be dealt with and, in successful governance, reconciled. An age of relative international calm, without great war and economic crisis, can be very challenging precisely because the leader has more difficulty in mobilizing and combining groups within society. Cataclysmic war involves terrible costs, literal life-and-death stakes, and enormous strain for the leader as well as the people, but has the compensation that the issues are clear-cut and appeals to patriotism and survival have great unifying effect. The United States has been fortunate that in the face of direct challenge to the survival of the nation, in both the Civil War and the Second World War, leadership was up to the task, able to use available advantages and resources to mobilize the nation, and redefine the calculus of politics and government as a result.

The challenge for America after the Cold War is therefore one of leadership in a non-crisis environment. The size and scale and diversity of the economy, military capabilities, international treaties and more informal involvement should facilitate, though not guarantee, United States influence around the globe. The attractiveness of a free society, the lure of economic betterment, the pervasiveness of the popular culture, the very diversity of the population should all assist the United States in working to recombine relations among industrialized nations after the Cold War. Yet there is also the challenge to leadership that there is no apparent great crisis, no immediate perceived threat to our way of life. There is not even the 'long twilight struggle', John F. Kennedy's reference to the Cold War in an effort to motivate and mobilize the nation to a more active posture. With the end of that twilight struggle, the challenge to American leadership is especially complex.

5 An American Worldview; An American World

NATIONAL INTEREST AND INTERNATIONAL COMMUNITY

At the beginning of this book a threefold division was drawn among intellectual, structural and sociological approaches to defining and analysing international relations. Britain and South Korea have been discussed because each seems to represent, though in different ways, characteristics of foreign policy and national development which have important lessons for the United States in the international system evolving in the wake of the Cold War. Britain and South Korea both have been extremely reliable allies of the USA, especially though not exclusively in wartime, and this is a consideration in attempting to address American foreign policy now and in the future. However, that is not the exclusive reason for giving these two nations special attention in this analysis. Both countries provide examples of behaviour which can be emulated by others – South Korea for developing states aspiring to enter the ranks of industrialized powers, Britain for the United States and other nations in a period when pursuit of flexible, pragmatic diplomacy seems very possible as well as desirable.

The Cold War was a distinctive defining experience, combining both intense conflict, which encouraged aggressiveness, and the very great military restraint imposed on each superpower thanks to the nuclear risk. That background is inescapable in shaping the perspectives of American leadership in the post-Cold War period. That experience may also be helpful to the United States in trying to cope with a contemporary international system that now offers little prospect of general war between great powers but endless challenge from limited crises and wars. The list of post-Cold War military conflicts is already noteworthy, including especially but not only the Gulf War. Meanwhile, the United States must continue to adjust to an environment of uncertainty, in which there is no longer the predictable and therefore strangely comforting confrontation of the Cold War era, where the enemy was a known quantity, the dividing lines in the international system rather clear, and future challenges presumably would be similar to those already experienced. Effectiveness in policy will be a function of managing an international environment comprised of influential concepts and ideas on which there is no consensus, shifting coalitions of states with no firm blocs to replace those of the Cold

War, other structures such as the private corporation, and the cumulative impact of people operating with great freedom beyond the boundaries of the traditional nation-state.

DEMOCRACY AND MARKETS

This unfolding of the twentieth century has witnessed the virulent growth of totalitarian ideologies in large and powerful nations, and also the decisive defeat and retreat of those same doctrines and their followers. The secular messianic movements of our times, fascism and communism, have both been effectively eliminated. In the case of communism, a substantial literature and community of support among professional intellectuals, especially but not exclusively in Europe, has made the waning of the doctrine particularly significant in terms of impact on education, research and those who think and write abstractly for a living. The end of communism as an alternative mode for the organization of society, at least in the western world, therefore has great implications for intellectual communities as well as the public at large.

China remains formally wedded to communism, but the doctrinal commitment is more and more removed from practical behaviour. That nation-state is undergoing change at the roots, including the slow-motion transition from the era of Deng Xiaoping, away from the forced-draft socialist development of industry, toward spreading market practices, with external investment spurring extraordinary economic expansion. In recent years China has had the most rapidly growing economy in the world, with all the dislocations and disruptions as well as opportunities entailed by such development. Whatever the future may bring for the economy and politics, the previous total control of the society by the state will be very difficult to re-establish. The process of foreign investment involves opening doors, in quite literal as well as figurative terms, which in the contemporary age will be virtually impossible to close. Even the surviving communist systems therefore are no longer secure in political regime or reliable in ideological commitment.

Whether open economic markets combined with general commitment to democracy will be sufficient for political stability outside the established free societies is a fundamental, and open, question. The only clear answer is that capitalism alone, without further compatible political content accepted as legitimate, is unlikely to be either satisfying to a democratic public or, closely related, politically durable. The most persuasive single argument for this point is the undeniable fact that capitalist literature is genuinely interesting only in a narrow economic sense. Marxists write plays, poetry, novels and, not least, histories. Capitalists make money. This may help explain why there is no outstanding literary tradition concerning the world of business. Novels about business tend to be flat, insufficient in interpreting the genuine drama of commercial quest, conflict, victory and defeat. Business executives talented as managers and entrepreneurs regularly demonstrate through memoirs and speeches that such abilities are not necessarily accompanied by literary or rhetorical skill.

The discredited hate doctrines mobilized people by providing a vision of the future which was gripping, absorbing and went well beyond such specific concerns as making a living. This is another way of stating that commercial life is not the basis of a fully comprehensive and satisfying political system. A prime incentive for earlier generations to embrace fascism and communism was realization that the market brought human misery as well as human wealth, but at no time fulfilled all human aspirations. Dictatorship's appeal involves removing precisely that worry and preoccupation from the hands of each individual, who is sacrificed to the unity of the whole. The twentieth-century totalitarian would add that the individual is sacrificed to the will of the whole.

The human drive for political community as well as commercial gain is unavoidable. Politics indeed circumscribes as well as facilitates commerce. Democracy may be necessary for any truly capitalist economic system to survive over the long term, but history has demonstrated in any case that capitalism alone is not sufficient for either political satisfaction or political stability. The end of the Cold War therefore returns attention to the future of domestic political regimes as well as the evolving and increasingly international market economies. In the former Soviet Union and Eastern Europe, the collapse of communism has brought widespread commitment to democracy as well as the market. Uncertainty about the future course of this development reflects the absence in many cases – though not all – of a democratic tradition, the evidence of history that democratic forms have been established before only to be overturned, and the turmoil that has attended the current experiments in freedom.

In Asia, questions arise about the compatibility of Eastern political cultures with Western forms and customs of democracy. Professor Samuel Huntington of Harvard has raised this subject provocatively, arguing that Western culture remains distinctive from others in the world, albeit in a period of exceptional transition, and that conflicts in the future will involve different civilizations more than nation-states. This is linked to the important political evolution now underway. 'World politics is entering a new phase, and intellectuals have not hesitated to proliferate visions of what it will be – the end of history, the return of traditional rivalries between nation states, and the decline of the nation state from the conflicting pulls of tribalism and globalism, among others.' He also sees opportunities for democracy in the non-Western context of Asia and has described China as moving in a democratic direction, though not right away. Speaking in early June 1995 at the inaugural meeting of the Association of Development and Industrial Banks in Asia in South Korea, he cautiously predicted democracy for the nation. 'The precondition to democratization usually is the coming to power of reform elements within an authoritarian system. Will this happen in China? Not I suspect in the first generation after Deng but quite possibly in the second.' He continued, underscoring independence from the West.

> For 2000 years, China was the pre-eminent power in East Asia. Chinese now increasingly assert their intention to resume that historic role and to bring to an end the overlong century of humiliation and subordination to the West and Japan that began with British imposition of the Treaty of Nanking in 1842.[1]

Professor Paul Krugman of Yale has further developed the theme that Asia is different from the West, drawing analogies between production gains in the dynamic Asian growth economies and perceptions of forced-draft progress in the communist command economies during the 1950s and 1960s.[2]

The uncertainty of the current situation relates directly to the fact that political liberty and democracy are neither so confidently embraced nor so easily managed as market economies. Uncertainty is inherent in the free way of life. This is a fundamental issue, given that even in China there is acceptance of economic freedom as well as commercial profit. A commercial market is compromised and restricted by a closed society, yet there is no guarantee that more open economies will necessarily lead directly to political democracy.

Here the Clinton administration has been very perceptive and persuasive with continued emphasis on the importance of democracy, even if criticism of other nations, notably China on human rights grounds, has not been handled smoothly. A particularly systematic and insightful treatment of the Clinton approach to foreign policy, and especially the role of democracy and related human rights concerns, was provided by Anthony Lake, National Security Adviser to the President, in a speech at the School for Advanced International Studies in Washington DC in the fall of 1993. To some extent, this theme has been characteristic of American foreign policy since the beginning of the republic, and certainly since the beginning of the Cold War. The special character, distinctiveness and perhaps unique spirit of the American experiment with liberty resonates across our history. The Cold War, following hard on the Second World War, interrupted American emphasis on democracy with the urgent need to bolster national security.

Lake addresses, and perhaps has helped to counter, the danger that a *laissez-faire* attitude would permit economics to have sway over politics, that markets would be emphasized more than freedom. He states that

> with the end of the Cold War, there is no longer a consensus among the American people around why, and even whether, our nation should remain actively engaged in the world . . . Calls from the left and right to stay at home rather than engage abroad are re-enforced by the rhetoric of Neo-Know-Nothings.

He counters:

> Those of us who believe in the imperative of our international engagement must push back.

Lake provides a counter-weight by balancing American commitment to capitalism and commerce with an equally strong political commitment to democracy and freedom. '*The successor to a doctrine of containment must be a strategy of enlargement – enlargement of the world's free community of market democracies*' (italics in the original). Lake enumerates four principles to the overall strategy: strengthen the 'major market democracies', 'help foster and consolidate new democracies and market economies', counter aggression, and pursue our 'humanitarian agenda'. He devotes particular attention to the former Soviet Union and Eastern Europe, where democracy can make a great difference and security concerns remain very influential. Lake is also especially concerned about the problem of 'backlash states' which reject both the market and democracy.[3]

United States history reflects the flexibility of a free people. American nationalism has served both imperialism and liberation; American freedom has served both exploitation of labour and democracy. Much of the older foreign policy debate in the USA, including the major one early in this century between Woodrow Wilson's 'New Freedom' and Theodore Roosevelt's 'New Nationalism', involved wrestling with these factors. The American sense of mission, however flawed in implementation in the past, can also provide very powerful resistance to the desire to stay aloof from what is happening with other countries and in other parts of the world. The American sense of mission, as long as this theme is not implemented in an imperialistic or purely military fashion, can provide stable undergirding of American foreign policy. The genius of America is precisely that we do not have a comprehensive, structured ideology in European terms. For this reason, the international system in its present state should be very congenial to the pragmatic and empirical American approach. Though we lack an ideology, we do have a faith – that democracy is inherently worthwhile – and recently that general commitment has been supplemented in policy and scholarly circles with the assertion that democracies are both reluctant to go to war and, relatedly, are not likely to fight one another. Social scientists have assembled arguments which include the proposition that most wars have involved dictatorships partly or exclusively. President Clinton has referred to this theme, increasingly popular in the academic and to some extent wider communities, that democracies 'do not fight' one another. This perspective tends to gloss over the basic reality that until very recent years in the history of the world truly representative government was extremely rare. The experiences of the few democracies with relatively long histories in fact are not reassuring on this point. Perhaps the enormous level of threat the democracies faced in the Second World War, which in turn brought them firmly together in alliance, explains why some contemporary analysts have been unpersuaded by the fact that over the longer term relations among Britain, Canada and the United States were characterized by almost constant tension and occasional armed conflict.[4]

IDEOLOGY AND LIBERALISM

Can we accurately speak of an 'end of ideology' thanks to the death of fascism and now communism? In many ways, this does seem to be exactly what is happening in the world today. President Kennedy remarked long ago, in 1962, that the great ideological debates were a thing of the past, that the most challenging problems of his age were complex administrative tasks. His own death and the aftermath seemed to undercut that proposition, literally as well as metaphorically. The assassination of President Kennedy on 22 November, 1963 was in retrospect the initial shock in a violent series that punctuated the social and racial turbulence of the 1960s. Yet in spite of these instabilities, and the tragedy of Vietnam for Southeast Asia and the US, from a longer time perspective JFK was quite accurate in his observation.[5]

Specifically, Kennedy was perceptive in that the old European class-based debate over allocation of resources had largely come to an end by the 1960s. The primary economic division that had defined political conflict in democracies as well as other political systems had faded, a change masked in part by the fact that they did not abruptly disappear but simply dissipated. Arguably, indeed, the new dichotomy between culture and 'counterculture' in the 1960s was a function of broad prosperity, in which people who were relatively secure economically for that very reason could undertake unconventional behaviour. Social non-conformity and political radicalism were highlighted by the mass media, which in turn provided conservatives with an opening to charge that the press and intellectuals were broadly sympathetic to these trends. Richard Nixon's election victory in 1968 was to some extent the result of a campaign designed to attract public hostility to the counterculture – 'hippies and demonstrators' – and all that movement seemed to represent in terms of challenge to the status quo.

As many social scientists and other observers have noted, American politics has never been class-based in the explicit, hostile terms that have been so important to European party division and competition. For this very reason, appeals along traditional class lines normally have not been sufficient for electoral or political victory; indeed they have often been counterproductive, and majorities have to be created laboriously through appeals to combinations of specific public or economic interests. Franklin Roosevelt in 1936 probably came closest of any major politician in either main party in the United States to developing and exploiting themes of class conflict and hostility. That period of the Great Depression may also be the one time in US history when the individualistic society was close to an actual revolution of poor against rich. Yet the moment passed without out a real revolution, New Deal reforms in retrospect bolstered rather than undermined the status quo, and the United States has gone on to a record of fundamental constitutional continuity with our own past.

This American history makes the nation especially important to the end of ideology debate and also the much-discussed 'end of history' theme of Francis Fukuyama's book, mentioned near the end of Chapter 4. Fukuyama, often misunderstood by critics who have not read past the title of his book, actually discusses the waning of traditional sorts of group and class conflict over resources, rather than any end of history in literal terms. The United States is the one industrial nation which from the start has been devoted formally to both liberty and equality. This nation is the one that has the strongest claim to embracing genuine democracy as a pragmatic ideal from the beginning. The French overthrew a conservative monarchy without establishing a stable successor, however attractive radical utopian democratic sentiments may have been to leaders and followers of the revolution. Germany and Japan struggle still with responsibilities for the

Second World War, with institutions of democracy constructed over un-democratic histories. The United States, therefore, remains distinctively prepared for and comfortable with the age in which broadly appealing extreme ideologies have become a thing of the past. Only Britain, the source of American legal and representative traditions and culture, is in a somewhat comparable position among the Western democracies, but with a long history of feudal institutions and customs, as well as intense class conflict. The USA's enormous economic and military capacities only reinforce a position of great influence. If ideology is truly ending, there is a new opportunity for the US to encourage the rest of the world to be more 'like us,' meaning more free, less predictable, more individualistic.[6]

The defeat and, also important, discrediting of the great totalitarian movements of the twentieth century has opened the door for promotion on a global scale of the liberal beliefs which informed political culture in England from the eighteenth century, following the terrible trauma of the Civil War and restoration of the monarchy. Divine right of monarchs in the traditional sense was ended, and the consent of Parliament became essential to the legitimacy of rule. John Locke argued more effectively and persuasively, if not more powerfully, than any other theorist of the time regarding the paramount importance of individual good, the essential role of public consent, and natural rights which predate the state. This general attitude, more than the specifics of his argument, informed Benjamin Franklin, Thomas Jefferson and other leaders of the revolutionary republican experiment in America. Adam Smith focused on individualism from a more strictly commercial perspective, laying out an argument that has become fundamental to much of American popular culture. The state should be strictly limited in order to permit the unrestricted pursuit of commercial gain. He provided as well, as mercantalism was being undercut by larger forces of trade, a practical tribute to market economics. In recent years, as in the years before the Great Depression, faith in the free market has become paramount in our society. Americans have consistently returned to his legacy, even if the commitment has not been continuous.[7]

Aristotle identified larger middle classes as associated with stable government, and hence the environment needed for effective long-term representative institutions. A growing and politically adept middle class was the key to Britain's gradual but steady and finally successful democratic reform process. The expansion of the middle class in England directly resulted in a wider suffrage and spreading democratic culture. Likewise, the middle class was crucial in South Korea in the 1980s in pressing the military regime to withdraw in favour of free elections and representative government. This expansion of the middle class among the growing market economies of the world is richly promising for American foreign policy. Above all, this population should be a source of democratic reform and resulting political stability once that is achieved. South Korea provides an especially strong example, far from Anglo-Saxon culture and history, of a country where these traditional British political and economic ideas are taking root. In both these countries and others, including the United States, the continuing importance of Aristotle's fundamental class insight appears to be confirmed.[8]

STRUCTURE

Nato: Arms and Influence

Regional organizations are an important component of the contemporary international system, and Europe, despite all the frustrations of the politics of collaboration and the diplomacy of using force, teaches some basic lessons. Discussion of alternatives to Nato, and the possible end of that alliance, has been confined primarily to academic circles because the organization has proven to be a tough survivor, despite the frustration attending involvement in the new Balkan war of the 1990s. Despite policy divisions among Nato members, the Alliance remains sufficiently strong that East European states are applying for membership. Reflecting the weakness, disintegration and then collapse of the Soviet system, there has been virtually no effort to maintain regional institutional co-operation among even the major members of the old Warsaw Pact military organization established by the Soviets to counter Nato.

Examining the reactions and stances of the more than twenty nations which have joined the Partnership for Peace proposed by the Clinton administration provides a flavour of the diversity as well as commitment involved. Poland has been seeking full participation under Article 5 of the treaty and would in fact bring relatively large military resources, including 250 000 troops and an extensive peacekeeping programme. After some initial scepticism, the Polish government came out for the Partnership, drawn in particular by the promise of the new arrangements to encourage cohesion in the Alliance. Among other nations which might be described as relatively close to Western Europe, reactions have varied. In the Czech Republic, President Vaclav Havel declared relatively early in favour of the pact. His statement in November 1993 underscored both the vulnerability of his people, positioned in Central Europe, should war break out, and also their basic accord with the values of Nato partners. In an interview early in 1995, he stated that, 'For reasons of security, being accepted into Nato is indeed more urgent for us than being accepted into the European Union.' In Hungary, attitudes have been considerably more ambiguous, reflected in a diverse continuing debate. In November 1994, Prime Minister Gyula Horn stressed European Union membership was the highest priority of the government, and proposed a referendum as a way of resolving and also avoiding political isolation on the issue.

Romania initially emphasized the Conference on Security and Co-operation in Europe as the mechanism that would solve problems and provide opportunities. This changed to a more realistic focus on the European Union, Nato and the Western European Union. There has been some pressure for clarification of the conditions for participation in the Partnership. With Poland, Romania is pivotal in regional impact. An analysis by the Institute for National Strategic Studies notes, 'If Romania and Poland (the "checkers") – the two most important states by population, armed forces, and geostrategic location – became *de jure* members of Nato, Ukraine and the other Central European states would become *de facto* members of Nato.'

Lithuania also has been especially anxious to join western institutions, including Nato, the European Union and the Western European Union. A history of domination by outside powers has persuaded the current national leadership that the Baltic states must be linked in formal institutional terms with central European states or risk a return of external domination in the future, perhaps soon. Perceived uncertainty and instability in Russia, in political as well as economic terms, has served significantly to reinforce this sentiment. Lithuania was very apparent in trying to follow up on European Union efforts to address and encourage the goal of associated states, including the December 1994 Essen Summit which endeavoured to work out a set of techniques for expanding the organization.

Ukraine, which had a visible independence movement under the old Soviet Union, has been distinctive in approaching the post-Cold War diplomatic and security environment, reinforcing Russian desires to keep this state as well as the Baltics from joining Nato. Further exacerbating frictions with Moscow, Ukraine did distance itself from the Commonwealth of Independent States, the confederation of former Soviet states, and has joined the North Atlantic Co-operation Council (NACC) of Nato, a forum for dialogue between Nato and Central and Eastern European states which first met in December 1991. Ukraine was an early supporter of the Partnership for Peace. The 1993 Military Doctrine statement was explicit in proclaiming the desirability of participating in Western European and Atlantic area organizations, and included defined language complaining that the WEU's 6+3 Associated Partner programme was too 'exclusive.' The Ukraine government has been anxious to avoid being a buffer between the Commonwealth of Independent States and the West, and has tried to encourage understanding between Nato and Russia even while pursuing comparatively distinctive goals.[9]

Russia, though extremely anxious concerning the implications of Nato enlargement, also has moved somewhat toward less belligerence regarding such a change, within limits, as an emerging reality that probably cannot be avoided. At the end of 1994, the Russian government reaffirmed a tough line concerning Nato expansion. The Foreign Minister, Andrei Kozyrev, bluntly urged, 'the Nato alliance not [to] . . . draw new dividing lines in Europe by expanding eastwards too rapidly'. Russian President Boris Yeltsin echoed the foreign minister, warning in the context of a meeting of the CSCE that expansion efforts by Nato could mean that the Cold War was succeeded by a 'cold peace'. He spoke sarcastically about the notion that Nato could 'export stability eastwards'. President Clinton at the same meeting had urged that the CSCE employ principles 'which can guard against the assertion of hegemony or spheres of influence'.

Even in this adversarial atmosphere, however, Yeltsin managed to sound somewhat conciliatory, with remarks geared to the perspectives of the West that emphasized the importance of European co-operation and eventual unity. He noted that the search for a new mission for Nato 'should avoid creating poles of division' and instead should be handled so the process 'brings European unity closer'. The Russian leader then provided a succinct but comprehensive insight into the fears that were informing his perspective: 'We hear the explanation that this is an "expansion of stability" in case of an undesirable turn of events in Russia. But, if for that reason they want to push the limits of Nato's responsibility to the borders of Russia, I will say one thing – it is too early to bury democracy in Russia.'[10]

At a comprehensive conference on the subject held in Washington in late April 1995, a Russian participant portrayed Nato enlargement as 'potentially very explosive to Russian society', and drew parallels between this state of affairs and the Cuban Missile Crisis of 1962. This sentiment is obviously a very extreme version of the unhappiness and occasional alarm which has characterized Russian reaction to the proposals for Nato enlargement, reflecting traditional anxiety about insecure western borders. Moscow also has expressed alarm, and made threats, about the reunification of Germany. Military action was not forthcoming, but anxiety over Germany is both clear and understandable.

Significantly, the government of Russia has also viewed Nato expansion as likely to occur. Various proposals have been made to soften the impact of further major change in the status quo in the eastern portion of Europe. These have included making sure the process of expansion is slow, moving into the twenty-first century; insistence that any enlargement should not border Russia directly and should not include deployment of nuclear weapons further eastward, or forward deployments of military forces; and a treaty of understanding between Nato and Russia.

Recently Russia has shown some signs of flexibility concerning Nato, in line with the fact that in recent years Moscow has expressed more alarm about developments in the former satellite states of Central and Eastern Europe in rhetoric than in practice. Serious threats concerning the reunification of Germany were not followed by any military action, for example. At the end of May 1995 there were indications that the Russians were clearly willing to compromise on the matter of Nato's role in Europe; a desire for recognition as a great power, collaborating with others, had overcome irritation and anxiety concerning expansion of the membership of the Alliance. A specific communication encouraged by a summit of Nato foreign ministers in Noordwijk, Holland was followed immediately by discussions between Nato representatives and counterparts from Eastern Europe and the former Soviet Union.[11]

There has been a diversity of views expressed concerning the desirability of expanding Nato in terms of the interests of US foreign policy, but the weight of opinion among prominent leaders has come down on the side of enlargement. The debate has been sufficiently comprehensive and visible to be carried out within the public domain. Journalist William Safire, blunt as usual, headlined one of his columns in early 1995 'Baltics Belong in a Big Nato'. He repeated the traditional American conservative note that the Russians cannot be trusted, and therefore favoured, 'supporting the expansion of the Nato alliance while we have the chance – now, with Russia preoccupied. If we wait until the bear regains both strength and appetite, the most vulnerable nations will never be protected . . .'. Advocates of expansion include Senators Richard Lugar and Mitch McConnell, former Secretary of State Henry Kissinger, former National Security Adviser Zbigniew Brzezinski, and Professor Samuel Huntington of Harvard. Gen. William E. Odom of the Hudson Institute, writing in *The National Interest*, has argued forcefully for enlarging Nato, regarding such an organization as more effective for the sort of intervention in the Balkans and elsewhere which he supports. Yet soon after in the same journal, Josef Joffe, editorial page editor and columnist for the *Suddeutsche Zeitung* in Munich, cautioned about inherent limits.[12]

Separate but closely associated with the debate over Nato expansion is the discussion of the best mechanism for keeping the peace, in Europe and possibly elsewhere, into the twenty-first century. Logically, rejecting Nato as the most desirable structure for peacekeeping does not mean rejecting the expansion of the Alliance. Expanding Nato, however, does imply using the Alliance for active peacekeeping, at least in Europe. Rejecting a peace-keeping role also returns discussion to the basic question – why does Nato exist?

Expanding Nato would unavoidably change the fundamental culture and character of the Alliance, which might be highly desirable, given the con-clusion of the Cold War and collapse of the Soviet Union which were the initial inspiration for forming the organization. Over time, an inclusive Nato might become a type of Concert or, more likely, 'Congress' of Europe, with even more emphasis on consultation and more caution in responding to armed conflict than has been the case in the past. This is not the same as arguing against Nato expansion or in favour of directly trying to organ-ize a new Concert of Europe; neither perspective is persuasive. Rather, the Partnership opens the prospect of using Nato to enhance co-operation in Europe, with an instrument having far more tested durability than any new institution which might be established. The arguments for expansion in important ways are fundamentally political as well as military. Enlarging Nato will help avoid war through encouraging congruence and collegiality of outlook and habits of consultation within a common framework; Nato supporters have to accept the possibility that the Alliance will become a different sort of organization as a result of taking in new members.

An essay by Edward Mortimer in the *Financial Times* in December 1994 explored the difficulties facing the Nato Alliance in the absence of the Soviet Union. In November 1991, Nato nations at the Rome summit had decided upon a new 'strategic concept' with four main elements. These were: (1) 'To provide one of the indispensable foundations for a stable security environment'; (2) 'a transatlantic forum for allied consul-tations'; (3) to deter and resist 'any threat ... of aggression against the territory of any Nato member state'; and (4) 'To preserve the strategic balance within Europe.' Mortimer reacted sceptically that, 'The lack of a clear direction was obvious. Only the third function has any concrete meaning, and that left it deliberately unclear against whom or what such deterrence and defence were now required ...' He dismissed the other three objectives as 'classic communique-speak. "Strategic balance" is a meaningless concept unless one defines the forces that need to be bal-anced; while to define an alliance as a forum for allied consultations is tautological. A "stable security environment" could mean anything or nothing.'[13]

This consideration leads directly to the fundamental dilemma of and challenge facing the Nato Alliance. If the Alliance is to continue to exist, a change in *de facto* purpose will have to be devised. Otherwise, gradual atrophy and decay will eliminate the organization even if a sudden shock crisis does not. In fact, the survival of the Alliance, despite exploration of other possibilities, including an enhanced security role for Nato, argues that the organization is stronger and more durable than many critics and advocates of reform have been willing to admit. The difficulty is articulating clearly, in a generally agreed manner, a rationale that is comprehensive enough to encompass all the members yet concrete enough to have meaning beyond the most abstract generalizations. Dulles, with a lawyer's literal-mindedness, took the Nato treaty and tried to write others around the globe that would have similar significance. His inability to appreciate the importance of congruence of interests beyond the details of specific contracts was his great failure. Eisenhower, who had the shrewdness worthy of the successful lawyer, kept his attention at all times on basic national interests, which was no doubt one motivation for imposing a strict construction on the Nato treaty. His success was to appreciate the inherent fragility of international order and the great danger of war. The pressing challenge for Atlantic area leaders today, so far not thoroughly addressed, is to define ways in which national interests best come together in the context of the Nato Alliance beyond the old Cold War context. The Clinton administration in very practical terms has effectively begun this process with the Bosnia peace settlement. If the agreement holds, the Nato Alliance probably will also.

European Union: Commerce and Finance

The European Union, by contrast, remains far from true political integration, and has only achieved partial economic integration, yet the incentives to pursue the latter remain strong, and a psychological commitment among many to achieve the former is still present. The dynamics of European community are independent of Cold War politics in a way that is not true of Nato. The European Union is implicitly related to the growth of democracy. Tommaso Padoa-Schioppa, Deputy Director General of the Banca d'Italia, has argued that, 'the firm desire of Greece, Spain, and Portugal to link the restoration of democracy to participation in the EC is a clear expression of the political, not just economic, value of the Community'. The Community has served the original goals of limiting and diluting traditional nationalism. The separate but related point, that the Community is directly associated with democratic sentiments and is especially attractive to democratic regimes, is much less frequently discussed. Democracies generally have relatively free economies. A free economy does not in pristine logic require democratic politics, but as Padoa-Schioppa indicates, the two forms of freedom are rather closely related; a free economy seems to involve a free polity, just as political freedom is hard to envisage without the economic independence from the state provided by the market.[14]

As with Nato, there has been a continuing debate over extension of the European Union eastward. The Copenhagen Summit in 1993 resulted in an accord that Central and Eastern European associated countries would have the opportunity to become members of the European Union. The 'Europe Agreements' committed the Union to industrial free trade with Bulgaria, the Czech Republic, Hungary, Poland, Romania and Slovakia. Slovenia and the Baltic republics were to become affiliated in the near future. Yet the Community has been cautious on this matter. The hesitation to take dramatic steps, no doubt unavoidable in a bureaucracy representing democratic states, has led to continuing criticism from elements of the media, intellectual circles and policymakers and politicians themselves. The *Financial Times* editorialized on 7 December 1994: 'Members of the European Union have been timid, where Eastern Europeans have been heroic'.[15]

The European Union, far more than Nato, has the potential to be reproduced elsewhere. Nato was based initially on a very distinctive confrontation. The European Community was inspired by the specific problems of European nationalism but involves the basic universal currency of commerce. Dulles tried and failed to reproduce Nato simplistically around the globe. Monnet's vision still has applicability elsewhere, even though other regional efforts have not shown the great success of the EU. In Asia, APEC provides not only a forum but also the institutional promise of greater regional integration. Driven by dynamic growth and expanding trade, the organization has the capability to involve Japan in a broader community of nations, something that would not be possible today in a Nato-style military security alliance.

The broader international co-operation at the top provided by the G-7 association of economic powers provides an opportunity for institutional expansion. Fresh opportunities, so far not exploited, exist to increase the mandate of such organizations beyond economics to more comprehensive diplomacy, including military security matters. William Odom has suggested, in addressing military security concerns, that a great power committee comprising Russia, Germany, France, Britain and the United States could be created within the OSCE, the successor to the CSCE. Further, Russia's

strong desire to join the G-7 suggests that if the limited expansion of Nato were coupled with both G-7 membership and a security committee in OSCE, Russian leaders might find Nato expansion less irritating. And it should not be overlooked that Russian democrats have actually favored Nato's expansion to prevent a devastating vacuum in Central Europe.[16]

Likewise, Japan–USA problems, addressed generally in bilateral terms, are nevertheless aided at least indirectly through the communication and co-ordination available through the G-7. Washington's hard line on international trade matters under Clinton, epitomized by Trade Representative Mickey Kantor, has led to virtually ignoring appeals to or complaints from such institutions. Professor Gary Saxonhouse of the University of Michigan has argued the case that an intense bilateral focus has hurt broader relationships:

> From the beginning of the Bush administration until the nearly final breakdown of the Uruguay Round negotiations in December, 1990, far more attention was devoted by the most senior U.S. government officials to managing economic relations with Japan than . . . to . . . the most comprehensive and complex of multilateral trading negotiations.

He also finds the multinational corporation an extremely important factor in this state of affairs:

> Indeed, the increasing confidence of many of the large, globally oriented U.S. corporations in the efficiency of such bilateral negotiations has gravely weakened domestic political support that is critical to congressional acceptance of whatever . . . is finally negotiated.

This leads directly into the subject of the relationship between public and private sectors, a source of public policy tension and sometimes great controversy throughout the history of the American republic. That relationship reflects the dual commitment in our political culture to liberty, which implies limited government and active commerce, and equality, which requires government activism and commercial restrictions.[17]

THE 'PRIVATE SECTOR' ON THE WORLD STAGE

The multinational corporation readily comes to mind when referring to the 'private' realm beyond government, because the global firm has become so important and also because in American common usage 'private enterprise' means commercial activity. In fact there are a vast range of enterprises beyond government and business, including religious institutions, philanthropic foundations, service organizations, interest groups and many others which have a great impact on international affairs. But the multinational corporation is none the less a major factor with growing political as well as economic importance. The social and cultural impact of international business is vast, reaching well beyond profits and markets to providing a source of social integration. A 1995 article in the *Wall Street Journal* states flatly that 'the day of the global executive is coming – and fast.' The piece cites dramatic evidence for the very steep increase in international business movement of people:

> Nearly every industry has spotlighted foreign markets as a major growth opportunity. The National Foreign Trade Council estimates that as many as 225 000 Americans will work overseas this year, up from 125 000 in 1993. And prestigious business schools such as Wharton and Indiana are now churning out instant global executives through internationally flavored MBA programs.[18]

United States' foreign policy can be effective through more explicit, thorough co-operation with both regional organizations and multinational corporations. The fact that the key to Asian stability appears to be through economic rather than military security organization further reinforces this point. The former Soviet Union illustrates both current problems and the potential for collaboration. For instance, the Ukraine developed a serious reform programme after President Leonid Kuchma took office and the United States accordingly has increased assistance, despite a shrinking overall aid effort to the former Soviet Union. David J. Kramer, writing in a critical vein in *The National Interest*, has argued that US government programmes to encourage investment in the former Soviet Union do not rely enough on the private sector. He stresses that the US government should be trying to encourage private investment, privatization and democracy there. Programmes of direct grants and insurance increase the role of the state when that should be reduced. Interestingly, in an article very critical of US government policy, there is support for exchange programmes: 'maintain funding for exchanges. This is the best way for Russians of all stripes – bankers, politicians, farmers, etcetera – to learn from us, and us to learn from them.'[19]

PEOPLE

Foreign policy was once rightly regarded as the preserve of social and economic elites, removed even in democratic systems from the mass of the population. The pace and tempo of contemporary life has also had a very dramatic related impact. George Kennan, whose career has spanned an exceptionally long period of time along with combining reflection, writing and policy action, has aptly described this phenomenon. The State Department at the turn of the century was comparable to a comfortable old-fashioned law office, with – literally – a grandfather clock ticking in the entryway. This is obviously the atmosphere no longer, and unhurried evaluation of policy is a luxury of diplomats of the past, not today's world. The pressure of very rapidly moving events, added to the pressure cooker of modern mass politics, creates an enormously difficult environment in which to define and carry out effective diplomacy.[20]

Yet for all the limitations of the contemporary period, there is the great promise of the communications, information and travel revolutions. There is more opportunity than ever before to create a community of people as well as international organizations of nations. The United States has special advantages thanks to the appeal of its popular culture, and here the experience of Britain and South Korea continue to be instructive. Both nations stand out in these human terms in relations with the United States. The 'special relationship' between the United States and Britain usually is meant primarily to refer to the close rapport that has existed between leaders of the two nations, an important dimension to be sure. The term also implies however a range of broader public associations, social as well as economic, among large numbers of people in both countries, a special quality of rapport that is one of the legacies of American involvement *in* Britain as well as *with* Britain during the Second World War.

The Korean–American relationship also was cemented in war, the Korea conflict of 1950–3, but has other dimensions, more contemporary and increasingly important. The tie between the two nations in addition is very greatly influenced by the large, growing and increasingly visible Korean population within the USA. British immigration was fundamental to the establishment and evolution of America as a British colony and then independent nation, rooted in liberal economic and political values characteristic of the mother country. Korea has provided a much more contemporary migration to America. The very large numbers of Korean immigrants to the USA have already created a most dramatic positive impact in educational as well as commercial life. The commitment visible in Korea and different parts of Asia to strong associations, starting with the family, will perhaps facilitate the spreading of democracy. Traditional liberal theory holds that voluntary groups, separate from the state, play an important role in the development of representative government. Certainly this was true in the evolution of the British political system, as well as our own. Associations as vehicles for public communication and involvement may be a very practical way of spreading the American message.[21]

The development of an international service economy, with the United States a principal factor, is also very significant. Workers are less isolated, more cosmopolitan, to some extent more mobile, and often better informed. Service employment tends to require a higher degree of education, information and technical skill than manufacturing, is more readily transportable to different regions and occupations, and is very congruent with an increasingly integrated world environment. The downside, with important political and social as well as economic implications, is that the expansion of the service economy works to shut out and isolate less well-educated workers who find job opportunities limited or non-existent. The negative impact of this trend on the already segregated ghettos of the inner city is self-evident.

The role of the mass media further underscores the influence of American popular culture and, ultimately, political culture and institutions. Earlier in the twentieth century, radio and film as well as newspapers were important mechanisms for totalitarian control. In the contemporary global market, with nearly pervasive television and computer networks, dictatorship becomes very hard to maintain, except in unusual, isolated cases. Opening the economy to foreign investment renders old-fashioned political information control virtually impossible. Great opportunities are provided, not for propaganda, but for the sharing of information among many different peoples from a range of different sources. Professor Carl J. Friedrich of Harvard recognized this point implicitly in his classic text *Constitutional Government and Democracy*, first published in 1937. In the 1949 edition, the author observed, 'The possibility of broadcasting the spoken word to the four corners of the globe has profoundly altered the realities of modern politics.' He noted that both democracy and dictatorship made use of the medium, but concluded insightfully that 'modern community' had been turned into 'a market place' through the capacity to reach millions of people in the direct, personal means of the spoken word. The same point can be made about the visual image, an equally and arguably more important tool in our own time.[22]

Relatively large numbers of people of all sorts – not just diplomats, military personnel and the wealthy – are spending much more time travelling internationally. The multinational corporation contributes to this state of affairs through diversity of personnel, lots of business travel, and leaping over national borders. As a result, the present as noted earlier resembles the situation in pre-nationalist eighteenth-century Europe, when diplomats and military officers changed posts with little consideration of national loyalties or commitments. Even more important is the fact that this is an age of mass travel as well as pervasive communication, a revolution which began in earnest with the advent of the jumbo jet in the early 1970s. Aristotle's middle class is not just expanding but also dispersing; large numbers of people are for the first time in history finding globetrotting relatively inexpensive.

People are also purchasing internationally in new ways. This goes well beyond, for example, mass production in factories in China of inexpensive consumer goods for export. In Japan, mail-order and related sales are becoming dramatically more popular as a direct function of restrictions in the home market. The *New York Times* reported in July 1995: 'From its headquarters in Freeport, Me., L.L. Bean sends thousands of catalogues to consumers throughout Japan, now Bean's largest foreign market. Sales last year reached $100 million, up 66 per cent from 1993.'[23] A global consumer society is increasingly familiar; the fact that this economic reality is finally beginning to penetrate the purchasing milieu of Japan in a significant way is especially noteworthy.

AN AMERICAN WORLDVIEW: AN AMERICAN WORLD

The world in the twentieth century has experienced both great expectations and great disillusionment. At the turn of the century, before the First World War, the idea of progress as reliable, immutable and steady was so firmly established that the great cataclysm of that war proved an almost unbearable shock to the nervous system of the West. The resulting disillusionment and uncertainty, among both the mass of the people and national leaders, means that the war provided an almost total break with the past. The reliability of progress was followed by a questioning of virtually all traditions and verities, at least by some segments of the population. Hopes for world organization to restrict war were destroyed, as the League of Nations was destroyed, by the unwillingness of a sufficiently strong coalition of nations to work together to thwart aggression. The grievances, real and imagined, of nations and populations, and the insecurity and pain of global economic depression, all encouraged the movement to aggressive dictatorships that once again resulted in world war. Throughout the period, up until Germany began combat in Europe in 1939, the United States remained generally aloof from events in terms of providing an effective international leadership role.

Given this history, there should be no surprise that many worry that the end of the Cold War has opened the door to further instability and perhaps more general war. The killing in the Balkans has provided ready evidence for this proposition. The inability of the UN and Nato to stop the fighting appeared to confirm, at least for some, that supranational institutions were as ineffective as ever when confronted with the brutal reality of war. The peace agreement reached among the warring factions at American initiative late in 1995, followed by the deployment of peacekeeping forces under Nato rather than UN command, has highlighted the important security roles incumbent on both the remaining superpower and the durable regional alliance.

Beyond the particulars of the Balkan conflict and American intervention there, two general factors militate against the pessimism associated with anticipation of continuing warfare. First, the industrial world, and increasing segments of the non-industrial world, enjoy virtually unprecedented prosperity. The growth in wealth, and in the well-being of the average citizen, in western democracies since the Second World War has been extraordinary and – one sign of general prosperity – has come to be taken for granted. A general cause of war has been the drive for territory and power justified by appeals for a better life for the people. Modern dictators have harnessed the fearsome tools of modern technology in pursuit of very traditional goals – land and treasure – along with mass murder, under the rationale of rendering the nation better off. Prosperity since the Second World War has steadily and without fanfare, or even much public recognition, removed this fundamental incentive of people to turn to dictators and to war. The traditional Liberal argument, that free trade and an expanding middle class are basically benign, appears to be vindicated.

Second, the communication and transportation revolutions have opened for the first time the possibility of having a relatively open global community. The revolution in inexpensive world travel which began in the 1970s has been joined by the personal computer revolution. Large numbers of people in industrial, and to some extent non-industrial, countries have opportunities never before experienced to communicate quickly, directly and effectively with others virtually anywhere in the world. Global travel, formerly open only to a very small wealthy class, is now generally available. Images and vicarious experiences of all kinds, including the powerful film and video entertainment media, as well as news and other information, are now affecting people worldwide to an unprecedented degree.

This state of affairs in turn provides very practical, universally valid advantages to the United States. Popular culture in the world is primarily American culture. Coca-Cola, Disneyland, rock music, the most popular movies, computer software of all kinds are primarily or exclusively American in origin. As consumer culture becomes more available, these aspects of American culture become more visible and influential. Consumer goods do not immediately translate into reflective, serious commitment to political democracy, but there is at least an indirect connection. Certainly the argument that a free society produces such generally popular goods and services cannot be denied, and that argument would be made more often if only intellectuals were more sympathetic to popular culture.

Additionally, such openness provides an antidote to the narrow misunderstandings, virulent nationalism and hatred of other groups on which dictatorships and war feed. For understandable reasons, Hitler and the Japanese warlords moved quickly once in power to segregate their people from others. The radio, newsreel and newspaper propaganda of the Second World War totalitarians provides evidence of human deception, human hate and human self-destructiveness that are both frightening and fascinating, and could only have taken place in the hermetically sealed environment of the twentieth-century dictatorship. The communications revolution which gave Hitler the means of total control and manipulation of a people also, when carried further, provides an openness and diversity that is the antidote to dictatorship and organized hate. The ultimate impact of the electronic communications revolution, which has moved steadily through the century, has been in combination with other forces to strengthen freedom, not dictatorship.

I had the opportunity to visit Hanoi, the capital of Vietnam, for the first time in 1994. The only uncomfortable incident on a fascinating and, in some ways, inspiring trip was at the Hanoi airport, where soldiers spent an exceptionally long time scrutinizing my travel documents while others on the plane, Europeans as well as Asians, were permitted to pass through with no problems. Immediately on arrival at the hotel, I turned on the television and saw Phil Donahue, icon of very low-brow, highly personal, consumer-driven daytime American television. Other fare was available as well, largely American in origin. Vietnam remains a one-party dictatorship, yet no traditional police state can survive when uncensored television is available to even a minority beyond the ruling party. The current drive to open the economy of Vietnam, as in China, at a minimum opens the doors and windows of the dictatorship to outside influences, largely Western in nature.

The world revolution toward greater individual freedom finally amounts to a complex and changing relationship between people and technology. President Kennedy's commitment to land a man on the Moon by the end of the decade of the 1960s, an effort criticized at the time and since as an impractical and utopian waste of resources, has had continuing technical consequences which by now influence the life of virtually every American and a growing percentage of the world's population. The most tangible product of that mammoth effort is the computer chip, which has generated the personal computer revolution of our time. Individual citizens are not only able to travel but also seek and collect amounts of specific information that are extraordinary by the standards of any earlier generation. The American space programme, now more prominent in Hollywood films than government policies, nevertheless remains the outstanding metaphor for the revolution which is still unfolding.

The communication and transportation revolutions have a direct bearing on not only such large-scale collective concerns as whether people will follow the path of dictatorship or democracy, but also on very particular individual concerns involving life-style and work opportunities available in daily life. The two dimensions are closely related. The same developments which have undercut dictators have provided extraordinary opportunities to individual citizens.

This revolution in individual freedom has undercut arguments, popular after the Second World War, that the future of industrial societies lay primarily in the hands of large organizations, public or private. John Kenneth Galbraith in the 1950s and 1960s persuasively defined an emerging society in which corporate structures, increasingly removed from outside control, including consumers, would effectively determine economic and social priorities. Vance Packard and other popular critics of an earlier Cold War age warned of insidious efforts at control of the public through subtle advertising techniques.[24] So far, broad social development in America indicates a reverse trend. The multinational corporation is a very powerful world economic force, but societies, especially our own, are characterized by greater and greater individual independence and freedom. Considerable attention in the western media has been devoted to the subject of corporate staff reductions – 'downsizing' – in the American economy in recent years. The human pain, and sometimes tragedy, of unemployment is self-evident. Corporate personnel reductions, however, also work to reduce the immediate control of the organization over individuals. The commercial power of the multinational is expanding in the world at the same time that the power of the large firm to control people directly, at least in industrial nations, is declining. Technology meanwhile has provided more opportunities than ever for Americans to do what they have traditionally done extremely well – launch individual business enterprises.

If we are challenged, it is to exercise enough discipline in our personal and social lives to maintain social cohesion and social stability. The new siren song of personal focus and personal gain may yet prove to be one of the most important genuine challenges confronting the security, meaning stability, of the West, though not the East. Managing ourselves, in a rich and unfettered age, is an accurate characterization of the contemporary social dilemma. Being dominated and manipulated by corporate forces is a threat of relatively small magnitude.

SECURITY THREATS, POLICY CHALLENGES

If general war seems less a threat now than at any time in this century, more specific menaces to national and international security can readily be found. These are likely to grow in significance and danger as the current century ends and the new one begins. Technology which enhances individual communication and other freedom, and ultimately undercuts state control, also provides new opportunities to terrorists, motivated either by ideological or criminal intent – or both.

This danger is married to the growth in support of extremist movements of various kinds, religions both secular and spiritual. The end of the international communist movement, combined with the earlier defeat of fascism, may actually give a spur to such splinter movements. They are not mass phenomena, but do not have to be, as long as technological power provides the ability to generate large-scale destruction from a few sources, or a single one. Such considerations return attention to the power and effectiveness of the United States as international policeman, in a truer sense of that word than is often intended in international politics.

There has also with contemporary prosperity been a basic shift in the cleavages of public policy debate, with significant international implications. In industrial nations generally, the inherent conflict between the rich minority and the rest of the population was the principal focus of domestic political debate. Even in the United States, normally free of European class-style politics, this fundamental division was present, and during the Great Depression reached extreme levels. Since the Second World War, however, the traditional division has been transformed. Poverty is the affliction of a distinct minority, but also one which is increasingly segregated from the rest of society. The severity and persistence of this problem, or set of problems, exacerbated by racial division in the United States, argues for co-operative efforts among industrial nations in future to compare and co-ordinate social policies. The European Union already does precisely this. Immigration, among other considerations, provides in any case an unavoidable international dimension to this social policy arena.

PUBLIC AND PRIVATE

Scholars and government people often look askance at the world of business, and the separation and at times hostility is often reciprocated by the other side. There truly is a problem of 'two cultures' which continues despite the United States experiencing a generally conservative pro-business political trend in the 1980s and 1990s. The benign and liberalizing effects of open markets, however, provide an opportunity and challenge to use foreign policy to bring the two cultures together. Perhaps Democratic Presidents indeed have special opportunities here, just as Republicans could more easily work with communist regimes during the Cold War with less fear of being called 'soft on communism'. Since the New Deal, assertive government at home and abroad has generally been equated with larger government budgets, necessary to fund both ambitious social programs and a very large military establishment.

A note of caution is required in considering partnerships between business and government. The 1980s and 1990s, like the 1920s, have been a time of generally pro-business attitudes on the part of the public. This has not always been the case, however, and history is instructive on this point. After the First World War, there was considerable sentiment in favour of the argument that arms merchants had been a major factor in bringing on the conflict. Harry Truman was selected as vice president for a failing FDR by Democratic Party leaders for a number of reasons, including his effective prominent leadership of special investigations of corporate profiteering during the Second World War. President Eisenhower, after two decades of Republican presidential losses, was careful to select one of the most able – and liberal – Republicans around, Herbert Brownell, to serve as his attorney general. He did not want to be found wanting in the policing of big business. The Kennedy brothers in office found that attacks on big business, specifically the steel industry, paid useful political dividends. Any new government-business partnerships will be vulnerable to a shift in public sentiment, something very possible in reaction to the next series of Wall Street or other commercial scandals, or a severe economic recession.

In future, when ever more complex economic calculations will be part of foreign policy at the highest level, as the global system becomes more integrated overall and more differentiated concerning particular products and services, interest groups will become an increasingly important part of the calculus. Democratic politics is by definition group politics, as citizens in their roles as producers and consumers band together to pursue particular interests and concerns they hold in common. Democratic theory has wrestled with the best way to address and manage the roles of interest, which seem antithetical to the broad interests of the population as a whole, the common good. The framers of the American Constitution spent considerable time on precisely this subject, their words and decisions reflecting a general suspicion of the impact of special 'interests' on effective republican government. True political realism, in foreign or domestic policy, is the recognition that interests are inevitably part of the policy calculus.

The international system now unfolding involves especially complex direct interplay between government agencies and interest groups that used to be seen as largely domestic in nature. Eric M. Uslaner, in an essay entitled 'All Politics Are Global, Interest Groups and the Making of Foreign Policy', makes the important point that public–private sector interchange is becoming increasingly important, thanks to the evolution of interest group concerns in the USA. 'There has been a sharp rise in the number of groups participating in foreign policy since the 1970s, even as there are no firm numbers . . .'. He mentions energy as a policy area viewed as domestic in nature before the 1973 oil shocks, with government decisions determined by the domestic politics of specific fuels. Thereafter, national security and producing nations were factored very consciously into federal decisions. The constellation of Washington lobbyists has changed profoundly: 'Japan alone spent up to $60 million in 1989 on lobbying, four times as much as in 1984 . . .'[25]

From time to time, recent presidents have experimented with efforts to put co-ordination of national economic policy on a par with national security policy. From the Truman administration, 'security' meant military affairs, and the formal organization of the National Security Council in the executive branch reflects this bias. Efforts to create a comparable economic policy council with an international mandate have proven far less successful. For this very reason, however, the president should endeavor to address interest group concerns not through a formal body, but through ensuring that this dimension is considered as part of the ongoing foreign policy review and evaluation process. Knowing which US corporations are most active in a particular part of the world would be helpful in achieving a full picture of American resources on the ground. Such firms could be consulted as part of the policy process. Some could be encouraged to expand investment in particular regions through loan and investment guarantees and underwriting, following a course already developed regarding the former Soviet Union.

The new world we now brave requires articulating our vision and principles in attractive and persuasive ways, making full use of the mass media, while serving as a catalyst between our own institutions and those of actual and potential allies. An earlier extended essay described steps to strengthen Nato as basically 'tactical' and 'technical' in nature, demonstrated during the last phase of the Cold War by contrasting yet equally effective leadership styles of Nato commanders Alexander Haig and Bernard Rogers. The current argument is very much the reverse for a very different world in which old barriers have fallen. Western Europe provides a congenial culture and habits of military as well as diplomatic co-operation.

Asia provides dramatic economic growth and increasing opportunities for greater co-operation in advancing trade and finance. Invigorating partnerships on both sides through imaginative leadership will bolster the United States in efforts to encourage stability and growth in Africa, Latin America, the Middle East, South Asia, and the specific trouble spots that are guaranteed to erupt in the future.[26]

The nation-state continues as the basic unit of international relations in areas where the stakes are highest, the use of force. This places the same premium on national political leadership that has always existed. The role and influence of the United States, now unique in the world, mean that the president of the United States is more important than ever, and political leadership is the vital ingredient to democratic success. In some ways, the dictators have the easier time, with a task that involves very direct communication with the people *en masse*. Democratic leadership involves a much more complex balancing and manoeuvre, an art form requiring handling myriad interests, inspiring the people without splintering constitutional restraints. In the most fundamental ways, at least today, dictators do not have things easy at all, for democracy in political terms and the open market in economic terms are the linked 'waves of the future', achieved in more nations than ever before, aspired to at least in limited forms even where they have not been achieved. 'Democracy Works Best', declared *The Economist* in a cover feature in the late summer of 1994, and the text went on to argue the case for positive association between political democracy and growth. The movement for centralized planning and regulation, whether of the European social democratic or more extreme dictatorial varieties, appears to be dead as the century ends.[27]

Britain and South Korea represent allies with special advantages for American foreign policy in the post-Cold War age of democracy. Germany and Japan are restricted still by the legacies of responsibilities for world war. China is still a communist state, and has the added double challenge of decentralization of authority at the same time that central direction is uncertain. France has found national redefinition thanks to de Gaulle, yet that renewal requires a distinctive stance in the world and some distance from the United States. In a world of regional alliances as well as blocs, where broadly complex patterns of international commerce and new technologies are knitting peoples together, the USA has a special opportunity, and Britain and South Korea should play special roles in our policies.

Samuel H. Beer closed his most influential book, *British Politics in the Collectivist Age*, with this observation: 'Happy the country in which consensus and conflict are ordered in a dialectic that makes of the political arena at once a market of interests and a forum for debate of fundamental moral concerns.' He received some criticism for an allegedly too positive, overly-optimistic evaluation of the British political system. The term 'happy', along with other emotive sentiments, is not the stuff of conventional social science treatises. Recent history underscores, however, as history more generally has confirmed, that stable, competitive democracy is indeed the most reliable road to what can reasonably be described as happiness for the majority of the population. The challenge to maintenance of a democratic society is recognition and acceptance that happiness, a life that is satisfying and both rewarding and rewarded, involves constant sensitivity to and acceptance of change. This involves a dynamic human process, not a static state of being. This insight informs the American Declaration of Independence, which refers to the 'pursuit' of happiness.[28]

Modern political democracy and relatively free economic markets, not dictatorship, have the capacity to accommodate and help drive the extraordinary pace of change in contemporary times. This observation may seem unexceptional to the committed democrat but represents a reversal of conventional wisdom for a diversity of people through a good part of this century. The legacy of the Great Depression was so significant, and so traumatic, that for many the image of the dominant, controlling state was at least reassuring and at most intoxicating, a structure capable of ordering society and delivering economic goods on a reliable basis. The belief that western capitalism was inherently unstable as well as unfair helped spur committed communists, even in the face of undeniable inefficiencies and inequities in their own system. The belief that bourgeois westerners, including especially Americans, were too 'soft' to fight helped spur German and Japanese militarists in hubris and lust for war. This century, after fearful wars and atrocities, has confirmed that in fact the strong and durable system is democracy. The United States, after winning the Cold War, now has the responsibility as well as the opportunity to use traditional diplomacy, economic persuasion, military means and political example to lead in ordering a more stable world. Happy the country that has that historic opportunity – no matter how frustrating, sloppy and bizarre the daily debates of democratic politics.

Epilogue to the 2000 Reprint: The Indispensability of Leadership

BILL CLINTON AND AMERICA'S GLOBAL ROLE

The past several years have brought no fundamental shifts in the currents of international change described and analyzed in this book, though there have been noteworthy developments. Surprisingly, in regard to the United States a tentative and hesitant evaluation of President Bill Clinton expressed earlier still seems largely justified, given that his administration is still in progress, along with the observation that effective handling of international financial matters has been combined with uneven performance elsewhere, including the Balkans. If this is a fair portrait, Clinton has largely failed as a foreign policy leader, in terms of both the clarity of vision expressed by President Ronald Reagan and the decisiveness in crisis demonstrated by President George Bush in the Persian Gulf.

Characteristically, the most striking and perhaps durable images of Clinton as leader are just that, visual images. Above all, he has consistently demonstrated a deft use of the mass media, especially television. This has been a consistent quality in his national political career. Immediately after he delivered a disastrous, overly long and dull speech at the 1988 Democratic convention, to nominate Michael Dukakis, he shrewdly appeared on the Johnny Carson television show, doubtless before a much larger audience than had been watching the party nomination show. Through a deft combination of charm, low-key good humour, and saxophone playing, he won over both Mr Carson and, presumably, the television audience.

Likewise, in the midst of the 1998 impeachment crisis, and related credibility crisis, foreign policy imagery was used as prop and shield. Clinton appeared at press conferences in tandem with leaders of other countries, including British Prime Minister Tony Blair and French President Jacques Chirac. Perhaps most telling of all, a hasty last-minute trip to Japan and Korea was put together in 1998. The fact that this was arranged to coincide with prosecutor/inquisitor Kenneth Starr's televised appearance to testify in the US House of Representatives can hardly have been pure chance or coincidence. In Tokyo, in the midst of ongoing economic recession and policy indecisiveness, a beleaguered government was forced to rearrange schedules, juggle other senior visitors from abroad, and sustain the pressure of yet another imposition from their impulsive American ally. The government in Seoul had to do the same. There was no apparent foreign policy goal to this visit; the domestic manoeuvring of the US President was all too apparent.

The American-led Nato air campaign against Serbia has resulted in similar expressions of cynicism; but this is not the real problem with US policy. The bombing of Serb military forces and infrastructure can be summed up as an American approach to war which endeavours to use technology as the solution to frustrations which are essentially diplomatic in nature, to rely on air power in order to avoid the risks of ground combat, and to put as much emphasis as possible on business as usual at home. The gradualism of the Nato air campaign reflected all the wrong incentives: the desires of politicians not to rock the boat of domestic comfort, the bias of diplomats to view military means as inferior to negotiation, and the lack of comprehensive long-term preparation which is a hallmark of democracies. History has been ignored in that no military campaign has ever been decided by air power alone; the Kosovo Liberation Army played a crucial role in this one. Cynicism is reinforced by a President who endeavours to wage war while not inconveniencing the people. Initial terms requiring Kosovar self-determination and Nato occupation of Serbia were dropped.

The problem is not shortage of statements of purpose and principles. The President throughout his tenure has delivered notable speeches on foreign policy issues. The 1993 APEC address in Seattle remains a masterful performance. Likewise, significant presentations have been made at the United Nations, the Council on Foreign Relations in New York and elsewhere. The problem is that these have not been woven together into any visibly integrated, comprehensive foreign policy theme or themes. There is no sense that Clinton is devoting sustained attention to international leadership on the part of the US. Journalist William Safire has caustically described a President who delivers foreign policy 'snack food', a variation on the term sound bytes, designed to impress and reassure the domestic audience, and at times threaten overseas enemies, usually Saddam Hussein in Iraq. A media-driven continuous domestic political campaign, enormously successful in two presidential campaigns, has become the basis of foreign policy as well. Critics are provided an opening to complain that high policy has been sacrificed in the scramble for victory at the polls, with the habit now so ingrained that the practice continues even when there are no more elections to be won.[1]

While President Clinton avoided conviction in the Senate impeachment trial, the fact that he was undeniably and admittedly guilty of lying to the people, in fairly dramatic public fashion, has directly undermined his credibility. This in turn means that doubts are now almost automatically expressed about any of his actions in foreign policy, especially the use of force. During the last months of 1998, bomb attacks on two United States embassies in Africa were linked by Washington to terrorist leader Osama bin Ladin. In retaliation, military air strikes were carried out against alleged terrorist base camps in Afghanistan and an alleged chemical weapons plant in the Sudan. Scepticism was immediately expressed about the justification, motives and timing of the US attacks. Even the normally friendly press in Britain has voiced continuing doubt on the matter. US air strikes against Iraq during the same period, in retaliation for noncompliance with United Nations weapons inspection efforts, generated similar scepticism. Republican Senate Majority Leader Trent Lott took the opportunity publicly to undermine the administration's declared reason for the attacks.

This state of affairs has placed significant initiative and responsibility in the hands of Cabinet members and other senior members of the administration. William Perry, a highly successful Secretary of Defense during the first term, has returned to duty as a troubleshooter dealing with the ongoing threat of North Korean nuclear weapons capabilities and related matters. Secretary of the Treasury Robert Rubin has had the challenging task of harnessing financial resources of industrial states and also private sources, in the never-ending task of leadership, liquidity maintenance, loan provision and overall stability in the international financial system. If the President's historic record is still uncertain at best, Secretary Rubin has by now become established as one of the most effective leaders of Treasury and international financial policy in the history of the country.

Likewise, while criticism of Clinton in terms of foreign policy effectiveness has been commonplace, the administration has been served by a number of capable individuals, with well-defined policy views. Balkan negotiator and troubleshooter Richard Holbrooke managed to harness Nato allies and oversee a fragile, but until recently largely successful, stabilization effort in that region. National Security Adviser Anthony Lake laboured to provide co-ordination in the administration of foreign policy, largely avoiding the turf battles and doctrinal clashes of earlier regimes. Joseph Nye in both the State and Defense departments provided a refreshing traditional picture of clarity of thought and skilful action in the service of the national interest, in particular in defining the dimensions of effective regional security policy in Asia.

These names are representative of a much broader pool of talent in the administration, but have been comparatively visible in part because of an absence of sustained leadership at the very top. Revealingly, none has served continuously throughout the tenure of the administration. Holbrooke has been a part-time negotiator in a full-time series of Balkan crises, following relatively brief service as Ambassador to Germany and Assistant Secretary of State. Nye was in the administration only two years before returning to Harvard as Dean of the Kennedy School. Lake served through Clinton's first term, then withdrew in the midst of partisan Congressional debate over his nomination to be Director of Central Intelligence.

While Clinton has been criticized from different directions concerning foreign policy effectiveness, one of the most interesting developments of the past several years has been the dramatic increase in public approval ratings in this very area. The 1999 edition of the foreign policy opinion report of the Chicago Council on Foreign Relations is based on public and leadership samples polled during October–December 1998. The Clinton administration received relatively low ratings in the earlier 1994 survey concerning overall foreign policy performance. In the 1998 poll, the rating went up 24 percentage points, with 55 per cent of the public concurring that the administration's handling of foreign policy had been 'excellent' or 'very good'. This rating is above comparable findings concerning the administrations of Presidents Ronald Reagan (53 per cent) and George Bush (45 per cent). Leaders were less enthusiastic about Clinton. A total of 44 per cent selected 'excellent' or 'good' to describe the foreign policy record overall, which is 14 percentage points above the earlier survey but still below the Reagan (47 per cent) and Bush (61 per cent) administrations.

The Clinton administration was not graded so highly concerning effectiveness in specific policy areas. Topics include economic and military issues; bilateral relations with China, Japan and Russia; the peace processes in the Middle East and Northern Ireland; and other matters. In no case did a majority of the public rate policy performance as 'excellent' or 'good'. The leadership group was even less sympathetic, with the notable exceptions of peacemaking efforts. These findings are summarized in Table E.1.[2]

What accounts for this relatively high but general public evaluation? Clinton's opinion poll ratings overall, not just in foreign policy, have been very favourable over approximately the past year. A common explanation has been that this directly reflects the extraordinary long-term growth of the economy and resulting broad prosperity, very low unemployment, absence of inflation and an astronomically spiralling stock market. This is no doubt a major factor. Additionally, the President's high poll ratings on

Table E.1 Evaluation of Clinton Administration Foreign Policies

Percentage rating the Clinton administration's handling of issues as 'excellent' or 'good'

Issue	Public	Leaders
Overall foreign policy	55	44
Relations with Russia	49	39
Overall trade policy	46	52
Relations with Japan	46	43
The Arab/Israeli peace process	44	68
Relations with China	41	35
International terrorism	39	42
Situation in Northern Ireland	33	78
Asia financial crisis	31	40
Nuclear proliferation	31	32
Situation in Iraq	30	27
Immigration policy	28	26
Situation in the former Yugoslavia	26	26

Source: Chicago Council on Foreign Relations, *American Public Opinion and U.S. Foreign Policy 1999*, p. 36.

foreign policy and in general may well be the public's way of indirectly expressing disagreement with the Republican impeachment offensive in the House of Representatives.

Wider domestic political and international economic contexts are also important. In late 1994, the Republicans won a major election victory, taking control of both houses of Congress. The House of Representatives had a Republican majority for the first time in approximately 40 years. Financial crisis in Asia, long-term recession in Japan and debt crisis in Brazil have not resulted in general recession in the US or Europe; Russian economic collapse has not resulted in a military coup or total anarchy; military duelling with Iraq has not resulted in a repetition of the Persian Gulf War; North Korean 'nuclear chicken' has led to confrontation, but fortunately so far, not armed conflict. The administration's high standing overall in the foreign policy poll may be one byproduct of the absence of general catastrophe in the world.

The Republican majority in Congress, moreover, has not provided alternative leadership and arguably has suffered as a result. At least in the House of Representatives, the pursuit throughout 1998 of impeachment of the President did little to enhance the standing of the party. Consequently in the elctions that year the Republicans, while still holding majority control, lost seats in the House and Senate. This was the first time since 1934 that the party in the White House gained seats in an off-year election. The Republican emphasis on the need for stronger national defence was muted, clearly overshadowed by the sporadic pressure for tax cuts. In a manner which has now become established custom, Clinton outmanoeuvred Republican critics by co-opting their policy positions, most recently by proposing a very significant $110 billion increase in military spending.

This state of affairs contrasts with the 1950s, when Republican President Dwight Eisenhower occupied the White House for two terms but the Democrats controlled both houses of Congress for nearly his entire term. There were a number of Democratic Congressional contenders for the 1960 presidential nomination, including Senators Hubert Humphrey, Lyndon B. Johnson and Stuart Symington as well as John F. Kennedy. Despite the competition among them, and other internal pressures, the Democrats were able to mount a coherent policy critique of the Eisenhower administration, with emphasis at the centre on greater defence spending and a more activist role in the world. By contrast, neither party today has a clear-cut foreign policy agenda, and Republican internal disagreements and disarray in Congress are apparent.

KOREA IN ASIA

The news from Asia has been dominated by economic crisis and pain, though not exclusively, while the mood in Europe is long-term uncertainty. The Asia financial crisis, which has had a harsh – though not completely negative – impact on the economy of South Korea, has also encouraged reform. Moving from economic to military security difficulties, the Korean Peninsula has also been a focus of attention, as the Pyongyang regime in North Korea has played variously games of attempted blackmail, cat and mouse, chicken – and, finally, a shell game – in the ongoing effort to use the threat of creation of a nuclear capability to both intimidate and cajole opposing powers into providing money and other forms of economic assistance. In the Atlantic region, Britain has continued to exercise a leadership role, through both close military co-operation with the United States in the Persian Gulf, and continuation of sceptical independence from the effort to create a common currency and related central bank for the European Union.

The financial collapse in 1997 and resulting recession in South Korea, as well as other parts of Asia, provided a stark challenge for not only the nations directly afflicted but also the leadership of the International

Monetary Fund, the United States government and those of industrialized nations generally. These entities were already wrestling with the riptides of rapidly shifting global financial uncertainty. Once currencies began dropping in value in Asia, with the notable exceptions of mainland China and Taiwan, the repercussions in Korea were enormous. In the Republic of Korea, a very heavy debt load had been tenuously maintained in times of rapid growth. With plummeting value of the South Korean *won*, there was a genuine danger that growing defaults in debt payments by corporations would lead in turn to a general national financial collapse.

The immediate effects were starkly apparent. National gross domestic product expanded by nearly 9 per cent in 1995 and 7 per cent in 1996. This slowed to under 6 per cent in the first three quarters of 1997, then 3.5 per cent in the fourth quarter, and slipped into contraction and recession in 1998. Industrial production slumped dramatically from 2.8 per cent in December 1997 to a worrisome negative 11.3 per cent in January 1998. Unemployment, which had been under 3 per cent for most of 1997, had climbed to over 7.5 per cent in mid-1998. The exchange rate, which had been 887.5 *won* to the US dollar in mid-1997, had moved to 1695 by early 1998. The composite price index on the Korean stock exchange had been at 765.2 in June 1997; by June 1998 the level was 313.3.

Nevertheless, and in part because of these dire statistics, a combination of circumstances provided for not only immediate financial rescue, but evidence of good potential for long-term economic recovery and perhaps a more effective political/governmental system as well. IMF assistance provided vital liquidity. By June 1998, foreign exchange reserves were back at $40 billion and by early 1999 approached $55 billion. South Korea's current account balance, which had been heavily negative through much of 1996 and 1997, was in the black at a level of approximately $4 billion per month by early 1998. The consumer price index, which had been increasing by nearly 8 per cent at the end of 1998, was down to under 1 per cent by March 1999, while industrial production was increasing at a rate of nearly 20 per cent and investment in new plant and equipment was up by approximately 25 per cent.[3]

On 18 December 1997, Kim Dae Jung, after years of imprisonment, exile, dissidence and opposition to the established regime, was elected at the age of 72 to the Presidency of the Republic of Korea. His opposition National Congress for New Politics, in alliance with smaller groups, secured a plurality of 40.3 per cent of the vote, edging out candidate Lee Hoi-chang of the ruling Grand National Party, who received 38.7 per cent of the vote. The basic test of democracy, rotation of political groups in power, had been met and passed.

Kim Dae Jung was an especially promising new President in terms of both personality and history. He is personally honest and uncorrupt; his hero is Abraham Lincoln. While a vast number of politicians have quoted, exalted and at times exploited the martyred American Civil War president, Kim arguably has actually tried to emulate him. Capping a lengthy political career that has demonstrated extraordinary determination and capacity to overcome adversity, he quickly displayed a forgiving nature as well. The new President pardoned two predecessors jailed for corruption, Chun Doo Hwan and Roh Tae Woo. They were part of a regime that had imprisoned Kim and that may have tried to kill him on at least one occasion. While his administration has been challenged from the start by opposing political and economic interests, he did succeed quickly in capturing the moral high ground, with the authority and respect that entails.

President Kim also moved quickly to press for domestic economic reforms. Transparency in the financial system, successfully resisted by commercial and government opponents before the crisis, was instituted in the wake of the collapse. The President went on record to declare that inefficient financial institutions and other firms would be allowed to fail. Meanwhile, beyond laudable pronouncements, the government worked with business to grapple day-to-day with the restructuring of established corporate conglomerates into more profitable entities. While the financial crisis in Asia has not been completely overcome, by 1999 the Republic of Korea could provide evidence of both recovery and reform.

BRITAIN AND EUROPE

In Britain, one of the noteworthy events of 1997 was the decisive general election victory of the Labour Party, under the leadership of Tony Blair. After nearly two decades of Conservative Party government, primarily under the leadership of Margaret Thatcher, Labour secured the largest parliamentary majority since the last Liberal government elected in 1906. With that mandate, the new leadership moved quickly to institute a noteworthy legislative agenda. This has been focused primarily on domestic rather than foreign policy concerns. The hereditary tradition of the House of Lords is being abolished and significant regional governments instituted in the United Kingdom. There has also been emphasis on social services reform, which is a perennial public policy concern, in contrast to the current dramatic efforts to restructure institutions of national government.

Foreign policy has also been important. Characteristically when there is an alternation in the party in power in Britain, there is a commitment to a thorough defence policy review. Historically, however, this has usually resulted in marginally more or less public spending, with no dramatic changes comparable to the major American escalations, both in spending and on new weapons systems, of the Kennedy or Reagan administrations. Tory complaints that a Labour government would be weak or ineffectual in defence commitments have been belied by Prime Minister Blair's consistent strong commitment to the American alliance, including actions against Iraq and very active participation in the US-led Nato air strikes against Serbia.

The Balkan conflict, dramatic as well as destructive, provided confirmation of the fundamental proposition that history remains important to policy, even through the great shifts represented by the Cold War and post-Cold War international systems. The Clinton administration has decided to intervene in an area that has been characterized for hundreds of years by brutal, murderous behaviour of populations emotionally divided by strong ethnic and religious identities, reinforced from time to time by ideological cleavages, notably in World War II. To some extent, as Prime Minister Blair has emphasized, this effort represents the much stronger commitment in our time to the rule of law. Yet morality has always been a dimension in evaluation of policy, even if not explicitly acknowledged. The unavoidable test of effective military action is whether the means are appropriate and proportionate and the ends realistic. History teaches that ethnic conflict, often bloody, is powerfully rooted in the Balkans and therefore highly unlikely to be overcome by the diplomatic moves of the moment.

Characteristic American emphasis on technology and air power has further complicated the situation. Unfortunately, there is no example in history of war being settled through air power alone, including this one. Retrospective analysis of World War II has concluded that the effectiveness of strategic bombing was significantly exaggerated at the time. Later, during the Vietnam War, the massive, sustained air attacks in Indochina over a period of years did not weaken North Vietnam's basic war-waging capabilities and almost certainly created hostility among the population of South Vietnam. Professor Michael Mandelbaum's criticism of the Clinton administration for confusing foreign policy with social work has been confirmed in various parts of the world. One result in the Balkans has been to increase human misery of the population in the region under the guise of pursuing the most high-minded and moral of goals.[4]

Yet the Clinton record is not entirely negative. The fragile Northern Ireland peace agreement brokered by former US Senator George Mitchell has indirectly contributed to reinvigorating the 'special relationship' between the two nations. This subject also demonstrates the complex ties between foreign and domestic policy realms, and the continuing significance of regional and ethnic conflicts in Europe.

Europe also continues to provide the most important arena for Britain's foreign policy leadership. The Labour government has come to reflect the caution of the contemporary Conservative Party concerning greater federal institutional independence for the European Union. The common European currency, introduced in accounting and administrative terms in 1999, to be followed by an actual tangible money in 2002, has received considerable fanfare but so far limited effectiveness, confirming at the moment the earlier observation that ready acceptance of a single European market has not been joined by a truly strong supranational currency. Financial markets have been cautious about the value of the initiative and have traded, but not embraced, the new unit. Britain has opted to remain out of the system, even though the nation held the rotating presidency of the European Union as final plans were being made and implemented for the change. So far, scepticism about the effectiveness of a regional currency unit continues to be justified. Institutional mechanisms have been put in place, but the ultimate test of putting European Union over national economic interests in the case of an economic downturn and recession has not yet been faced. The corruption scandal in early 1999, and resignation of the entire European Commission, has not helped the cause of Europe-wide financial policy.[5]

ALLIES

Significantly, when focused on the dimension of leadership, both Britain and Korea continue to stand out in the context of their respective regions. Both have strong chief executives, willing to stake out well defined and largely consistent positions in confronting the most important policy challenges. In each, government has been willing to address military security questions head-on, concerning both North Korean nuclear facilities and commitment to support both the US and Nato in the Balkans and the Persian Gulf. Each administration has been willing to address economic questions of paramount importance. In the case of Korea, economic survival has been at stake, which nevertheless did not guarantee the effective policies which have so far been implemented. In the case of Britain, scepticism concerning the new *euro* currency has so far been justified, with markets hardly rushing to embrace the new monetary unit. In this sense, traditional British emphasis on the importance of the nation–state, and scepticism concerning truly independent supranational European institutions, continues to be justified. Justified or not in regard to a specific policy, one test of leadership is decisiveness, and by this measure Britain remains well defined as a leading Atlantic area power.

The greatest questions concern the United States. With unprecedented prosperity and steady long-term economic growth without inflation, the Clinton administration has enjoyed a very strong base for political action. Arguably relatively open markets and a productive work force are primarily responsible for this state of affairs. Nevertheless, the administration has not been reluctant in claiming credit for the people's accomplishments. Concerning the test of real leadership, defining broad national goals and drawing the people to them, the Clinton regime has been remarkably deficient. A president lacking in personal credibility enunciates a series of discrete policies, with no consistent sustained effort at public education.

Given this situation, the talents of subordinates, such as Secretary of the Treasury Rubin, and independent public executives, such as Federal Reserve Board Chairman Alan Greenspan, become relatively important – and for that matter, so do those of business leaders such as Bill Gates of Microsoft, or senior statesmen such as Henry Kissinger. The United States, founded as the quintessential liberal democracy, with fundamental scepticism of government authority, has moved at the century's end to a state of affairs where the centre of action and centre of gravity increasingly is in the private sector. A President who in some ways personifies the temptations as well as opportunities of comfortable prosperity has not focused attention or inspiration, in a serious and durable way, on the important positive dimensions of our public space.

In this sense, the US has abdicated leadership. Both Britain and South Korea provide important examples of leaders who directly personify their roles, possessing in each case the potential of transcending the limitations of national experience. That is certainly true of President Kim Dae Jung and perhaps also of Prime Minister John Major. Certainly, undeniably, that is not the case with President Bill Clinton of the United States.

Significantly, international leadership on the world stage remains grounded in the nation–state, despite regular predictions through history that this traditional entity is going to be replaced by international institutions of various kinds. The nation–state continues as the basic repository of power in the international system, a concluding point of emphasis in the earlier edition of this book. Secretary-General Kofi Annan of the United Nations is undeniably an influential leader on the world stage, with an influence that is perhaps uniquely associated with the goals of global cooperation and community. Yet for any use of coercive force in the world, the UN remains dependent on the contributions of militaries from the nation–states which comprise the membership of the organization. A similar point can be made regarding Nato and the intervention in the Balkans. Military force, however, is not the only measure of either power or influence. Robert O. Keohane and Joseph S. Nye Jr have written insightfully on the very diverse dimensions of interdependence in the contemporary world. In a recent article, they have written on the extraordinary speed and range of the communications revolution: 'Internet traffic doubles every 100 days. Communications bandwidths are expanding rapidly, and . . . costs continue to fall. As late as 1980, phone calls over copper wire could carry one page . . . per second; today a thin strand of optical fiber can transmit 90,000 volumes in a second.'[6]

Democracies, and arguably market economies, have special advantages in this environment. The unpredictability of representative government is a direct function of the constant interplay among different versions of the most desirable policies. The often bizarre specifics of partisan competition are transcended by the institutional strength of free institutions and the inventiveness of free citizens. The unfettered flow of information is not threatening to such governments and is an essential lubricant to efficient markets. In a self-reinforcing process, lower prices increase growth. Keohane and Nye observe that, 'As Adam Smith would have recognized, the value of information increases when the costs of transmitting it decline, just as the value of a good increases when transportation costs fall, increasing demand by giving its makers a larger market.'[7] In this world, the 'big lie' of the dictator becomes ultimately an inefficient and self-defeating set of blinders.

This means that international leadership is up for grabs in a way that was not the case during the Cold War. The United States has at present a remarkable position of strength in the telecommunications, communications, computer, education and associated industries. Economic developments are ever-shifting, however, and arguably both Britain and South Korea are in good positions to expand national roles in this global environment in the next century. In each case, strong established alliances with the American superpower, and associated strong military traditions, are complemented by willingness to address and grapple with the demands of an open and competitive marketplace. In each of these three countries, today as through history, effective domestic political leadership is essential to playing an effective international role.

Notes

Chapter 1

1. Arthur Cyr, *U.S. Foreign Policy and European Security, passim* and especially ch. 2.
2. Arthur Cyr, *Liberal Politics in Britain, passim* and especially ch. 6 on the social changes which are influencing British party politics and, by implication, might also have a significant impact on foreign policy and international relations as well, discussed below in the context of sociological change and the international system.
3. Ibid., chs 2, 6. See also Samuel H. Beer, *British Politics in the Collectivist Age.*
4. Political science has experienced since the 1950s a proliferation of efforts to provide conceptual and at times theoretical frameworks to explain international relations and foreign policy, some useful to instruction, some useful to research. There is no effort to describe comprehensively or employ such efforts in this study, beyond a few relatively straightforward concepts such as bipolarity. At the same time, there is no implication that the threefold analytic scheme employed represents more than a useful, pragmatic way to order and analyze political developments. The work of Stanley Hoffmann, Robert Jervis, Robert Keohane and Joseph Nye has been especially instructive for me; useful works are cited in the bibliography. Each author is notable for use of theory to clarify international developments and foreign policies, and avoidance of elaborate theory removed from policy analysis.
5. Joan Edelman Spero, *The Politics of International Economic Relations*, p. 1.
6. Ibid., p. 106.
7. John E. Rielly (ed.), *American Public Opinion and U.S. Foreign Policy* (The Chicago Council on Foreign Relations: 1975–1999 editions).
8. The most comprehensive discussion of the foreign policy of the Reagan administration by an insider is George P. Shultz, *Turmoil and Triumph – My Years as Secretary of State.*
9. Ibid., ch. 19, on Central America. On the 'Reagan Doctrine', see Peter W. Rodman, *More Precious Than Peace – The Cold War and the Struggle for the Third World*, pp. 259 ff. He describes the 'Doctrine' as 'a case study of how historical forces and purposeful leadership sometimes converge to produce major international change' (p. 260).
10. See Samuel Lubell, *The Future of American Politics*, pp. 248–53 on the role and style of President Eisenhower, and in total on the changing roles of parties in American politics.
11. A discussion of the future course of the European Union from the perspective of an institutional optimist, with some consideration of military security dimensions, is provided by William James Adams (ed.), *Singular Europe – Economy and Polity of the European Community After 1992.*
12. '[Adviser Bob] Zoellick and I had discussions at Treasury in 1988 with one of my key international aides, Bob Fauver, about developing this idea of a

Pacific organization further. At State, we brought Fauver into the East Asia and Pacific Bureau . . . Consequently, when Bob Hawke, the Australian Prime Minister, proposed APEC . . . we welcomed his initiative . . .' James A. Baker III, *The Politics of Diplomacy – Revolution, War and Peace, 1989–1992*, pp. 44–5. Baker goes on to note from his very long-term experience at the very top: 'The relative paucity of working institutions is often overlooked when discussing international relations. In domestic society, institutions are so prevalent that we take them for granted, but in the global arena, there are really not that many, the United Nations and NATO being the most prominent. Without institutions, it's hard to get work done . . .' (p. 45).

13.   On this broad theme in Britain, see also Samuel H. Beer, *Britain Against Itself – the Political Contradictions of Collectivism*.

14.   William Pfaff, *The Wrath of Nations*, provides stimulating background discussion of nationalism and migration, with particular attention to the Balkans.

15.   'Pragmatic internationalism' is the term used in the 1995 edition of the Chicago Council on Foreign Relations report, *American Public Opinion and U.S. Foreign Policy 1995*, p. 6, to capture this sentiment, discussed at greater length later in this book.

16.   For two insightful perspectives on changing recent German opinion and policy trends, by two of the most effective younger American specialists on the subject, see Ronald D. Asmus, *Germany's Geopolitical Maturation: Public Opinion and Security Policy in 1994*, and Daniel Hamilton, *After the Revolution: The New Political Landscape in East Germany*.

Chapter 2

1.   For the atmosphere and tone of the time, reflecting the journalistic conventional wisdom, see Theodore H. White, *The Making of the President 1964*. A characteristic quote: 'For mismanagement, blundering and sheer naiveté, Goldwater's New Hampshire campaign was unique in the campaigns I have seen' (p. 108).

2.   There were certainly major differences between the candidates in 1980, with the Iran crisis providing immediate opportunity for Reagan, and Carter's emphasis on detente highlighting the contrast with the Republican candidate: 'Ronald Reagan had been identified for fifteen years as an unbending foe of Soviet expansionism and ideology, going so far as to tell the *Wall Street Journal*, "if it weren't for the Soviet Union, there wouldn't be any hot spots in the world"' (p. 27). Rather, Reagan was clearly more comfortable with domestic issues and topics: 'A . . . serious mistake . . . came when the Republican nominee sought to paint himself as a reassuring performer in the area where his experience was weakest: that of foreign affairs.' The author went on to describe a gaffe in which Reagan dispatched running mate George Bush to Japan and China, was reminded he had long supported strong ties with Taiwan, and responded vaguely when asked what Bush would tell the Chinese. Jeff Greenfield, *The Real Campaign – How the Media Missed the Story of the 1980 Campaign*, pp. 276–7.

3.   'I was pleased that Governor Reagan was the nominee. With him as my opponent, the issues would be clearly drawn. At the time, all my political team believed that he was the weakest candidate the Republicans could have

chosen. My campaign analysts had been carefully studying what he had been saying during the Republican primary elections, and it seemed inconceivable that he would be acceptable as President when his positions were exposed clearly to the public', Jimmy Carter, *Keeping Faith – Memoirs of a President*, p. 542. Reagan seems to have been quite relaxed about his own alleged relaxed work habits, and sometimes surprising lack of information. In his memoirs, he indicates relying on films rather than briefing books in the White House: 'Before most of my major foreign trips, the National Security Council prepared a short film that gave me a preview of the places I would be visiting and the people I would be meeting', Ronald Reagan, *An American Life*, p. 368.

4. Townsend Hoopes, *The Devil and John Foster Dulles*, chs. 21–3. Henry Kissinger is insightful concerning Eisenhower – and Reagan: 'Eisenhower embodied that strange phenomenon of American politics by which presidents who appear to be the most guileless often turn out to be the most complex. In this sense, Eisenhower was a precursor of Ronald Reagan', *Diplomacy*, p. 631.

5. Hoopes, pp. 427 ff. on pressures on Eisenhower to be more overtly aggressive toward the perceived Soviet threat; on the President's strong preference for restraint, see also Stephen E. Ambrose, *Eisenhower – Soldier and President*, pp. 517–18 and *passim*.

6. Reagan saw the theme of morale or self-confidence as important, not surprisingly. He reflects on his memoirs concerning the end of his first year in office: 'And I think the nation had begun the process of spiritual revival that was so badly needed. It was once again striving to live up to that special vision of America . . .', Ronald Reagan, op. cit., p. 299. Reagan confided to his diary about Helmut Kohl: 'We did hit it off and I believe we'll have a fine relationship' (p. 560). Thatcher on Reagan, who clearly charmed her: 'In addition to inspiring the American people, he went on later to inspire the people behind the Iron Curtain by speaking honest words about the evil empire that oppressed them', Margaret Thatcher, *The Downing Street Years*, p. 157.

7. On Carter and Schmidt, for example, see John Vinocur, 'The Schmidt Factor', *New York Times Magazine*, 21 September 1980, p. 112.

8. One of the most interesting and revealing of the many Kennedy administration memoirs, in ways unintended as well as intended, is Arthur Schlesinger Jr., *A Thousand Days – John F. Kennedy in the White House*. Reagan's emphasis on defence was reminiscent of Kennedy's, and the Carter administration like the Eisenhower administration had also been moving in this policy direction toward the end. 'Trends within the United States which had been discernible for several years were focused by events in 1979 towards a consensus in favour of increased military spending and a more assertive American presence abroad' (International Institute for Strategic Studies (IISS), *Strategic Survey 1979*, p. 33).

9. On the proposition that Reagan was in fact a candidate supported because people understood and agreed with his ideas, rather than because of any smooth media image, see Greenfield, op. cit., pp. 82 ff.; 'the ability of Reagan to convey a clear, coherent sense of what he was seeking to do that accounted . . . for his nomination . . .', p. 83.

10. Ibid., chs 13–15.

11. 'Concern about nuclear war and nuclear threat emerged as a major item here and throughout the survey' (Chicago Council on Foreign Relations, *American Public Opinion and U.S. Foreign Policy 1983*, p. 9).

12. Foreign policy address to the Chicago Council on Foreign Relations, 17 March 1980 ('Totalitarian Marxists are in control of the Caribbean island of Grenada . . .').

13. Reagan, op. cit., pp. 234–5. Defence spending percentages of GNP are from IISS, *The Military Balance 1981–1982*, p. 5, and 1983–1984, p. 4.

14. Ibid., pp. 547 ff. McGeorge Bundy, *Danger and Survival – Choices About the Bomb in the First Fifty Years*, provides excellent capsule discussion of the Committee on the Present Danger, pp. 556 ff., and SDI, pp. 570 ff. The evolving debate over nuclear strategy in the face of an ongoing Soviet strategic buildup resulted in a large number of publications. Two useful pieces among many which could be cited: Bernard Brodie, 'The Development of Nuclear Strategy', *International Security*, vol. 2, no. 4 (Spring 1978) pp. 65–83, and also essays by Robert Ellsworth, Stanley Sienkiewicz, and Louis B. Sohn in the same issue; Desmond Ball, 'Strategic Forces: How Would They Be Used?', *International Security*, vol. 7, no. 3 (Winter 1982/ 1983) pp. 31–60, and also essays by Donald W. Hanson and Robert Jervis in the same issue.

15. Shultz, op. cit., pp. 717–18.

16. Reagan, op. cit., pp. 449 ff.

17. Shultz, op. cit., pp. 135–45. Alexander M. Haig, Jr., *Caveat – Realism, Reagan, and Foreign Policy*, pp. 252 ff. See also for example Giovanni Agnelli, 'East–West Trade: A European View', *Foreign Affairs*, vol. 58, no. 5, (Summer 1980) pp. 1016–33.

18. Haig, p. 27

19. Ibid., ch. 14, is revealing concerning Haig's state of mind and point of view in the intense conflict with senior members of the White House staff.

20. Ibid., pp. 111 ff. Speech on the Middle East at the Chicago Council on Foreign Relations, 26 May 1982. He stated: 'Lebanon today is a focal point of danger . . . Lebanon, once extolled as a model in a region of suffering minorities, is now a byword for violence . . .'.

21. Shultz, op. cit., pp. 227 ff. regarding the US role in Lebanon; pp. 686–7 regarding the Libya air strike, including Reagan's determination in making this decision, although Shultz is critical of publicity which gave advance warning.

22. William Niskanen, *Reaganomics – An Insider's Account of the Policies and the People*, pp. 173 ff. provides an interesting account of James Baker's role as Secretary of the Treasury, with specific discussion of the Plaza accords of November 1985: 'Baker decided to make a major change in U.S. policy. In secret negotiations . . . Baker won the agreement of the other G-5 governments to devalue the dollar' (p. 176); also Baker, op. cit., p. 606. Baker notes that the Brady Plan which followed his own also emphasized the importance of reform.

23. Elizabeth Drew, *Campaign Journal – The Political Events of 1983–1984*, pp. 227–9.

24. Schultz, op. cit., p. 673.

25. Reagan, op. cit., pp. 484–6.

26. Shultz, op. cit., pp. 814, 816.

27.   Reagan, op. cit., 'At Reykjavik, my hopes for a nuclear-free world soared briefly, then fell during one of the longest, most disappointing – and ultimately angriest – days of my presidency' (p. 675). Reagan goes on to express his unhappiness when Gorbachev 'threw us a curve' by insisting any comprehensive arms cut accord had to include abandoning SDI (p. 677). The President reconfirms through the remainder of his memoirs great disappointment that the START treaty was not finally concluded before he left office; see pp. 697, 699, 701, 702, 709, 716, 720.

28.   IISS, *Strategic Survey 1989–1990*, provides useful specific information on the decline and collapse of the Soviet Union, including economic deterioration across the board; for example, 1989 growth of national income of 2.4 per cent, GNP 3 per cent, industrial production 1.7 per cent, compared with 4.4 per cent, 5.5 per cent, 3.6 per cent respectively in 1988. 'Five years after *perestroika* and economic reform began, these are shocking results . . . the old economic system no longer functions . . .', pp. 15–16.

29.   Peter Collier and David Horowitz, *The Kennedys – An American Drama*, p. 293; 'Joe Kennedy saw that his son had somehow acquired a "universal appeal" that no other politician came close to. "Jack is the greatest attraction in the country," he said to an interviewer. "I'll tell you how to sell more copies of a book. Put his picture on the cover . . . He can draw more people to a fund-raising dinner than Cary Grant or Jimmy Stewart"' (pp. 292–3). Provocative discussion of the Kennedys as well as Reagan and other American politicians in relation to the media is found in Garry Wills, *Reagan's America – Innocents at Home*.

30.   'For de Gaulle, nothing mattered more than for the French to see themselves and to be perceived by others as acting for their own free will. De Gaulle regarded the humiliation of 1940 as a temporary setback to be overcome by stern and uncompromising diplomacy', Kissinger, *Diplomacy*, p. 605.

31.   The Chicago Council on Foreign Relations, *American Public Opinion and U.S. Foreign Policy 1995*, pp. 6–7, 33 ff.

32.   Richard D. Challener, 'The Moralist as Pragmatist: John Foster Dulles as Cold War Strategist', in Gordon A. Craig and Francis L. Lowenheim (eds), *The Diplomats 1939–1979*, p. 160.

Chapter 3

1.   Lou Cannon, *Reagan*, provides one of the most insightful available biographies of the President and his political career. Shultz, op. cit., has interesting very positive evaluative commentary about his former boss, including, 'Reagan as president was a Republican, a conservative, a man of the right. But these labels will mislead historians who do not see beyond them, for Americans could see some of Ronald Reagan in themselves' (p. 1136); see also pp. 1134–6. For a very critical view of Reagan from a fine historian, see Robert Dallek, *Ronald Reagan – The Politics of Symbolism*.

2.   The *New York Times*/CBS News Poll had the approval rating of President Bush at 84 per cent in January 1991 and 41 per cent by March 1992. See report for 26–29 March 1992, p. 1.

3.   *New York Times*, 21 January 1989, p. 10.

4.   *Wall Street Journal*, 30 November 1989, p. A9.

5. Bob Woodward, *The Commanders*, generally confirms this point, though with a Washington cynic's cast, in his informative account of the Persian Gulf crisis and war; for example, 'From his nine months in the Bush administration, [Admiral William] Crowe knew its obsession with consensus, and with loyalty to the President and his positions' (p. 38). Terry L. Deibel, *Foreign Policy*, no. 84 (Fall 1991), quotation from p. 5, pp. 3–23; see also articles same issue by Ted Galen Carpenter and William S. Lind.

6. Schlesinger, op. cit., pp. 312 ff. on McNamara's role; Henry Kissinger, *White House Years*, pp. 38 ff. on going to work for President Nixon.

7. Carter, op. cit., provides his perspective on the conflict, which might be termed the power of positive thinking: 'The different strengths of Zbig and Cy matched the roles they played, and also permitted the natural competition between the two organizations to stay alive' (p. 54). Reagan, op. cit., is more candid: 'Two of my cabinet members whom I admired most, Cap Weinberger and George Shultz, never got along especially well together' (p. 511).

8. Woodward, op. cit., pp. 355–62.

9. Adams, op. cit., p. 7.

10. Ibid., pp. 7, 9. The European Community, now the European Union, has a fundamental tension between the goals of political integration and the unwillingness of nation-states to sacrifice basic sovereignty in such areas as national security, military forces and related matters. The Adams volume examines this subject most effectively and the reader is urged to review the volume, in particular the chapter by Joseph H.H. Weiler.

11. Ibid., p. 62.

12. Reagan, op. cit., pp. 680–3.

13. *Wall Street Journal*, 14 November 1989, p. 1.

14. Ibid., p. A22. Baker, op. cit., develops a lengthy and persuasive case that the administration had a comprehensive plan and an active, aggressive foreign policy in dealing with the revolution in the former Soviet bloc and other developments in other parts of the world. Baker as memoirist contrasts with Kissinger in marshaling details but avoiding broad conceptualizations. Baker argues that 'Our push for democratization in Eastern Europe . . . was more pronounced . . .' than what was possible in dealing directly with Moscow. (p. 45). He is also justly proud of the arms control record, regarding both conventional and nuclear forces, of the Bush administration (p. 473 ff.). With the end of the Cold War, such accords seem to have less visible public impact.

15. See, for example, David Broder's column regarding John W. Gardner's ruminations on the quality of leadership in the *Chicago Tribune*, 6 December 1989, p. 25.

16. On Japan, the USA and the automobile industry; see, for example, *Wall Street Journal*, 19 November 1991, pp. A1, A8, an article which begins with discussion of the Ford–Mazda joint venture; *The Economist*, 1 February 1992, pp. 25–6 on the importance of Japanese investment in the US Middle West, a significant phenomenon masked by the noisy complaints of Lee Iacocca of Chrysler, who had received an ovation at the Detroit Economic Club for denouncing Japan's alleged economic destructiveness; *New York Times*, 27 December 1992, p. F7 provides a profile of Jiro Yanase, head

of Yanase & Company, the main General Motors dealer in Japan since 1915.

17. *International Herald Tribune*, 19 September 1992, p. 4. The Bush arms control record is solid; lack of public credit reflects the President's lack of drama as well as the end of the Cold War.

18. *Wall Street Journal*, 7 October 1992, p. A16.

19. An excellent review of the Balkans is provided by Susan L. Woodward, *Balkan Tragedy – Chaos and Dissolution After the Cold War*.

20. *A National Security Strategy of Engagement and Enlargement* (The White House: February 1995) especially pp. 26–7.

21. *Financial Times*, 3–4 December 1994, p. 1.

22. *Chicago Tribune*, 19 September 1994, p. 25.

23. Focus on the Balkans in the context of the political debate in Washington was not unprecedented but was no doubt increased by the capture of both houses of Congress by the Republicans in the November 1994 elections, while the White House remained in the hands of the Democrats. The Croatian offensive in Bosnia in the summer of 1995 muted somewhat the intensity of the debate.

24. President Bush had been criticized for loyally remaining committed to Gorbachev over Yeltsin even as the Soviet leader's position crumbled with the Soviet Union; in the case of Yeltsin, there has been no equally obvious likely successor. Baker, op. cit., especially ch. 28, is helpful in providing an almost daily chronicle of unfolding events; see pp. 623–5 on Bush and Yeltsin.

25. *Strategic Forum*, Institute for National Strategic Studies, no. 31 (May 1995) p. 2.

26. *Business Week*, 10 July 1995, pp. 32–3.

27. *Wall Street Journal*, 26 July 1995, p. A12.

28. See, for example, 'US–North Korea Sign Nuclear Accord in Geneva', *Korea Update*, vol. 5, no. 20 (31 October 1994) pp. 1–2. North Korea agreed, among other concessions, to abandon a 5-megawatt experimental reactor at a nuclear complex in Yongbyon and cease construction on two new 50-megawatt and 200-megawatt nuclear reactors.

29. Press criticism of the administration for waffling and indecisiveness, combined with the loss of 18 American Army Rangers in combat in Somalia, was no doubt the combination that led to the removal of Defense Secretary Les Aspin from office in 1995. On broader strategic implications, including cooperation with allies in 'third area' conflicts, see IISS, *Strategic Survey 1994/95*, pp. 206 ff.

30. *New York Times*, 21 January 1993, p. A15.

31. John H. Mearsheimer provides a stimulating discussion of the uncertainties of the post-Cold War world in 'Why We Will Soon Miss the Cold War', *Atlantic Monthly* (August 1990) pp. 35–50.

32. Chicago Council on Foreign Relations, *American Public Opinion and U.S. Foreign Policy 1995*, pp. 6–8, 13, 24–5, 30, 33, 35, 36 and *passim*.

Chapter 4

1. Shultz, op. cit., pp. 991–1015 provides an interesting commentary on his growing impression of the enormous pressure on Gorbachev in the fall

of 1987, with nevertheless no interruption in the Washington summit in December.

2. 'America and the World 1990/91', *Foreign Affairs*, vol. 70, no. 1, pp. 1–48 provides insightful articles on the end of the Cold War, with Michael Mandelbaum in 'The Bush Foreign Policy' arguing that the apparently 'passive' role of the Bush administration was in fact sensible prudence, Charles Krauthammer in 'The Unipolar Moment' that the United States can and must exercise unparalleled power, and William Pfaff in 'Redefining World Power' that 'superpower' status requires the existence of an equal rival.

3. 'Unlike the states of Western Europe, which Russia simultaneously admired, despised, and envied, Russia perceived itself not as a nation but as a cause, beyond geopolitics, impelled by faith, and held together by arms . . . After the Revolution, the passionate sense of mission was transferred to the Communist International', Kissinger, *Diplomacy*, p. 143. Regarding the background and career of Ho Chi Minh, see Bernard Fall, *The Two Viet-Nams – A Political and Military Analysis*, pp. 81–103.

4. See, for example, Zbigniew Brzezinski, *Power and Principle – Memoirs of the National Security Adviser 1977–1981*, pp. 178 ff.

5. While Eisenhower worked to undermine Senator Joseph McCarthy, he refused to confront the Senator directly, and in the important 1952 Wisconsin primary election avoided defending his mentor General George Marshall, then under scurrilous and unfair attack by McCarthy. Eisenhower did defend Marshall vigorously in an early campaign press conference. Fred I. Greenstein, *The Hidden-Hand Presidency – Eisenhower As Leader*, p. 161.

6. 'X', 'The Sources of Soviet Conduct', *Foreign Affairs* (July 1947), reprinted in Hamilton Fish Armstrong (ed.), *Fifty Years of Foreign Affairs*, pp. 189–205. George F. Kennan, *Memoirs 1925–1950*, especially ch. 15, provides both the background and the aftermath to the 'X' article.

7. Kissinger, *Diplomacy*, p. 785.

8. The views expressed also had an impact on Richard Nixon and the Republican Party platform in 1960, but in a different way reflecting the direct political pressure of Governor Nelson Rockefeller of New York. See Theodore H. White, *The Making of the President 1960*, ch. 7.

9. President Kennedy's rhetoric, which was soaring or excessive depending on your point of view, was a considerable contrast with the more explicit and negative anti-Communist and anti-Soviet tone of the Eisenhower years. Part, though only part, of the continuing difficulty in evaluating Kennedy's tenure in office may be the different ways in which such a tone strikes people who otherwise occupy the same place on the political spectrum. American liberals who felt the nation had to be more assertive militarily against Communism reacted fundamentally differently from those who believed that American military and covert actions abroad were counterproductive or wrong. The basic division in perspective split the Democratic Party in the late 1960s, just as the Vietnam War split the nation. This in turn was undeniably a factor in the Republican return to the White House in 1968, ushering in an era of executive branch control and increasing strength in the Congress.

10. Raymond L. Garthoff, *Detente and Confrontation – American–Soviet Relations from Nixon to Reagan*; see also the review of Garthoff by Walter LaFeber, *Political Science Quarterly*, vol. 110, no. 1 (Spring 1995) pp. 125–6.

11. Garry Wills, *Lincoln at Gettysburg*, is exceptionally illuminating on the revolutionary character of Lincoln's message and on the mechanisms of communication in the mid-nineteenth century. 'Lincoln is here not only to sweeten the air of Gettysburg, but to clear the infected atmosphere of American history itself . . .', p. 38.

12. Hoopes, op. cit., is extremely informative on the treaty efforts of the time, especially in chs 14 and 27.

13. Cited in Edwin H. Fedder, *Nato: The Dynamics of Alliance in the Postwar World*, p. 10, quoting from André Beaufré, *Nato and Europe*, p. 29. This bureaucracy has also had the consequence, doubtless not directly intended at the outset, of establishing habits of consultation, a sense of collegiality and a source of institutional continuity among the participants, all very useful in maintaining the alliance after the Cold War.

14. Hoopes, op. cit., ch. 14.

15. *Nato Handbook*, pp. 20 ff.

16. Bureau of Public Affairs, US Department of State, *Dispatch* (10 January 1994) pp. 13–18, statements by Vice President Al Gore and Secretary of State Warren Christopher. See the detailed discussion of Nato expansion in ch. 5.

17. See, for example, Saadia Touval, 'Why the U.N. Fails', *Foreign Affairs*, vol. 73, no. 5 (Sept./Oct. 1994) pp. 44–57.

18. Charles Glaser, 'Why Nato is Still Best: Future Security Arrangements for Europe', *International Security*, vol. 18, no. 1 (Summer 1993) p. 7.

19. Ibid., p. 35; Richard Rosecrance, 'A Concert of Powers', *Foreign Affairs*, vol. 71, no. 2 (Spring 1992) pp. 64–82. He is no utopian regarding an earlier age: 'the Concert of Europe functioned effectively from 1815 to 1822, and desultorily thereafter' (p. 65). See also his *Action and Reaction in World Politics – International Systems in Perspective*.

20. See Roy Pryce, *The Politics of the European Community*, for basic background on the origins and fate of the European unity movements.

21. See John Newhouse, *Collision in Brussels*, on the gamble in the mid-1960s to give the Commission of the Community independent authority.

22. Despite various proposals over time to increase the security role of the European Union, and predictions of Nato's demise with the end of the Cold War, the division of labour between the two entities has so far remained remarkably consistent. The Western European Union (WEU) has been promoted as a security arm of the EU, but with indecisive consequences to date. A humanitarian task force was established, and there have been successful efforts to enlarge participation, but a French proposal for a satellite initiative received mixed reactions. Various bilateral efforts seem more promising, including especially now well-established French–German forces integration, and recent initiatives for British–French air forces collaboration, a Dutch–German army corps, and a French–Italian–Spanish air–maritime brigade. The decision by France to return to ministerial and military committees of Nato is a major achievement for the Alliance, reversing the French policy of aloofness which dates from 1966. See IISS, *Strategic Survey 1994– 1995*, pp. 113–17.

23. Adams, op. cit.

24. Ibid.; Ernst-J. Mestmacker, 'The New Germany in the New Europe', pp. 43–54.

25. See, for example, US Department of State, Bureau of Public Affairs, *Dispatch* (31 July 1995), statements by Secretary of State Warren Christopher *et al.*, pp. 591 ff.

26. Robert Scalapino and Lewis Coleman, co-chairs, *America's Role in Asia – Interests and Policies* (San Francisco: Center for Asian Pacific Affairs, The Asia Foundation, nd).

27. Hoopes, op. cit., pp. 247–8 for example on Adenauer and Dulles.

28. Ambrose, op. cit., pp. 45 ff. is insightful on the complex relationship between Eisenhower and MacArthur, which had an influence on the former's approach to administration and leadership, and was certainly reflected in the contrasting American approaches in post-war Germany and Japan.

29. An excellent summary of fairly recent statements regarding APEC as a source of institutional integration in the Pacific region, including statements by President Clinton and Secretary of State Christopher, is found in US Department of State, Bureau of Public Affairs, *Dispatch* (29 November 1993), especially pp. 813–21.

30. See, for example, the set of articles on 'America in Asia', including the featured piece by Secretary of State James A. Baker, *Foreign Affairs*, vol. 70, no. 5 (Winter 1991–92) pp. 1–18; also, Scalapino and Coleman, op. cit.

31. Kissinger, *Diplomacy*, p. 829.

32. Baker, *Foreign Affairs*, op. cit., pp. 1–18, plus personal interview. 'In January 1992, at the special meeting of the UN Security Council, Li Peng met President Bush; immediately thereafter China announced its intention of adhering to the Missile Technology Control Regime. In turn, President Bush decided, despite strong Democratic Congressional opposition, to support China's MFN status and to lift sanctions on the sale of sensitive technology to China. U.S.–Chinese relations were moving to a new plane, but because of its weakened bargaining position, Beijing had to pay for this advance with actions it might not have endorsed happily . . .' IISS, *Strategic Survey 1991–1992*, pp. 122–3.

33. *The Economist*, 12 November 1994, p. 24.

34. Spero, op. cit., chs 4, 8; Peter F. Cowhey and Jonathan D. Aronson, *Managing the World Economy – The Consequences of Corporate Alliances*, especially Part III on specific recommendations for managing the multinational corporation.

35. Jeffrey T. Bergner, *The New Superpowers – Germany, Japan, the U.S., and the New World Order*, p. 221.

36. Bergner is worth reviewing with this consideration in mind.

37. The importance of such symbolism as hosting the Olympic Games in 1988 might be viewed as a modern confirmation of the strength and independence symbolized by the turtle ships. *The Economist* drew such inferences in a lead article on the approaching 1988 Olympics: 'South Korea has vaulted from near-medieval conditions – 95 per cent of Koreans were farmers in 1935 – into the ranks of middle-income countries during the lifetime of people like its retiring President [formerly General] Chun Doo Hwan' (20 June 1987), p. 19.

38. Kennan, op. cit., pp. 485 ff. on the defining experience of the Korean War.

39. An earlier version of this discussion appeared in Arthur Cyr, *British Foreign Policy and the Atlantic Area – The Techniques of Accommodation*, pp. 10 ff.

Notes

40. Kenneth Waltz, *Foreign Policy and Democratic Politics*, pp. 7–8.
41. Kissinger, *Diplomacy*, pp. 95–6.
42. David Fromkin, *In The Time of the Americans – FDR, Truman, Eisenhower, MacArthur, Marshall – The Generation That Changed America's Role in the World*, is especially effective in description of the profound changes in international relations which developed rather than emerging abruptly as a result of the Second World War.
43. The decline of Britain was of course not visible to most of the British, in particular Churchill; the loss of the 1945 general election by his Tory Party was in this sense a blessing in shielding the great wartime leader from grappling with an end of empire for which he was singularly unequipped.
44. *Wall Street Journal*, 3 March 1995, p. A6.
45. Jonathan Clarke, 'Repeating British Mistakes', *The National Interest*, no. 39 (Spring 1995) pp. 69–70.
46. Fromkin, op. cit., p. 458.
47. Lawrence B. Krause and Fun-koo Park (eds), *Social Issues in Korea: Korean and American Perspectives*, p. 12; Robert Solomon, *The Transformation of the World Economy, 1980–93*, p. 156.
48. *Business Week*, 31 July 1995, pp. 56 ff.
49. Christopher J. Sigur (ed.), *Continuity and Change in Contemporary Korea* (New York: Carnegie Council on Ethics and International Affairs, 1994) p. 58.
50. David I. Steinberg, 'The Transformation of the South Korean Economy', in Donald N. Clark (ed.), *Korea Briefing 1993 – Festival of Korea*, pp. 31–2.
51. One example of both the opportunities and pitfalls of rapidly growing diverse enterprises, harnessed to one leader's drive and ego, is provided by Korea's Samsung Corporation. Commitment to the organization, reminiscent of Japan's business culture, is also blended with a freewheeling entrepreneurial drive that seems more like the United States.

> Industrialists from rival conglomerates, betraying a hint of envy, call Samsung more cult than conglomerate. They refer to it as 'The Republic' because of its growing size and its employees' fierce devotion to the chairman. 'The problem with Samsung is it neglects the individual's personality,' says the chairman of a midsize conglomerate. 'It lacks human relationships.'
> Yet Samsung has impressive achievements, and foreign bankers praise its executives. At a meeting . . . the conversation drifted to Samsung's money-losing petrochemicals affiliate. Not to worry, a group official said: The world's petrochemical plants are aging, and demand will eventually outstrip supply.
> 'He quoted us chapter and verse on every petrochemical plant in the world,' a participant recalls. 'He knew each plant in Japan, the U.S. and every other country . . . . and he knew the number of nuts and bolts it took to build them': *Wall Street Journal*, 2 March 1995, pp. A1, 6.

Despite this powerful position, Samsung was reportedly in difficulty with the government within six months of the appearance of this article. See *Wall Street Journal*, 18 August 1995, p. A1.

52. *Pacific Economic Outlook 1995–1996* (San Francisco: The Asia Foundation, 1995) p. 38.
53. Pamela Cox, 'Three Decades of Growth: Korea Graduates From World Bank Lending', *Korea's Economy 1995* (Washington, DC: Korea Economic Institute of America, 1995) p. 6; *Business Week*, 31 July 1995, p. 58.
54. *South Korea and the United States*, a report on a conference sponsored by The Asia Society, The Seoul Forum for International Affairs, and The Johnson Foundation, at Wingspread Wisconsin, 20–22 April 1988 (New York: The Asia Society, 1988) p. 8. The report is revealing concerning interest-group interplay on both sides of the Pacific.

   Several Koreans criticized the United States' product-by-product approach to trade negotiations, saying that the list from beef to cigarettes to frozen potatoes seemed never-ending. The product-by-product approach appears to the Korean public as 'ad hoc, random, adversarial, and without intellectual justification,' said one. Moreover, even completely liberalizing agricultural trade, the most sensitive issue in Korea, will not solve the trade imbalance, others argued (p. 9).

55. 'Democracy Under the Sixth Republic', by Kim Dalchoong, in *Democracy in Korea: The Roh Tae Woo Years*, papers from 22 June 1992 Merrill House Conference sponsored by the Carnegie Council on Ethics and International Affairs (New York: Carnegie Council on Ethics and International Affairs, 1992) p. 32.
56. *Hankook Ilbo* (7 March 1995) p. 105; *Korea Focus on Current Topics*, vol. 3, no. 2 (Mar.–Apr. 1995).
57. *Korea Update*, vol. 5, no. 20 (31 October 1994) p. 1.
58. See *Korea Focus* (Mar./Apr. 1995) on intra-Korean trade. South Korea has reached beyond Moscow and Beijing in using economic influence to good diplomatic effect. Vietnam has also been a beneficiary of this sort of attention:

   Vietnam opened diplomatic relations with South Korea in 1992, and they have since exchanged prime ministerial visits. South Korea provides a modest technical assistance and training programme valued at US$50m. and, in August 1994, Vietnam and South Korea signed an agreement on cultural and educational exchange. South Korean trade and investment figures are more substantial and South Korea maintains a huge trade surplus with Vietnam. In 1993, South Korea sold goods valued at US$730m while importing only US$90m. South Korean investment, involving 85 projects valued at US$782m, is concentrated in hotel construction, steel mills and manufacturing plants (Carlyle A. Thayer, *Beyond Indochina*, Adelphi Paper 297, London: IISS, 1995, p. 51).

59. Francis Fukuyama, *The End of History and the Last Man*, p. xi.
60. *New York Times*, 21 January 1989, p. 10.
61. *New York Times*, 21 January 1993, p. A15.

Chapter 5

1. Samuel P. Huntington, 'The Clash of Civilizations', *Foreign Affairs*, vol. 72, no. 3 (Summer 1993) p. 22, and also pp. 22–49; *Korea Times*, 3 June 1995, p. 1.

2. Paul Krugman, 'The Myth of Asia's Miracle,' *Foreign Affairs*, vol. 73, no. 6 (Nov./Dec. 1994) pp. 62–78.

3. Remarks of Anthony Lake, Assistant to the President for National Security Affairs, 'From Containment to Enlargement,' delivered at Johns Hopkins University School of Advanced International Studies, Washington, DC (21 September 1995) especially pp. 1, 5, 8, 9. Lake devotes focused attention to Nato and the approaching Partnership for Peace proposal:

> The military problem involves Nato. For half a century, Nato has proved itself the most effective military alliance in human history. If Nato is to remain an anchor for European and Atlantic stability, at the President believes it must, its members must commit themselves to updating Nato's role in this new era. Unless Nato is willing over time to assume a broader role, then it will lose public support, and all our nations will lose a vital bond of transatlantic and European security. That is why, at the Nato summit that the President has called for this January, we will seek to update Nato, so that there continues behind the enlargement of market democracies an essential collective security (p. 7).

4. See as examples David Lake, 'Powerful Pacifists: Democratic States and War', *American Political Science Review*, vol. 86, no. 1 (March 1992) pp. 24–37; William J. Dixon, 'Democracy and the Peaceful Settlement of International Conflict', *American Political Science Review*, vol. 88, no. 1 (March 1994) pp. 14–32. Alexis de Tocqueville, the French aristocrat who toured and described the United States early in the nineteenth century, provides more sensitive insights than some contemporary analysts. He argues (*Democracy in America*, New American Library edition, 1956) that 'democratic' peoples are less inclined to war, weak at the start of war thanks to lack of emphasis on the military in peace time, but more likely to prevail in war because of the diverse talents brought to bear. 'Hence . . . the selfsame democratic nations which are so reluctant to engage in hostilities, sometimes perform prodigious achievements when once they have taken the field' (p. 282). His points could be applied directly to the experience of the democracies in the Second World War. He also reasons, in a restatement of nineteenth-century Liberal faith in free trade, that 'Neighboring democratic nations not only become alike in some respects, but they eventually grow to resemble each other in almost all' (p. 284). He does not, however, draw a direct powerful correlation between democracy and peace.

5. Schlesinger, op. cit., p. 644. Kennedy made the comment during a Sunday lunch at his country estate with the French intellectual André Malraux, and the President returned to the theme in more public forums following. He remarked, with no apparent sense of irony, that only medical care for the aged seemed to get people passionately aroused.

6. Samuel B. Beer, *To Make a Nation – The Rediscovery of American Federalism*, for a superb, sophisticated discussion of the ideas and interests which informed the process of creating the American Constitution.

7. One of the most informative and stimulating treatments of the subject is provided in Harold J. Laski, *Political Thought in England from Locke to Bentham*, especially pp. 26–61 on Locke.

8. Regarding Aristotle, see the discussion in the provocative, stimulating blending of mathematics and political theory provided by Hayward R. Alker, Jr., *Mathematics and Politics*, p. 17 and *passim*. Aristotle in his *Politics* urged 'to endeavour either to mingle together the multitude of the poor and that of the wealthy or to increase the middle class (for this dissolves party factions due to inequality)' (p. 427).

9. Institute for National Strategic Studies, *Strategic Forum*, no. 31 (May 1995) p. 3. based on a large international conference held 24–5 April 1995 in Washington DC. Other citations below, including the Russian reference to the Cuban Missile Crisis of 1962, are from this document. Also very useful is James W. Morrison, *Nato Expansion and Alternative Future Security Alignments*, McNair Paper 40 (Washington D.C.: National Defense University, April 1995); *Nato Handbook*, pp. 50 ff. See also Roy Allison, *Military Forces in the Soviet Successor States*, Adelphi Paper 28, IISS, 1993.

   By early 1995, twenty-five countries had joined the Partnership for Peace. They were: Albania, Armenia, Austria, Azerbaijan, Belarus, Bulgaria, Czech Republic, Estonia, Finland, Georgia, Hungary, Kazakhstan, Kyrgyzstan, Latvia, Lithuania, Moldava, Poland, Romania, Russia, Slovakia, Slovenia, Sweden, Turkmenistan, Ukraine and Uzbekistan.

10. *Financial Times*, 6 December 1994, p. 1; see also *Financial Times*, 2 December 1994, p. 1: 'Mr. Andrei Kozyrev, the Russian foreign minister, last night warned the Nato alliance not to draw new dividing lines in Europe by expanding eastwards too rapidly.'

11. *Korea Times*, 31 May 1995, p. 2.

12. *New York Times*, 16 January 1995, p. A11; William Odom, 'Nato's Expansion – Why the Critics are Wrong', *The National Interest*, no. 39 (Spring 1995) p. 48 and pp. 38–49. Josef Joffe, 'Is There Life After Victory? What Nato Can and Cannot Do', *The National Interest*, no. 41 (Fall 1995) pp. 19–25.

13. *Financial Times*, 7 December 1994, p. 15.

14. Adams, op. cit., p. 62.

15. *Financial Times*, 7 December 1994, p. 15.

16. Odom, op. cit., p. 46.

17. Adams, op. cit., p. 349; the essay by Gary Saxonhouse, 'Europe's Economic Relations With Japan', pp. 347–69, provides an interesting treatment, marshaling statistical analysis, that Japanese trade with the European Union is lower than would be expected in the absence of discrimination. His observations about the influence of the multinational corporation take on added significance in this context.

18. *Wall Street Journal*, 25 July 1995, p. B1.

19. David J. Kramer, 'Russian Aid (II)', *The National Interest*, no. 39 (Spring 1995) p. 82 and pp. 78–82.

20. George Kennan, *American Diplomacy*, pp. 91–2.

21. Ho-Youn Kwon and Shin Kim (eds), *The Emerging Generation of Korean-Americans*, ch. 5 and *passim*.

22. Carl J. Friedrich, *Constitutional Government and Democracy*, p. 529. The enormous and growing capacity of the communications industry in total – including traditional print media – is a very powerful factor shaping perceptions of our world at large, one which largely promotes an American view of the world, ranging from consumer products to diplomacy. During the

1991 Persian Gulf War, there was considerable attention devoted to the importance of CNN television to decisionmakers as well as the public. Colin Powell noted in his memoirs, *My American Journey*:

> I was watching CNN's Bernard Shaw, Peter Arnett, and John Holliman, like current-day Edward R. Murrows, broadcasting from the ninth floor of the Rasheed Hotel, speculating over the meaning of sudden streaks. I knew the answer . . . Iraqi air defense emplacements were lashing out blindly (p. 506).

The analogy with Murrow broadcasting from London during the German bombing blitz of the Second World War is most apt.

23. *New York Times*, 3 July 1995, p. 1.
24. John Kenneth Galbraith, *The Affluent Society* develops the theme that Americans have excessively favored the private sector, *The New Industrial State* develops the case for an increasingly powerful and removed corporation; Vance Packard, *The Hidden Persuaders*, had a marked impact, though in the post-Second World War 1950s and 1960s rather than more recently, with his devil theory that Satan is working on us directly through the medium of the advertising agency.
25. Eric M. Uslaner, 'All Politics are Global: Interest Groups and the Making of Foreign Policy', in Allan J. Cigler and Burdett A. Loomis, *Interest Group Politics*, pp. 371–2.
26. Cyr, *U.S. Foreign Policy*, ch. 6.
27. *The Economist*, 27 August 1994, pp. 9, 15–17. Paul Kennedy, *The Rise and Fall of the Great Powers*, provides a 'wealth' of information on the revolutionary increase in industrial production in our time, relying heavily on the work of economic historians, including W.W. Rostow. Kennedy, normally restrained, refers to a 'dizzy rise': using 1900 as a base year with total world production of manufacturing at 100, the total by 1973 was measured as 1730.6 and by 1980 as 3041.6. Recovery from world war, move from agriculture to industry, related industrialization of the Third World, mobilization of resources in planned economies, and new technologies were factors cited for this global transformation; p. 414.
28. Beer, *British Politics*, p. 390. Also, 'What Future For the State?,' *Daedalus*, vol. 124, no. 2 (Spring 1995).

Epilogue

1. William Safire, 'Essay – So Govern Already', *The New York Times*, 25 February 1999, p. A27.
2. *American Public Opinion and U.S. Foreign Policy 1999*, pp. 35–6.
3. Korea Economic Institute of America, *South Korea Responds to the Crisis – Economic Data*, September 1998; Embassy of Korea, Washington, D.C., *The Korean Economy is Bouncing Back – A Statistical Glance*, 30 April 1999.
4. Michael Mandelbaum, 'Foreign Policy as Social Work', *Foreign Affairs*, vol. 75, no. 1 (January/February 1996), pp. 16–32.
5. 'Ready or Not, Here Comes EMU', *The Economist*, 11 October 1997, pp. 23–7. A characteristic comment: 'It would be wrong to say that Europe's

governments have set at naught their doubts about the principle of the single currency. To set something at naught you first have to recognise it – and doubts about the euro, it seems, have simply failed to register with most EU leaders.' (p. 23).

6.   Robert O. Keohane and Joseph S. Nye, Jr, 'Power and Interdependence in the Information Age', *Foreign Affairs*, vol. 77, no. 5. (September/October 1998), p. 83. Among US political scientists, Keohane and Nye, along with Stephen Krasner of Stanford University, have been especially insightful in relating the continued importance of the nation–state to the present and future trends in the international economy.

7.   Ibid., p. 93.

Bibliography

This list has been assembled to indicate works consulted in writing this book and also to provide suggested background reading for the interested serious general reader. Among periodicals, *The Economist* is to be commended, along with *Foreign Affairs*, *Foreign Policy*, *The National Interest* and *ORBIS*. Reading these journals on a fairly regular basis will provide solid grounding for understanding and analysis of developments in the international system.

Abel, Elie, *The Shattered Bloc – Behind the Upheaval in Eastern* Europe (Boston: Houghton Mifflin Company, 1990).

Adams, William James (ed.), *Singular Europe – Economy and Polity of the European Community After 1992* (Ann Arbor: The University of Michigan Press, 1992).

Aho, C. Michael and Marc Levinson, *After Reagan – Confronting the Changed World Economy* (New York: Council on Foreign Relations, 1988).

Alker, Hayward R., Jr, *Mathematics and Politics* (New York: The Macmillan Co.; London: Collier-Macmillan Limited, 1965).

Allison, Graham T., *Essence of Decision – Explaining the Cuban Missile Crisis* (Boston: Little, Brown and Co., 1971).

Ambrose, Stephen E., *Eisenhower – Soldier and President* (New York, London, Toronto, Sydney, Tokyo, Singapore: Simon & Schuster, 1990).

Aristotle (trans. H. Rackham), *Politics* (Cambridge, Mass. and London: Harvard University Press and William Heinemann, Ltd., 1932 and 1950).

Armstrong, Hamilton Fish (ed.), with James Chace, Carol Kahn, and Jennifer Whittaker, *Fifty Years of Foreign Affairs* (New York, Washington, London: Praeger Publishers for the Council on Foreign Relations, 1972).

Aron, Raymond (trans. Stephen Cox), *In Defense of Decadent Europe* (South Bend Indiana: Regnery/Gateway, Inc., 1977).

—— (trans. Terence Kilmartin), *On War* (Garden City, New York: Doubleday Anchor Books, Doubleday & Company, Inc., 1959).

—— (trans. Terence Kilmartin), *The Opium of the Intellectuals* (New York: The Norton Library, W.W. Norton & Co., Inc., 1957, 1962).

—— (trans. Richard Howard and Annette Baker Fox), *Peace and War – A Theory of International Relations* (Garden City, New York: Doubleday & Co., Inc., 1966).

Aslund, Anders, *How Russia Became a Market Economy* (Washington, DC: The Brookings Institution, 1995).

Asmus, Ronald D., *Germany's Geopolitical Maturation: Public Opinion and Security Policy in 1994* (Santa Monica, Calif.: RAND Corporation [prepared for the Friedrich Naumann Foundation, Office of the Secretary of Defense, United States Army, United States Air Force], 1995).

Bailey, Harry A. Jr (ed.), *Classics of the American Presidency* (Oak Park Illinois: Moore Publishing Company, Inc., 1980).

Baker, James A. (with Thomas M. DeFrank), *The Politics of Diplomacy – Revolution, War & Peace, 1989–1992* (New York: G.P. Putnam's Sons, 1995).

Barnet, Richard J., *The Alliance – America Europe Japan – Makers of the Postwar World* (New York: Simon & Schuster, 1983).

Beer, Samuel H., *Britain Against Itself – The Political Contradictions of Collectivism* (New York and London: W.W. Norton & Company, 1982).

——, *British Politics in the Collectivist Age* (New York: Alfred A. Knopf, 1967).

——, *To Make A Nation – The Rediscovery of American Federalism* (Cambridge Mass. and London: The Belknap Press of Harvard University Press, 1993).

Berger, Henry W. (ed.), *A William Appleman Williams Reader – Selections from His Major Historical Writings* (Chicago: Ivan R. Dee, 1992).

Bergner, Jeffrey T., *The New Superpowers – Germany, Japan, the U.S. and the New World Order* (New York: St. Martin's Press, 1991).

Beschloss, Michael R., *The Crisis Years – Kennedy and Khrushchev 1960–1963* (New York: Edward Burlingame Books/HarperCollins Publishers, 1991).

Blight, James G., Bruce J. Allyn, and David A. Welch, *Cuba on the Brink – Castro, the Missile Crisis, and the Soviet Collapse* (New York: Pantheon Books, 1993).

Blight, James G., and David A. Welch (with a Foreword by McGeorge Bundy), *On the Brink – Americans and Soviets Reexamine the Cuban Missile Crisis* (New York: Hill and Wang, 1989).

Blumenthal, Sidney, *Pledging Allegiance – The Last Campaign of the Cold War* (New York: HarperCollins, 1990).

Borneman, John, *After the Wall – East Meets West in the New Berlin* (New York: Basic Books, 1991).

Boulding, Kenneth E., *Conflict and Defense – A General Theory* (New York: Harper & Row, 1962, 1963).

Brandt, Willy (trans. Joel Carmichael), *A Peace Policy for Europe* (New York, Chicago, San Francisco: Holt, Rinehard & Winston, 1969).

Brzezinski, Zbigniew, *Alternative to Partition – For A Broader Conception of America's Role in Europe* (New York, Toronto, London: McGraw Hill Book Company, 1965).

——, *The Grand Failure – The Birth and Death of Communism in the Twentieth Century* (New York: Charles Scribner's Sons, 1989).

——, *Out of Control – Global Turmoil on the Eve of the 21st Century* (New York, Oxford, Singapore, Sydney, Toronto: Charles Scribner's Sons and Maxwell Macmillan Canada and International, 1993).

——, *Power and Principle – Memoirs of the National Security Adviser 1977–1981* (New York: Farrar Straus Giroux, 1983).

Buckley, Tom, *Violent Neighbors – El Salvador, Central America, and the United States* (New York: Times Books, 1984).

Bundy, McGeorge, *Danger and Survival – Choices About the Bomb in the First Fifty Years* (New York: Random House, 1988).

Burnett, Alan, *The A–NZ–US Triangle* (Canberra: Strategic and Defence Studies Center, Australian National University, 1988).

Burstein, Daniel, *Turning The Tables – A Machiavellian Strategy for Dealing With Japan* (New York, London, Toronto, Sydney, Tokyo, Singapore: Simon & Schuster, 1993).

Cahn, Anne Hessing and Joseph J. Kruzel, Peter M. Dawkins, Jacques Huntzinger, *Controlling Future Arms Trade* (New York, St. Louis, San Francisco, others: McGraw-Hill Book Company, 1977).

Califano, Joseph A. Jr., *Governing America – An Insider's Report for the White House and the Cabinet* (New York: Simon & Schuster, 1981).

Calleo, David, *The German Problem Reconsidered – Germany and the World Order, 1870 to the Present* (Cambridge, London, New York, Melbourne: Cambridge University Press, 1978).

Campbell, Edwina S., *Germany's Past and Europe's Future – the Challenges of West German Foreign Policy* (Washington, New York, London, Oxford, Beijing, Frankfurt, Sao Paulo, Sydney, Tokyo, Toronto: Pergamon–Brassey's International Defense Publishers, Inc., 1989).

Cannon, Lou, *Reagan* (New York: G.P. Putnam's Sons, 1982).

Caporaso, James A., *The Structure and Function of European Integration* (Pacific Palisades, Ca.: Goodyear Publishing Co., 1974).

Carter, Jimmy, *Keeping Faith – Memoirs Of A President* (Toronto, New York, London, Sydney: Bantam Books, 1982).

Case, John, *From the Ground Up – The Resurgence of American Entrepreneurship* (New York, London, Toronto, Sydney, Tokyo, Singapore: Simon & Schuster, 1992).

Chace, James, and Earl C. Ravenal, *Atlantis Lost – U.S.–European Relations After the Cold War* (New York: A Council on Foreign Relations Books, Published by New York University Press, 1976).

Chubb, John E., and Paul E. Peterson (eds), *The New Direction in American Politics* (Washington, DC: The Brookings Institution, 1985).

Cigler, Allan J., and Burdett A. Loomis (eds), *Interest Group Politics* (4th edn, Washington, DC: Congressional Quarterly, Inc., 1995).

Clark, Donald N. (ed.), *Korea Briefing, 1993 – Festival of Korea* (Boulder, San Francisco, Oxford: Westview Press, 1993).

Claude, Inis L., Jr, *Power and International Relations* (New York: Random House, 1962).

Cline, William R., Noboru Kawanabe, T.O.M. Kronsjo, and Thomas Williams, *Trade Negotiations in the Tokyo Round – A Quantitative Assessment* (Washington DC, The Brookings Institution, 1978).

Cockburn, Andrew, *The Threat – Inside the Soviet Military Machine* (New York: Vintage, 1983).

Coffey, Joseph I., *Arms Control and European Security – A Guide to East–West Negotiations* (New York and London: Praeger, 1977).

Cohen, William S., and George J. Mitchell, *Men of Zeal – A Candid Inside Story of the Iran-Contra Hearing* (New York: Viking, 1988).

Collier, Peter and David Horowitz, *The Kennedys – An American Drama* (New York: Warner Books, 1984).

Cook, Don, *Charles de Gaulle – A Biography* (New York: G.P. Putnam's Sons, 1983).

——, *Forging the Alliance – Nato, 1945–1950* (New York: Arbor House/William Morrow, 1989).

Cottrell, Alvin J., and James D. Theberge, *The Western Mediterranean – Its Political, Economic and Strategic Importance* (New York, Washington, London: Praeger Publishers, 1974).

Cowhey, Peter F., and Jonathan D. Aronson, *Managing the World Economy – The Consequences of Corporate Alliances* (New York: Council on Foreign Relations Press, 1993).

Craig, Gordon A., and Francis L. Loewenheim (eds.), *The Diplomats – 1939–1979* (Princeton, New Jersey: Princeton University Press, 1994).

Cumings, Bruce, *War and Television* (New York: Routledge, Chapman & Hall, Inc., 1994).

Cyr, Arthur, *British Foreign Policy and the Atlantic Area – The Techniques of Accommodation* (London and Basingstoke: Macmillan, 1979).

——, *Liberal Politics in Britain* (New Brunswick: Transaction Press, 1977, 2nd edn 1988).

——, *U.S. Foreign Policy and European Security* (London and New York: Macmillan and St. Martin's Press, 1987).

Dallek, Robert, *Ronald Reagan – The Politics of Symbolism* (Cambridge, Mass. and London: Harvard University Press, 1984).

Dam, Kenneth W., *The Rules of the Game – Reform and Evolution in the International Monetary System* (Chicago and London: The University of Chicago Press, 1982).

Davis, Paul K. (ed.), *New Challenges for Defense Planning – Rethinking How Much is Enough* (Santa Monica, Ca.: RAND, 1994).

de Gaulle, Charles, *The Complete War Memoirs of Charles de Gaulle* (New York: Clarion Books, Simon and Schuster, 1954, 1955, 1956, 1959, 1960).

DePorte, A.W., *Europe Between the Superpowers – The Enduring Balance* (2nd edn, New Haven and London: Yale University Press, 1986).

De Rose, François (trans. Richard Nice, foreword by Henry A. Kissinger), *European Security and France* (London and Basingstoke: Macmillan (IISS), 1984).

de Saint Phalle, Thibaut, *Trade, Inflation, and the Dollar* (New York and Oxford: Oxford University Press, 1981).

de Tocqueville, Alexis (ed. Richard D. Heffner), *Democracy in America* (New York: Mentor Books/The New American Library, 1956).

Destler, I.M., *Presidents, Bureaucrats and Foreign Policy – The Politics of Organizational Reform* (Princeton NJ: Princeton University Press, 1972, 1974).

——, Leslie H. Gelb, and Anthony Lake, *Our Own Worst Enemy – The Unmaking of American Foreign Policy* (New York: Simon & Schuster, 1984).

Dietrich, William S., *In the Shadow of the Rising Sun – The Political Roots of American Economic Decline* (University Park, Pennsylvania: Pennsylvania State University Press, 1991).

Drew, Elizabeth, *Campaign Journal – The Political Events of 1983–1984* (New York: Macmillan Publishing Co., 1985).

——, *Portrait of an Election – The 1980 Presidential Campaign* (New York: Simon & Schuster, 1981).

Eden, Douglas, and F.E. Short, *Political Change in Europe – The Left and the Future of the Atlantic Alliance* (Oxford: Basil Blackwell, 1981).

Editors of *Time* Magazine, *Mikhail S. Gorbachev – An Intimate Biography* (New York: Time Book/New American Library, 1988).

Epstein, Joshua M., *Conventional Force Reductions – A Dynamic Assessment* (Washington, DC: The Brookings Institution, 1990).

ESECS (Report of the European Security Study), *Strengthening Conventional Deterrence in Europe – Proposals for the 1980s* (New York: St. Martin's Press, 1983).

Fall, Bernard, *The Two Viet-Nams – A Political and Military Analysis* (revised edn, New York: Frederick A. Praeger, 1963, 1964).

Fallows, James, *National Defense* (New York: Vintage, 1981).

Fedder, Edwin H., *Nato: The Dynamics of Alliance in the Postwar World* (New York and Toronto: Dodd, Mead & Co., 1973).

Fisher, Louis, *Presidential War Power* (Lawrence, Kansas: University Press of Kansas, 1995).

Flynn, Gregory, and Hans Rattinger (eds), *The Public and Atlantic Defense* (London and Canberra: Rowman & Allanheld, Croom Helm, 1985).

Foster, Richard B., André Beaufré, Wynfred Joshua, *Strategy for the West – American–Allied Relations in Transition* (New York: Crane, Russak & Co., Inc., 1974).

Franck, Thomas M. and Edward Weisband, *Foreign Policy By Congress* (New York and Oxford: Oxford University Press, 1979).

Friedrich, Carl J., *Constitutional Government and Democracy – Theory and Practice in Europe and America* (revised edn, Waltham, Mass., Toronto, London: Blaisdell Publishing Co., 1937, 1950).

Fromkin, David, *In The Time of the Americans – FDR, Truman, Eisenhower, MacArthur, Marshall – The Generation That Changed America's Role in the World* (New York: Alfred A. Knopf, 1995).

Fukuyama, Francis, *The End of History and the Last Man* (New York: Avon Books, 1992).

Galbraith, John Kenneth, *A Life In Our Times – Memoirs* (Boston: Houghton Mifflin Co., 1981).

——, *The Affluent Society* (4th edn, Boston: Houghton Mifflin Co., 1958, 1969, 1976, 1984).

——, *The New Industrial State* (Boston: Houghton Mifflin Co., 1967).

Garthoff, Raymond L., *Detente and Confrontation – American–Soviet Relations from Nixon to Reagan* (Washington, DC: The Brookings Institution, 1985).

——, *The Great Transition – American–Soviet Relations and the End of the Cold War* (Washington, DC: The Brookings Institution, 1994).

Garton Ash, Timothy, *In Europe's Name – Germany and The Divided Continent* (New York: Random House, 1993).

Geipel, Gary L. (ed.), *Germany in a New Era* (Indianapolis, Indiana: Hudson Institute, 1993).

Germond, Jack W., and Jules Witcover, *Mad as Hell – Revolt at the Ballot Box, 1992* (New York: Warner Books, 1993).

——, *Whose Broad Stripes and Bright Stars – The Trivial Pursuit of the Presidency 1988* (New York: Warner Books, 1989).

Godson, Joseph (ed.), *35 Years of Nato – A Transatlantic Symposium on the Changing Political, Economic and Military Setting* (New York: Dodd, Mead & Co., 1984).

Golden, Peter, *Nato Burden–Sharing – Risks and Opportunities* (Washington, DC: Praeger, 1983).

Goldman, Peter, Tom Mathews, and the *Newsweek* Special Election Team, *The Quest for the Presidency – the 1988 Campaign* (New York, London, Toronto, Sydney, Tokyo: Simon & Schuster Inc., 1989).

Goldsborough, James Oliver, *Rebel Europe – How America Can Live with a Changing Continent* (London and New York: Collier Macmillan Publishers, Macmillan Publishing Co., Inc., 1982).

Goldstein, Walter (ed.), *Reagan's Leadership and the Atlantic Alliance – Views from Europe and America* (Washington, New York, London, Oxford, Beijing, Frankfurt, Sao Paulo, Sydney, Tokyo, Toronto: Pergamon–Brassey's International Defense Publishers, Inc., 1986).

Goodpaster, General Andrew J., General Franz-Joseph Schulze, Air Chief Marshal Sir Alasdair Steedman, Dr William J. Perry, *Strengthening Conventional Deterrence in Europe – A Program for the 1980s, European Security Study Report of the Special Panel* (Boulder and London: Westview Press, 1985).

Goodwin, Richard N., *Remembering America – A Voice from the Sixties* (New York, Grand Rapids, Philadelphia, St. Louis, San Francisco, London, Singapore, Sydney, Tokyo: Harper & Row, 1988).

Gordon, Lincoln, with J.F. Brown, Pierre Hassner, Josef Joffe, Edwina Moreton, *Eroding Empire – Western Relations with Eastern Europe* (Washington, DC: The Brookings Institution, 1987).

Gore, Senator Al, *Earth in the Balance – Ecology and the Human Spirit* (Boston, New York, London: Houghton Mifflin Co., 1992).

Graebner, Norman A. (ed.), *An Uncertain Tradition: American Secretaries of State in the Twentieth Century* (New York, Toronto, London: McGraw-Hill Book Co., Inc., 1961).

Graham, General Daniel O., *The Non-Nuclear Defense of Cities: The High Frontier Space-Based Defense Against ICBM Attack* (Cambridge, Mass.: Abt Books, 1983).

Graubard, Stephen R., *A New Europe? A Timely Appraisal* (Boston: Beacon Press, 1963, 1964).

Gray, Colin S., *War, Peace, and Victory – Strategy and Statecraft for the Next Century* (New York, London, Toronto, Sydney, Tokyo, Singapore: Simon & Schuster, 1990).

Greenfield, Jeff, *The Real Campaign – How the Media Missed the Story of the 1980 Campaign* (New York: Summit Books, 1982).

Greenstein, Fred I., *The Hidden-Hand Presidency – Eisenhower as Leader* (New York: Basic Books, Inc., 1982).

Grosser, Alfred (Foreword by Stanley Hoffmann, trans. Michael Shaw), *The Western Alliance – European-American Relations Since 1945* (New York: Continuum, 1980).

Gunther, Richard, Giacomo Sani, Goldie Shabad, *Spain After Franco – The Making of a Competitive Party System* (Berkeley, Los Angeles, London: University of California Press, 1986).

Hasse, Rolf H., with contributions by Werner Weidenfeld and Reinhold Biskup, *The European Central Bank: Perspectives for a Further Development of the European Monetary System* (Gutersloh: Bertelsmann Foundation, 1990).

Haig, Alexander M. Jr., *Caveat – Realism, Reagan and Foreign Policy* (New York: Macmillan Publishing Co., 1984).

Halle, Louis J., *The Cold War As History* (New York and Evanston: Harper & Row, 1967).

Hamilton, Daniel S., *After the Revolution: The New Political Landscape in East Germany* (Washington, DC: American Institute for Contemporary German Studies, 1990).

——, *Beyond Bonn – America and the Berlin Republic* (Washington, DC: Carnegie Endowment for International Peace, 1994).

Hanrieder, Wolfram, *The United States and Western Europe* (Cambridge, Mass.: Winthrop Publishers, Inc., 1974).
——, *West German Foreign Policy: 1949–1979* (Boulder, Colo.: Westview Press, 1980).
—— and Graeme P. Auton, *The Foreign Policies of West Germany, France, and Britain* (Englewood Cliffs, NJ: Prentice-Hall, 1980).
Heilbroner, Robert, *Visions of the Future – The Distant Past, Yesterday, Today, and Tomorrow* (New York and Oxford: The New York Public Library, Oxford University Press, 1995).
Hinsley, F.H., *Power and the Pursuit of Peace* (Cambridge University Press, 1963).
Hoffmann, Stanley (ed.), *Contemporary Theory in International Relations* (Englewood Cliffs, NJ: Prentice-Hall, Inc., 1960).
——, *Decline or Renewal? France Since the 1930s* (New York: The Viking Press, 1974).
——, *Gulliver's Troubles, Or the Setting of American Foreign Policy* (New York, Toronto, London, Sydney: McGraw-Hill, for the Council on Foreign Relations, 1968).
——, *Primacy or World Order – American Foreign Policy Since the Cold War* (New York, St. Louis, San Francisco, *et al.*: McGraw-Hill, 1978).
——, *The State of War – Essays on the Theory and Practice of International Politics* (New York, Washington, London: Frederick A. Praeger, 1966).
——, Charles P. Kindleberger, Laurence Wylie, Jesse R. Pitts, Jean-Baptiste Duroselle, François Goguel, *In Search of France – The Economy, Society, and Political System in the Twentieth Century* (New York: Harper Torchbooks/The Academy Library, Harper & Row, 1963).
Hofheinz Jr., Roy, and Kent E. Calder, *The Eastasia Edge* (New York: Basic Books, Inc., 1982).
Hogan, Michael J., *The Marshall Plan – America, Britain and the Reconstruction of Western Europe, 1947–1952* (Cambridge, New York, New Rochelle, Sydney, Melbourne: Cambridge University Press, 1987).
Holsti, Ole R., Randolph M. Siverson, Alexander L. George (eds), *Change in the International System* (Boulder Colo.: Westview Press, 1980).
Hoopes, Townsend, *The Devil and John Foster Dulles* (Boston, Toronto: An Atlantic Monthly Press Book, Little, Brown & Co., 1973).
Hunter, Robert E. (ed.), *Grand Strategy for the Western Alliance* (Boulder and London: Westview Press, 1984).
—— (ed.), *Nato – The Next Generation* (Boulder, Colo.: Westview Press, 1984).
Huntington, Samuel P., *Political Order in Changing Societies* (New Haven: Yale University Press, 1968).
——, *The Third Wave – Democratization in the Late Twentieth Century* (Norman and London: University of Oklahoma Press, 1991).
Iklé, Fred Charles, *How Nations Negotiate* (New York, Washington, London: Frederick A. Praeger, 1964).
Isaacson, Walter, and Evan Thomas, *The Wise Men – Six Friends and the World They Made* (New York: Simon & Schuster, 1986).
Jentleson, Bruce W., *With Friends Like These – Reagan, Bush, and Saddam, 1982–1990* (New York/London, W.W. Norton & Co., 1994).
Jervis, Robert, *The Illogic of American Nuclear Strategy* (Ithaca and London: Cornell University Press, 1984).

——, *Perception and Misperception in International Politics* (Princeton, NJ: Princeton University Press, 1976).

Joffe, Joseph, *The Limited Partnership – Europe, the United States, and the Burdens of Alliance* (Cambridge, Mass.: Ballinger Publishing Co., 1987).

Johnson, Paul, *Modern Times – The World from the Twenties to the Eighties* (New York, Cambridge, Philadelphia, San Francisco, London, Mexico City, Sao Paulo, Singapore, Sydney: Harper & Row, 1983).

Johnson, Stuart E., with Joseph A. Yager, *The Military Equation in Northeast Asia* (Washington, DC: The Brookings Institution, 1979).

Johnstone, Diana, *The Politics of Euromissiles – Europe's Role in America's World* (London: Verso, 1984).

Kahan, Jerome H., *Security in the Nuclear Age – Developing U.S. Strategic Arms Policy* (Washington, DC: The Brookings Institution, 1975).

Kanter, Arnold, *Defense Politics – A Budgetary Perspective* (Chicago and London: The University of Chicago Press, 1975, 1979).

Kaplan, Morton A., *The Rationale for Nato – European Collective Security, Past and Future* (Stanford and Washington DC: American Enterprise Institute for Public Policy Research and Hoover Institution on War, Revolution and Peace, 1973).

——, *System and Process in International Politics* (New York: John Wiley & Sons, Inc., Science Editions, 1957, 1964).

——, and Nicholas deB. Katzenbach, *The Political Foundations of International Law* (New York, London: John Wiley & Sons, Inc., 1961).

Kelleher, Catherine M., and Gale A. Mattox, *Evolving European Defense Policies* (Lexington, Mass. and Toronto: Lexington Books and D.C. Heath and Co., 1987).

Kemp, Geoffrey, Robert L. Pfaltzgraff, Jr, and Uri Ra'anan, *The Superpowers in a Multinuclear World* (Lexington, Mass., Toronto, London: Lexington Books, D.C. Heath and Co., 1973).

Kennan, George F., *American Diplomacy* (expanded edn, Chicago and London: The University of Chicago Press, 1984).

——, *The Decline of Bismarck's European Order – Franco-Russian Relations, 1875–1890* (Princeton, N.J.: Princeton University Press, 1979).

——, *Memoirs 1925–1950* (Boston and Toronto: Little, Brown & Co., 1967).

Kennedy, Paul, *The Rise and Fall of the Great Powers – Economic Change and Military Conflict from 1500 to 2000* (New York: Random House, 1987).

Keohane, Robert and Stanley Hoffmann (eds), *The New European Community: Decisionmaking and Institutional Change* (Boulder, Colo.: Westview Press, 1991).

Kernell, Samuel, *Parallel Politics – Economic Policymaking in Japan and the United States* (Tokyo and Washington: Japan Center for International Exchange and Brookings Institution, 1991).

Kim, Elaine H., and Eui-Young Yu, *East to America – Korean American Life Stories* (New York: The New Press, 1996).

Kim, Kyung-Won, *Revolution and International System* (New York and London: New York University Press and University of London Press, 1970).

Kissinger, Henry A., *A World Restored – The Politics of Conservatism in a Revolutionary Age* (New York: Grosset & Dunlap, 1964).

——, *American Foreign Policy – Three Essays* (New York: W.W. Norton & Co., Inc., 1969).

——, *Diplomacy* (New York, London, Toronto, Sydney, Tokyo, Singapore: Simon & Schuster, 1994).

——, *The Troubled Partnership – A Re-appraisal of the Atlantic Alliance* (Garden City, New York: Anchor Books, Doubleday & Co., Inc., 1965, 1966).

——, *White House Years* (Boston and Toronto: Little, Brown & Co., 1979).

Kleiman, Robert, *Atlantic Crisis – American Diplomacy Confronts a Resurgent Europe* (New York: W.W. Norton & Co., Inc., 1964).

Klunk, Brian, *Consensus and the American Mission* (Lanham, New York, London: University Press of America, 1986).

Knorr, Klaus, and Sidney Verba (eds), *The International System – Theoretical Essays* (Princeton, NJ: Princeton University Press, 1961).

Kolodziej, Edward A., *French International Policy under de Gaulle and Pompidou – The Politics of Grandeur* (Ithaca and London: Cornell University Press, 1974).

Krause, Lawrence B., and Fun-koo Park (eds), *Social Issues in Korea: Korean and American Perspectives* (Seoul: Korea Development Institute, 1993).

Krause, Axel, *Inside the New Europe* (New York: Cornelie & Michael Bessie Books, HarperCollins Publishers, 1991).

Krepon, Michael, *Strategic Stalemate – Nuclear Weapons and Arms Control in American Politics* (New York: St. Martin's Press, 1984).

Kwon, Ho-Youn, and Shin Kim (eds), *The Emerging Generation of Korean-Americans* (Kyung Hee University Press, 1993).

Laski, Harold J., *Political Thought in England From Locke to Bentham* (London: Thornton Butterworth Ltd., 1920).

Lewis, Flora, *Europe – A Tapestry of Nations* (New York, London, Toronto, Sydney, Tokyo: Simon & Schuster, 1987).

Lincoln, Edward J., *Japan – Facing Economic Maturity* (Washington, DC: The Brookings Institution, 1988).

Liska, George, *Imperial America – The International Politics of Primacy* (Baltimore: The Johns Hopkins Press, 1967).

——, *Nations in Alliance – The Limits of Interdependence* (Baltimore: The Johns Hopkins Press, 1962, 1968).

Lorenz, Konrad (trans. Marjorie Kerr Wilson), *On Aggression* (New York: Harcourt, Brace & World, Inc., 1963).

Lubell, Samuel, *The Future of American Politics* (Garden City, New York: Doubleday & Co., Inc., 1955).

Lukacs, John, *The End of the Twentieth Century and the End of the Modern Age* (New York: Ticknor & Fields, 1993).

Luttwak, Edward N., *The Pentagon and the Art of War* (New York: Institute of Contemporary Studies/Simon & Schuster, 1984).

Makin, John H., and Donald C. Hellmann (eds), *Sharing World Leadership – A New Era for America and Japan* (Washington DC: American Enterprise Institute for Public Policy Research, 1989).

Malcolm, Noel, *Bosnia – A Short History* (New York University Press, 1994).

Mandelbaum, Michael, *The Nuclear Question – The United States and Nuclear Weapons, 1946–1976* (Cambridge, London, New York, New Rochelle, Melbourne, Sydney: Cambridge University Press, 1979).

—— (ed.), Pierre Hassner, Stanley Hoffmann, Edwina Moreton and Gregory Treverton, *Western Approaches to the Soviet Union* (New York: The Council on Foreign Relations, 1988).

Marks, Anne W. (ed.), *NPT: Paradoxes and Problems* (Washington, DC: Arms Control Association, Carnegie Endowment for International Peace, 1975).

Mattox, Gale A., and John H. Vaughan, Jr. (eds), *Germany Through American Eyes – Foreign Policy and Domestic Issues* (Boulder, San Francisco & London: Westview Press, 1989).

May, Ernest R., *'Lessons' of the Past – The Use and Misuse of History in American Foreign Policy* (London, Oxford, New York: Oxford University Press, 1973).

Mayer, Jane, and Doyle McManus, *Landslide – The Unmaking of the President 1984–1988* (Boston: Houghton Mifflin Company, 1988).

McClelland, Charles A., *Theory and the International System* (New York and London: The Macmillan Company, Collier-Macmillan Limited, 1966).

Mearsheimer, John J., *Conventional Deterrence* (Ithaca and London: Cornell University Press, 1983).

Morgenthau, Hans, *Politics Among Nations – The Struggle for Power and Peace* (5th edn, revised, New York: Alfred A. Knopf, 1978).

Mueller, John, *Retreat from Doomsday – The Obsolescence of Major War* (New York: Basic Books, Inc., 1989).

Nacht, Michael, *The Age of Vulnerability – Threats to the Nuclear Stalemate* (Washington, DC: The Brookings Institution, 1985).

Neustadt, Richard E., *Alliance Politics* (New York and London: Columbia University Press, 1970).

Newhouse, John, *Cold Dawn – The Story of SALT* (New York, Chicago, San Francisco: Holt, Rinehart & Winston, 1973).

——, *Collision in Brussels – The Common Market Crisis of 30 June 1965* (New York: W.W. Norton and Co. Inc., 1967).

——, with Melvin Croan, Edward R. Fried, and Timothy W. Stanley, *U.S. Troops in Europe – Issues, Costs, and Choices* (Washington, DC: The Brookings Institution, 1971).

Nicholas, Herbert, *Britain and the U.S.A.* (Baltimore: The Johns Hopkins Press, 1963).

Niskanen, William A., *Reaganomics – An Insider's Account of the Policies and the People* (New York and Oxford: Oxford University Press, 1988).

Nixon, Richard, *The Real War* (New York: Warner Books, 1980, 1981).

Nye, Joseph S. Jr, *Bound to Lead: The Changing Nature of American Power* (New York: Basic Books, 1991).

Osgood, Robert E., and Robert W. Tucker, *Force, Order, and Justice* (Baltimore: The Johns Hopkins University Press, 1967).

——, Francis E. Rourke, Herbert S. Dinerstein, Laurence W. Martin, David P. Calleo, Benjamin M. Rowland, George Liska, *Retreat From Empire? The First Nixon Administration* (Baltimore and London: The Johns Hopkins University Press, 1973).

Oye, Kenneth A., Robert J. Lieber, Donald Rothchild (eds), *Eagle Defiant – United States Foreign Policy in the 1980s* (Boston and Toronto: Little, Brown & Co., 1983).

—— (eds), *Eagle Resurgent? The Reagan Era in American Foreign Policy* (Boston and Toronto: Little, Brown & Co., 1987).

Packard, Vance, *The Hidden Persuaders* (revised edn, New York: Washington Square Press/Pocket Books, 1957, 1980).

Parmet, Herbert S., *Richard Nixon and His America* (Boston, Toronto, London: Little, Brown & Co., 1990).

Paterson, Thomas G. (ed.), *Kennedy's Quest for Victory – American Foreign Policy, 1961–1963* (New York and Oxford: Oxford University Press, 1989).

Payne, Stanley G. (ed.), *The Politics of Democratic Spain* (The Chicago Council on Foreign Relations, 1986).

Pelkmans, Jacques and Alan Winters, *Europe's Domestic Market*, Chatham House Papers, 43 (London: The Royal Institute of International Affairs, Routledge, 1988).

Pfaff, William, *Barbarian Sentiments – How the American Century Ends* (New York: Hill & Wang, 1989).

——, *The Wrath of Nations – Civilization and the Furies of Nationalism* (New York, London, Toronto, Sydney, Tokyo, Singapore: Touchstone Books, Simon & Schuster, 1993).

Phillips, Kevin, *The Politics of Rich and Poor – Wealth and the American Electorate in the Reagan Aftermath* (New York: HarperPerennial/Division of HarperCollins Publishers, 1990).

Pierre, Andrew J., *The Global Politics of Arms Sales* (Princeton University Press, 1982).

Powell, Colin (with Joseph E. Persico), *My American Journey* (New York: Random House, 1995).

Preeg, Ernest H., *Traders and Diplomats – An Analysis of the Kennedy Round of Negotiations Under the General Agreement on Tariffs and Trade* (Washington, DC: The Brookings Institution, 1970).

Pryce, Roy, *The Politics of the European Community* (London: Butterworths, European Community Studies, 1973).

Reagan, Ronald, *An American Life* (New York, London, Toronto, Sydney, Tokyo, Singapore: Simon & Schuster, 1990).

Reich, Robert B., *Tales of A New America* (New York: Times Books, 1987).

Remnick, David, *Lenin's Tomb – The Last Days of the Soviet Empire* (New York: Random House, 1993).

Revel, Jean-François (with Branko Lazitch; trans. William Byron), *How Democracies Perish* (Garden City, New York: Doubleday & Company, Inc., 1983).

Richardson, James L., *Germany and the Atlantic Alliance – The Interaction of Strategy and Politics* (Cambridge, Mass.: Harvard University Press, 1966).

Rodman, Peter, *More Precious than Peace – The Cold War and the Struggle for the Third World* (New York, London, Toronto, Sydney, Tokyo, Singapore: Charles Scribner's Sons, 1994).

Rosecrance, Richard N., *Action and Reaction in World Politics – International Systems in Perspective* (Boston and Toronto: Little, Brown & Co., 1963).

Rush, Kenneth, Brent Scowcroft, Joseph J. Wolf (rapporteur and ed.), *Strengthening Deterrence – Nato and the Credibility of Western Defense in the 1980s* (The Atlantic Council, Cambridge Mass.: Ballinger Publishing, Harper & Row, Inc., 1981).

Rustow, Dankwart A., *Turkey – America's Forgotten Ally* (New York: The Council on Foreign Relations, 1987).

Sakaiya, Taichi, *What is Japan? Contradictions and Transformations* (New York, Tokyo, London: Kodansha International, 1993).

Schelling, Thomas C., *Arms and Influence* (New Haven and London: Yale University Press, 1966).

——, *The Strategy of Conflict* (New York: Oxford University Press, 1963).
Schlesinger, Arthur M. Jr, *A Thousand Days – John F. Kennedy in the White House* (Boston and Cambridge, Mass.: Houghton Mifflin Co. and the Riverside Press, 1965).
Schlossstein, Steven, *The End of the American Century* (New York and Chicago: Congdon & Weed, Inc., 1989).
Schmidt, Helmut (ed./introduction by Wolfram Hanreider), *Perspectives on Politics* (Boulder, Colo.: Westview Press, 1982).
Schwartz, David N., *Nato's Nuclear Dilemmas* (Washington, DC: The Brookings Institution, 1983).
Servan-Schreiber, J.-J., *The American Challenge* (New York: Atheneum, 1968).
Shapley, Deborah, *Promise and Power – The Life and Times of Robert McNamara* (Boston, Toronto, London: Little, Brown & Co., 1993).
Shogan, Robert, *The Riddle of Power – Presidential Leadership from Truman to Bush* (New York: A Dutton Book, 1991).
Shultz, George P., *Turmoil and Triumph – My Years As Secretary of State* (New York: Charles Scribner's Sons, 1993).
Sigal, Leon V., *Nuclear Forces in Europe – Enduring Dilemmas, Present Prospects* (Washington, DC: The Brookings Institution, 1984).
Silk, Leonard, *Economics in the Real World – How Political Decisions Affect the Economy* (New York: Simon & Schuster, 1984).
Singer, Max, and Aaron Wildavsky, *The Real World Order: Zones of Peace/Zones of Turmoil* (Chatham, New Jersey: Chatham, 1993).
Sloan, Stanley R. (ed.), Foreword by Sen. William V. Roth, Jr, *Nato in the 1990s* (Washington, New York, London, Oxford, Beijing, Frankfurt, Sao Paulo, Sydney, Tokyo, Toronto: Pergamon-Brassey's International Defense Publishers, Inc., 1989).
——, *Nato's Future – Toward a New Transatlantic Bargain* (Washington, DC: National Defense University Press, 1985).
Smith, Hedrick, *The Power Game – How Washington Works* (New York: Random House, 1988).
Snyder, Jed C., and Samuel F. Wells, Jr (eds), *Limiting Nuclear Proliferation* (Cambridge, Mass.: Ballinger Publishing Co., 1985).
Solomon, Richard H. (ed.), *Asian Security in the 1980s – Problems and Policies for a Time of Transition* (Cambridge, Mass.: Oelgeschlager, Gunn & Hain, Inc., 1979, 1980).
Solomon, Robert, *The Transformation of the World Economy, 1980–93* (Basingstoke and London: Macmillan, 1994).
Spanier, John and Eric M. Uslaner, *American Foreign Policy Making and the Democratic Dilemmas* (4th edn, New York, Chicago, San Francisco, Philadelphia, Montreal, Toronto, London, Sydney, Tokyo, Mexico City, Rio de Janeiro, Madrid: Holt, Rinehart & Winston, 1985).
Spero, Joan Edelman, *The Politics of International Economic Relations* (4th edn, New York: St. Martin's Press, 1990).
Stacks, John F., *The Campaign for the Presidency 1980* (New York: Times Books, 1981).
Stares, Paul B. (ed.), *The New Germany and the New Europe* (Washington, DC: The Brookings Institution, 1992).
Steinbruner, John D. (ed.), *Restructuring American Foreign Policy* (Washington, DC: The Brookings Institution, 1989).

——, and Leon V. Segal (eds), *Alliance Security: Nato and the No-First-Use Question* (Washington, DC: The Brookings Institution, 1983).

Szulc, Tad, *The Illusion of Peace – Foreign Policy in the Nixon Years* (New York: Viking, 1978).

——, *Then and Now – How The World Has Changed Since World War II* (New York: William Morrow and Co., Inc., 1990).

Tachau, Frank, *Turkey – The Politics of Authority, Democracy, and Development* (New York, Philadelphia, Eastbourne, Toronto, Hong Kong, Tokyo, Sydney: Praeger Special Studies/Praeger Scientific, 1984).

Talbott, Strobe, *Deadly Gambits – The Reagan Administration and the Stalemate in Nuclear Arms Control* (New York: Alfred A. Knopf, 1984).

——, *The Master of the Game – Paul Nitze and the Nuclear Peace* (New York: Alfred A. Knopf, 1988).

——, Foreword by Cyrus Vance, *The Russians and Reagan* (New York: Council on Foreign Relations/Vintage Books, 1984).

Thatcher, Margaret, *The Downing Street Years* (New York: HarperCollins, 1993).

Thompson, Kenneth W. (ed.), *Community, Diversity, And a New World Order – Essays in Honor of Inis L. Claude, Jr.* (Lanham, New York, London: University Press of America, 1994).

——, *Political Realism and the Crisis of World Politics – An American Approach to Foreign Policy* (Lanham, New York, London: University Press of America, 1982).

—— (ed.), *The Carter Presidency – Fourteen Intimate Perspectives of Jimmy Carter* (Lanham, New York, London: University Press of America, 1990).

Tolchin, Martin and Susan, *Buying Into America – How Foreign Money is Changing the Face of Our Nation* (New York: Times Books, 1988).

Waltz, Kenneth N., *Foreign Policy and Democratic Politics* (Boston: Little, Brown & Co., 1967).

——, *Theory of International Relations* (Reading Mass., Menlo Park Ca., London, Amsterdam, Don Mills Ontario, Sydney: Addison-Wesley Publishing Co., 1979, 1983).

Wattenberg, Ben J., Introduction by Richard M. Scammon, *The Real America – A Surprising Examination of the State of the Union* (New York: Capricorn Books, G.P. Putnam's Sons, 1974, 1976).

White, Theodore H., *The Making of the President 1960* (New York: Atheneum Publishers, 1961).

——, *The Making of the President 1964* (New York: Atheneum Publishers, 1965).

Wiarda, Howard J., *Foreign Policy Without Illusion – How Foreign Policy-Making Works and Fails to Work in the United States* (Glenview, Ill. and London: Scott, Foresman/Little, Brown Higher Education, 1990).

Wills, Garry, *Lincoln at Gettysburg – The Words That Remade America* (New York, London, Toronto, Sydney, Tokyo, Singapore: Simon & Schuster, 1992).

——, *Reagan's America – Innocents At Home* (Garden City, New York: Doubleday & Company, Inc., 1987).

Wittkopf, Eugene R., *Faces of Internationalism – Public Opinion and American Foreign Policy* (Durham and London: Duke University Press, 1990).

Woodward, Bob, *The Commanders* (New York, London, Toronto, Sydney, Tokyo, Singapore: Simon & Schuster, 1991).

Woodward, Susan L., *Balkan Tragedy – Chaos and Dissolution After the Cold War* (Washington, DC: The Brookings Institution, 1995).
Young, John W., *Britain, France and the Unity of Europe 1945–51* (Leicester University Press, 1984).
Yu, George (ed.), *Asia's New World Order* (London: Macmillan, 1996).
Zeiner-Gundersen, H.F., Sergio A. Rossi, Marcel Duval, Donald C. Daniel, Gael D. Tarleton, Milan Vego, *Nato's Maritime Flanks: Problems and Prospects* (Institute for Foreign Policy Analysis, Inc.; Washington, London, New York, Oxford, Toronto, Sydney, Frankfurt: Pergamon-Brassey's International Defense Publishers, 1987).

The Notes should be consulted for specific journal as well as additional monograph references. The publications of the Chicago Council on Foreign Relations play a special role. Other material of particular usefulness has included:

Nato: Facts and Figures (Brussels: Nato Information Service, 1976).
Nato Handbook (Brussels: Nato Office of Information and Press, 1995).
Report of the Japan–United States Economic Relations Group (Prepared for the President of the United States and the Prime Minister of Japan, 1981).
DePorte, A.W., *The Atlantic Alliance at 35*, Headline Series no. 268 (New York: Foreign Policy Association, 1984).
Western Defense: The European Role in NATO (Eurogroup, 1988).

Periodicals
Specific references are in note citations in the text

Adelphi Papers (IISS)
American Political Science Review
Asian Perspective (Institute for Far Eastern Studies, Kyungnam University)
Asian Security (Research Institute for Peace and Security)
Chicago Tribune
Dispatch (Department of State)
The Economist
Financial Times
Foreign Affairs
Foreign Policy
International Herald Tribune
International Security
Korea Focus (The Korea Foundation)
Korea Times
Korea Today
Korea Update
The Military Balance (IISS)
The National Interest
New York Times

ORBIS
Strategic Survey (IISS)
Survival (IISS)
The Times (London)
Wall Street Journal
World Politics

Index

205